Living Transnationally between Japan and Brazil

NEW STUDIES OF MODERN JAPAN

Series Editors: Doug Slaymaker and William M. Tsutsui

New Studies of Modern Japan is a multidisciplinary series that consists primarily of original studies on a broad spectrum of topics dealing with Japan since the mid-nineteenth century. Additionally, the series aims to bring back into print classic works that shed new light on contemporary Japan. The series speaks to cultural studies (literature, translations, film), history, and social sciences audiences. We publish compelling works of scholarship, by both established and rising scholars in the field, on a broad arena of topics, in order to nuance our understandings of Japan and the Japanese.

Advisory Board
Michael Bourdaghs, Rebecca Copeland, Aaron Gerow,
Yoshikuni Igarashi, Koichi Iwabuchi, T. J. Pempel,
Julia Adeney Thomas, Dennis Washburn, Merry White

Titles in the Series

Living Transnationally between Japan and Brazil

Routes beyond Roots

Sarah A. LeBaron von Baeyer

LEXINGTON BOOKS

Lanham • Boulder • New York • London

Published by Lexington Books
An imprint of The Rowman & Littlefield Publishing Group, Inc.
4501 Forbes Boulevard, Suite 200, Lanham, Maryland 20706
www.rowman.com

6 Tinworth Street, London SE11 5AL, United Kingdom

British Library Cataloguing in Publication Information Available

Library of Congress Cataloging-in-Publication Data Available

ISBN: 978-1-4985-8036-6 (cloth)
ISBN: 978-1-4985-8037-3 (electronic)

Contents

Glossary of Key Japanese Terms

Dekasegi 出稼ぎ = Temporary migrant worker; in recent decades, the term has come to refer specifically to a person of Japanese descent, often from Latin America, who works as a labor migrant in Japan

Gaikokujin/gaijin 外国人・外人 = Lit. an outsider; used by people in Japan to mean anyone who is a foreigner, and among Japanese-Brazilians to mean anyone who is not of Japanese descent

Hāfu ハーフ = From the English word "half," this term refers to someone who is half Japanese and half another nationality or ethnicity, usually Western and/or English-speaking

Haken gaisha 派遣会社 = See meaning of the Portuguese word *empreiteira*, in the next section

Ijime 苛め = The Japanese word for bullying

Issei 一世 = First generation Japanese emigrant from Japan

Nikkei 日系 = General adjective/noun for all emigrants and descendants of emigrants from Japan

Nikkeijin 日系人 = General noun for all emigrants and descendants of emigrants from Japan

Nisei 二世 = Second generation descendant of a Japanese emigrant from Japan

Sansei 三世 = Third generation descendant of a Japanese emigrant from Japan

Seishain 正社員 = Regular, full-time employee of a company (in contrast with a contract worker, or *keiyakushain* 契約社員)

Yakin 夜勤 = Night shift

Yonsei 四世 = Fourth generation descendant of a Japanese emigrant from Japan

Zainichi 在日 = Long-term foreign resident of Japan, usually used in reference to ethnic Koreans and Chinese who have lived in Japan for generations

Zangyō 残業 = Overtime work

Glossary of Key Portuguese Terms

Amarelo/a = Lit. yellow, one of the five official categories of "color" and/or "race" on the Brazilian National Census; usually used to refer to anyone of East Asian descent

Brasileiro/a = Brazilian; usually refers to any and all Brazilians, but among my interlocutors the term was also used specifically to signal a non-Japanese Brazilian

Descendente = Lit. a descendant; among Japanese-Brazilians, the term is used to refer specifically to someone of Japanese descent, regardless of generation or mixed/non-mixed heritage

Empreiteira = An employment brokerage firm; by the time I conducted fieldwork, most *dekasegi* continued to find work in Japan via these mediating institutions

Interior = The "interior" of Brazil refers to both large cities and rural areas, but not state capitals, and often connotes rurality, small-town life, and/or a lack of cosmopolitanism

Japa/japinho/a = The familiar or diminutive (and in some contexts pejorative) form of "Japanese" (see the next entry)

Japonês/japonesa = Lit. Japanese; used among Japanese-Brazilians to mean someone of Japanese descent and/or a native of Japan

Mestiço/a = Lit. mixed; used among Japanese-Brazilians in reference to someone who is of partial (as opposed to "full") Japanese descent

Puro/a = Lit. pure; used among Japanese-Brazilians to distinguish someone of "full" versus "mixed" Japanese descent

Acknowledgments

I am forever indebted to my interlocutors, whom I cannot name here, for so generously letting me into their lives in Japan and Brazil.

This work would not have come to be without the tireless support and dedication of my doctoral advisor and the chair of my dissertation committee, William W. Kelly. Dr. Kelly has guided my intellectual development ever since I began graduate school, shaping and reshaping my understanding of both anthropology and Japan, and serving as a mentor and mensch well beyond the call of duty. I owe equally heartfelt thanks to my professors and classmates in the Department of Anthropology at Yale University for helping me learn the ways and words of our craft. Special thanks to Helen Siu, Joseph Errington, Karen Nakamura, Kathryn Dudley, Kenneth David Jackson, Stuart Schwartz, and Tania Martuscelli for their teachings at Yale; Anne Aronsson, Annie Claus, Elizabeth Miles, Ellen Rubinstein, Isaac Gagné, Heidi Lam, Nana Okura Gagné, Nathaniel Smith, and Ryan Sayre for their insights in Zemi; and Jeffrey Lesser of Emory University for his warmth and generosity in helping me steer both fieldwork in Brazil and the earlier drafts of my dissertation. Over the last several years, students in my classes at Yale University, especially my seminar on Transnational Migration and East Asia, provided invaluable comments on my book manuscript.

Over the years I received generous support for research and writing from the Council on East Asian Studies and the McMillan Center for International and Area Studies at Yale University, the Japan Foundation, and Fulbright IIE. Bela Feldman-Bianco, Chiyoko Mita, Ethel Kosminsky, Glenda Roberts, Koichi Mori, Rose Hikiji, and Tamaki Watarai all helped me navigate the transnational terrain of my fieldwork, and Benjamin Junge, Daniel

Linger, Elisa Sasaki, Harald Fuess, Joshua Roth, Maxine Margolis, Nobuko Adachi, and Takeyuki Tsuda offered important insights at various stages of my work.

This book is dedicated to Diego Werneck Arguelhes, who was there for me at every step of this journey, from the introduction to the conclusion, and to my family, who provides me with so much in the way of both routes and roots.

Primary field site locations in Japan.

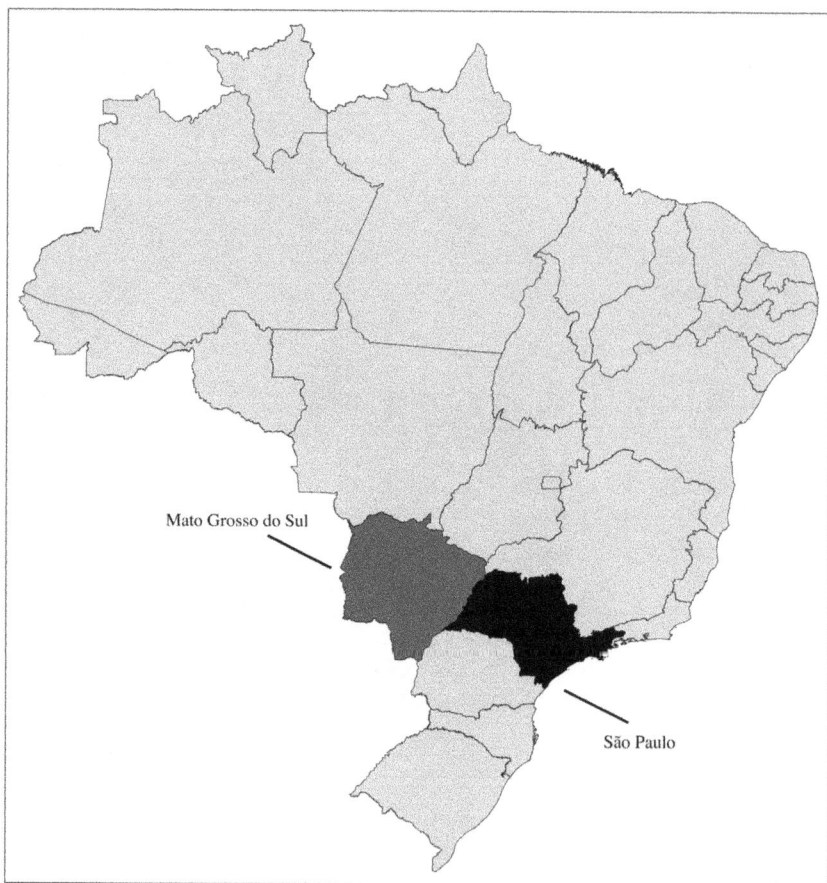

Primary field site locations in Brazil.

Introduction

Growing up in Quebec, in a small town a half an hour drive from Vermont, I crossed the US-Canadian border with my family as regularly as some people cross city or state limits. This was of course an easier thing for many people to do in the years before 9/11. My mother dipped into Vermont every week to fill up the car with cheap American gas, procure as many bricks of cheese as customs would allow us, and check her US post office box for the magazines she could not justify buying at Canadian subscription rates. Within minutes, kilometers morphed into miles, and French signs shifted to English, only to revert again as soon as we looped around and headed home.

Did my family's frequent border crossings mean we were "living transnationally"? Certainly, we bridged national and even linguistic and cultural boundaries on a regular basis. We contended with two different national legal frameworks—taking care not to bring too much Vermont cheese into Quebec territory, for example—as well as two different languages, currencies, and economic structures. We experienced the privilege of this kind of mobility because of the passports (in my case, both Canadian and American ones) and backgrounds we happened to have, and the particular geopolitical context and point in history in which we lived. This did not mean, however, that we consistently navigated affective relations, institutional realities such as immigration policy, school, or work, or even imagined or desired futures across national boundaries. In moving across physical borders, we did not encounter either significant barriers or breakthroughs in social mobility.

As I hope to demonstrate in this book, living transnationally is a particular way of experiencing the world, and one that is becoming more common as temporary labor migration continues to rise (Choo 2016) and people move and maintain ties across national boundaries at increasingly frequent and rapid rates (Castles & Davidson 2000; Glick Schiller et al. 1992; Ong 1999). At the same time, however, not all migrants are transnational; in fact, as Stephen Castles et al. (2014) point out, the majority of the world's migrants are not transnational. Living transnationally is about more than just physically crossing borders. It involves the social, institutional, and aspirational "scapes" (Appadurai 1996) that people—whether cosmopolitan elites or less flexible migrants—both regularly shape and navigate as a result of transnational movement.

While there exists a great wealth of macro-level data on international migration such as distribution of economic activity, amount of remittances, and gender differentials, less is known about what it means to live a transnational life day-to-day, outside of official surveys or statistics. How do migrants who live supposedly betwixt and between nation-states forge a sense of belonging for themselves in practice? What frictions occur in the process? These are the questions that led me to pursue a PhD in anthropology, as well as over two years of dissertation fieldwork, not in my own backyard of Quebec or Vermont but in various parts of Japan and Brazil. I have long been interested in the various borders that migrants cross, often multiple times throughout their lives, besides the legal ones: cultural borders, linguistic borders, class borders, generational borders, and so on. Building on theories of globalization, migration, and ethnicity and diaspora, I use the term "transnational living" as a means of articulating the ongoing processes through which transnational migrants and their families create and express multiple forms of belonging across these various boundaries.

Though I myself was not a child of transnational labor migrants, as a dual Canadian/American citizen growing up Anglophone but English/French bilingual in a politically and culturally divided region of rural Canada (particularly around the height of Quebec's last referendum for separation, in the mid-1990s), I was necessarily preoccupied with the contentious, shifting concepts of ethnic and national membership. The cultural and linguistic, as well as the class migrations of my childhood in Quebec sparked an interest in issues of ethnicity and belonging across a variety of national settings, which I would eventually focus on Japan and Brazil.

Furthermore, from a young age, I was aware that my father had been born in Germany, and that his mother—Jewish by both descent and Nazi standards—had escaped to the United States with him in 1938, when he was still just an infant. My grandmother's sister, meanwhile, escaped to Brazil, where together with another Jewish refugee, she had children and put down roots in Rio de Janeiro. Thus, I grew up cognizant of the fact that my father's side of the family had fled persecution based on ideas of race and ethnicity—because she was considered "mixed-race," my grandmother was not legally allowed to marry my grandfather in Germany, for instance—and that, though I had never met or communicated with them, I also had close Brazilian relatives as a result of my family's displacement. As a graduate student at Yale University, I was able to formally study Portuguese and track down and meet these family members for the first time in 2009.

Before I ever learned Portuguese, though, I was drawn to Japanese language and culture. In high school, I happened to have a Japanese friend who invited me to stay with her family in Japan for a few weeks over summer vacation. At seventeen, after finishing high school in Quebec, I moved to Fukui to live with that same friend's mother and attend public Japanese high school for eight months. Then, at Oberlin College in the United States, I majored in East Asian Studies, with a particular focus on Japanese language and literature. It was only during a college study abroad program—first the Japan-America Student Conference, and then a semester exchange at Kansai Gaidai University in Ōsaka, home to significant Buraku (historical outcaste) as well as ethnic Korean, Chinese, and Okinawan populations—that I became especially intrigued by the topics of ethnic minorities and foreign labor in Japan.

Japan, famous in the postwar period for its image as an enclosed and homogenous unit, has, since the 1980s, gradually opened its doors—or, rather, a series of side doors—to foreign labor. The Japanese government and private companies initially conceived of this as a temporary solution to labor shortages across a variety of sectors. However, many of these international migrants have since settled long term in Japan, raising families there while continuing to cultivate ties with places like China, the Philippines, and Brazil.

This book is an ethnographic account of one such population, which for the last several decades has remained among the most sizable ethnic minorities in Japan. As many people know, Brazil is home to the world's largest population of people of Japanese descent outside Japan. Less well known is the fact that Brazilians of Japanese descent, also referred to as Nikkei-Brazilians, are the largest population to migrate to Japan from outside of Asia and have, since the late 1980s, constituted the country's main source of nonnative labor. As early studies revealed (e.g., Linger 2001; Roth 2002; Tsuda 2003), despite identifying strongly with their Japanese heritage in Brazil, many Nikkei-Brazilians neither felt nor were considered Japanese when they first arrived in Japan. Instead, they tended to emphasize their Brazilian-ness, as well as their attachments to Brazil. Over the last three decades, however, even as they have continued to work primarily as brokered laborers on temporary contracts in Japan, an increasing number of Nikkei-Brazilian labor migrants and their families have grown to regard cities such as Minokamo and Toyohashi as their home—or one of several possible homes.

In the chapters that follow, I show how Nikkei-Brazilians now use language, dress, diet, work routines, leisure habits, migration patterns, and other elements of lifeways in intricate and shifting combinations to express a range of ethnic identities and national orientations. For Nikkei-Brazilians living transnationally between Japan and Brazil, the question is not one of simple assimilation versus ethnic segregation, or of perpetual in-betweenness. They are an important example of how Japan, despite its official stance as a homogenous and nonimmigrant receiving country "from above," is in fact "transnational from below" (Smith & Guarnizo 1998). As I demonstrate, over the years Nikkei-Brazilians have found multiple, shifting ways of being *both* Japanese and Brazilian, and *both* migrants (on the move) and immigrants (long-term settlers).

Like transnational populations elsewhere in the world—Mexicans in New York or Filipinas in Hong Kong, for example—Brazilians in Japan actively forge various forms of belonging across national boundaries. At the same time, they run into significant barriers in terms of both local and global mobility. These barriers in mobility prevent them from belonging quite so flexibly. The aim of this book is to reveal the structures through which transnational labor migrants become simultaneously emplaced and displaced, and through which they both express new forms of identification and run up against inflexibilities in belonging. In this way, it is a departure from the earlier accounts that describe transnational Nikkei-Brazilian labor migrants as "doubly homeless" or somehow lost between national, cultural, and linguistic settings. Rather, I argue, over the past nearly three decades, Nikkei-Brazilian labor migrants and their families have achieved multiple forms of belonging even as they have faced significant barriers to mobility and incorporation—both within and across national borders.

ETHNIC MINORITIES AND "NEWCOMERS" IN JAPAN

As Dru Gladney (1998) points out, ethnic minorities everywhere tend to be defined in terms of an accepted majority, which itself is constructed and "invented" over time (Hobsbawm & Ranger 1983). In Japan, the notion of a single and homogenous "Japanese" majority has been widely problematized in recent decades by Japanese and non-Japanese scholars alike (e.g., Befu 2001; Graburn et al. 2008; Low 2012; Morris-Suzuki 1998; Murphy-Shigematsu 1993; Nakamura 2006 & 2013; Oguma 1995 & 1998). At the same time, and especially since the original publication of Michael Weiner's *Japan's Minorities: The Illusion of Homogeneity* (1997), studies of ethnic minorities in Japan have gained increasing traction internationally. As these studies show, there are various ethnic minorities in Japan, but their statuses are incommensurate. Instead, there are multiple peripheral statuses, including the Indigenous Ainu, the historical outcastes known as Burakumin, the Zainichi, or descendants of former colonial subjects (primarily from what is now South and North Korea), and the more recently incorporated foreign residents (mostly from relatively nearby countries such as China and the Philippines). Some of these minority groups—such as the Ainu and Burakumin—are granted Japanese citizenship from birth; others—including both the "oldcomer" Zainichi and "newcomer" foreign residents[1]—are not. Some of them, for example, the Ainu, might be considered "involuntary minorities" (Ogbu & Simons 1998), "national minorities" (Kymlicka 1995), or "internal Others" (Ohnuki-Tierney 1998) due to a history of colonization and forced assimilation, while those who were incorporated into Japanese society largely of their own volition—for example, many of the more recent foreign arrivals—can be seen as "voluntary minorities" (Ogbu & Simons 1998) or "external Others" (Ohnuki-Tierney 1998), though, as Edward Fischer (2014) so persuasively demonstrates, what we think of as agency is itself often limited by the opportunity structures that are available to us.

Noncitizen residents of Japan occupy different positions vis-à-vis the state depending on their visa status, which in turn depends on their origins, length, and purpose of stay in Japan, and the skills they are presumed to bring with them. At the end of 2016, of the nearly 2.5 million registered foreign residents living in Japan, the largest visa-holding groups consisted of: (1) permanent residents, the majority of whom are from China, the Philippines, and Brazil; (2) "special permanent residents," made up of Zainichi, or former colonial subjects and their descendants, primarily from what is now South and North Korea; (3) international students, the bulk of whom are from China and Vietnam; and (4) technical trainees, also primarily from China and Vietnam.[2]

These legal groupings reveal little about the state's actual approach to immigration, however. Officially, Japan is not a "nation of immigration." In the face of a rapidly aging population, declining birth rate, and severe labor shortages across many sectors, the government continues to push the idea that more women in the workforce and/or increasingly sophisticated robots represent the answer to this conundrum. In practice, though, with the exception of "special permanent residents" (or Zainichi "oldcomers"), many of the "newcomer" foreign residents in Japan—from those who arrived several decades ago and are now permanent residents to the more recently arrived students and technical trainees—serve as an unofficial side-door for foreign labor.

As can be seen from figure I.1, in 2016 the five largest groups of foreign residents in Japan were nationals of China, South and North Korea
(grouped together under "Korea"), the Philippines, Vietnam, and Brazil.
Koreans constituted the largest group of foreign residents in Japan from the
end of the Second World War until the year 2007, when the number of Chinese surpassed Koreans for the first time since Japan's annexation of Korea
in 1910. While they remain the second-largest group of foreign residents in
Japan today, the number of Korean citizens has steadily declined in recent
decades, due in part to naturalization (Asakawa 2003; Graburn et al. 2008;
Htun 2012; Motani 2002). The majority of Koreans in Japan are "special
permanent residents" whose families have been in Japan for generations. In
2016, for example, of the 485,557 registered Koreans in Japan, 335,163 (or
approximately 70 percent) held the status of "special permanent resident"
(Ministry of Justice, Japan). They are, for the most part, an "oldcomer"—as
well as involuntary (Ogbu & Simons 1998)—minority who, as a result of
Japan's colonial past, possess special legal status and are incorporated linguistically and culturally into mainstream Japanese society. However, they
do not serve as a significant source of foreign side-door labor for Japan.
To understand who does, I now turn to the other major groups of foreign
residents in Japan: the Chinese, Filipino, Vietnamese, and Brazilian "newcomers" (figure I.1).

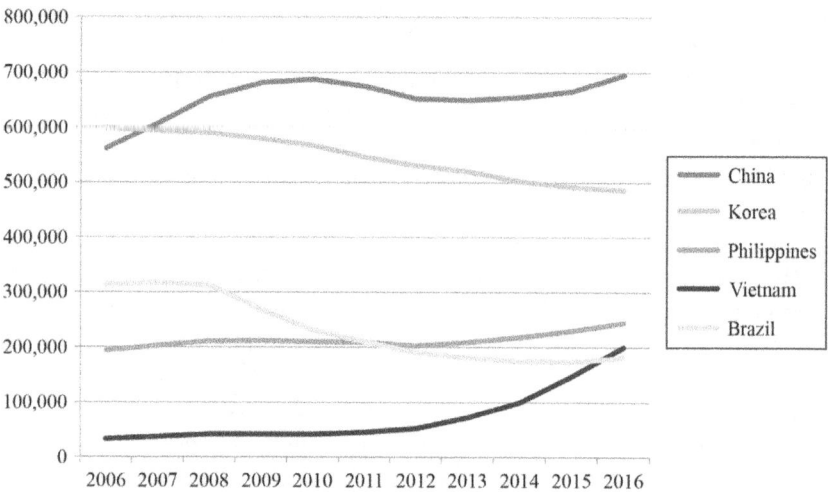

Figure I.1   Largest Groups of Foreign Residents in Japan by Nationality, 2006–2016.
Source: "Foreign Resident Statistics [*Zairyū Gaikokujin Tōkei*]," compiled by the author.
Yearly statistics accessible online at Japan's Ministry of Justice's website: http://www.moj.
go.jp/housei/toukei/toukei_ichiran_touroku.html.

China

Like other newcomer minorities in Japan, most Chinese nationals arrived after the mid-1980s (Liu-Farrer 2013). While there were 74,924 Chinese in 1985, by 2005 this number had leaped to 519,591, and in 2016 it stood at 695,522—by far the largest group of foreign residents in Japan (Ministry of Justice, Japan). The Chinese in Japan constitute a very diverse group, including both established newcomers—long-term and permanent residents who first began arriving in the 1980s—and Chinese nationals who have arrived more recently in Japan as students, trainees, skilled and highly skilled workers, and marriage and family migrants (Liu-Farrer 2013). As Gracia Liu-Farrer (2013) notes, although Chinese are increasingly choosing to settle down in Japan, many maintain significant social and economic ties with China, and can be characterized as a transnationally oriented community. Chinese university students (who constitute between 60 and 70 percent of all international students in Japan) in particular tend to remain in Japan long after their studies are completed and, thanks to their social and cultural capital, knowledge of the Japanese language, university degrees, and transnational business ties with China, fill an important occupational niche that has emerged as a result of China's growing importance as a market to Japanese companies (Chiavacci 2016).

The Philippines

Like the Chinese in Japan, citizens of the Philippines, too, have seen their numbers jump significantly since the 1980s—from 12,261 in 1985 to 187,261 in 2005. By 2016 there were 243,662 Filipino nationals in Japan, nearly three-quarters of whom were women (Ministry of Justice, Japan). As Lieba Faier (2009) explains, in this highly feminized migration flow, Filipina women tend to enter Japan on "entertainer visas" and are technically hired to work as cultural dancers and singers. In reality, however, the majority of them are employed as "hostesses" in Filipina bars and clubs throughout the country in what is known as the *mizu shōbai*, or sex industry. While a number of them go on to marry Japanese men and settle in Japan, many continue to cultivate transnational ties with the Philippines. Like Filipina migrants in Hong Kong (Constable 1999), Filipinas in Japan also construct a dynamic and shifting sense of home out of both sending and receiving countries.

Vietnam

In contrast to the more established Chinese and Filipino—and as we will soon see, Brazilian—transnational communities who have been in Japan since the 1980s, Vietnamese nationals have only very recently begun arriving in Japan in significant numbers. In 2006, there were just 32,485 Vietnamese nationals registered in Japan, many of whom originally entered Japan as refugees or were descendants of refugees from the 1970s; by 2016, that number had increased sixfold, and stood at 199,990 (Ministry of Justice, Japan). For the most part, Vietnamese enter Japan as technical trainees or students. As has been well documented, technical trainees and students (who can work part-time) are an increasingly popular, though not officially acknowledged, source of cheap foreign labor in Japan (Chiavacci 2016; Haines et al. 2007; Liu-Farrer 2013). Besides the Vietnamese, significant numbers of Chinese, Nepalese, Cambodian, Indonesian, Korean, and Filipino nationals also enter Japan as students and technical trainees. While from the state's point of view they too are meant to be only a temporary presence in Japan, over time these "new newcomers" may well establish longer-term, transnational ties bridging Japan and their various "home" countries.

Brazil

Japan's revised Immigration Control and Refugee Recognition Act (ICRRA) came into effect in 1990 in response to the persistent demand for laborers in certain sectors of the economy as well as the state's desire to curtail illegal workers. The first feature of the law was that it stiffened the penalties for both the employers of illegal and undocumented workers and the workers themselves. The second characteristic of the ICRRA was that it made people of Japanese descent (up to the third generation and provided they could prove they had at least one Japanese grandparent) and their spouses eligible for long-term residence and employment in what is deemed unskilled labor in Japan (Kondo 2005). Since 1990, people of Japanese descent can apply for a renewable visa valid for six months to three years with no stipulation on the type of activities they may carry out while in Japan. This so-called Nikkei provision in the newly revised ICRRA thus created a legitimate avenue for the Japanese government to hire unskilled foreign workers, albeit only those of Japanese descent.

The result of the reforms in immigration policy was a staggering increase in the number of Nikkei-Latin Americans, particularly Brazilians, registered as residents in Japan. Because Brazil is home to the world's largest population of people of Japanese descent outside Japan, Brazilians account for the majority of Nikkei workers in Japan. In the early to mid-1990s, a combination of hyperinflation, low salaries, and general lack of opportunities in Brazil led many Nikkei-Brazilians and their families to take advantage of Japan's revised immigration policy. Even for those Nikkei-Brazilians who previously held white-collar jobs, then, working in unskilled labor in Japan allowed them to earn significantly higher wages than what they were used to in Brazil.

In 1985, there were only 1,955 Brazilian residents in Japan, but by 2007, at their peak, there were 316,967, representing a significant majority of Japan's nearly 400,000 Latin American residents registered that year (Chiavacci 2016; Ministry of Justice, Japan). This number started to decline in 2008–2009, following the global financial crisis, and continued to do so in the years immediately following the Fukushima disaster of 2011 when, concomitantly, Brazil's economy and overall political situation looked increasingly bright. In recent years, however, the Brazilian population in Japan has stabilized at around 180,000, and in 2016, nearly two-thirds were registered as permanent residents, compared with less than a third in 2006, just ten years earlier (Ministry of Justice, Japan).

Today, as we conclude the third decade of labor migration from Brazil to Japan, or the so-called contemporary *dekasegi*[3] movement, the horizon of possibilities for Nikkei workers and their families includes permanent settlement and naturalization in Japan, circular (or repeat) migration between the two countries, and temporary or potentially final return to Brazil. The landscape of *dekasegi* life in Japan has also broadened to include significant variations in experience depending on the time Brazilians arrived or were born in Japan. Since the beginning of their migration to Japan, the population of Brazilians has included relatively balanced numbers of women and men, many of them accompanied by their young children (Roth 2002; Toma 2000; Yamanaka 2003). While youth under twenty have, since the early 1990s, represented from a fifth to a quarter of the overall population of Brazilians in Japan, they have until recently remained largely underrepresented in literature on the subject. Many of the Brazilians in their twenties and thirties in Japan today in fact spent a significant amount of their childhood and adolescence there. Thus, their identities and experiences differ not only from those Brazilians who arrived more recently in Japan but also from their parents or other family members who migrated to Japan as adults.

What is more, according to data from the mid-1990s, when Daniel Linger, Joshua Roth, and Takeyuki Tsuda conducted their pioneering studies on the topic, close to half of Nikkei-Brazilians were marrying outside their ethnic group. Most Nikkei-Brazilians were second-generation *nisei* (30.9 percent) or third-generation *sansei* (41 percent), with an increasing population of *yonsei* (fourth generation), roughly 62 percent of whom were of mixed descent. Because Nikkei-Brazilians up to the third generation could legally work in Japan with their spouses (who may or may not themselves be Nikkei), an additional 4 to 8 percent of the Brazilians in Japan were not of Japanese descent whatsoever (Tsuda 2003). Thus, a significant number of Brazilians in Japan appeared either "mixed" or non-Japanese, though this aspect of ethnicity has not, with the exception of Green (2010), been highlighted as a salient marker of identity in previous studies of Brazilians in Japan. In Paul Green's work, having found the majority of his interlocutors to be of mixed descent, many of whom did not readily identify with Nikkei heritage, he suggests, therefore, that it is more appropriate to refer to people as Brazilian rather than specifically or exclusively Nikkei-Brazilian.

In my own research, women and girls made up about half of the Brazilians I worked with, and second-generation *nisei* and fourth-generation *yonsei* each accounted for approximately a fifth of key interlocutors, while third-generation *sansei* accounted for over half. Just under a tenth of my interlocutors were non-Nikkei and, of the rest, more than half were of mixed descent. Following Green's example, then, except where necessary, I too try to refer to my interlocutors simply as Brazilian, regardless of the degree to which they identified as Nikkei, Japanese, Brazilian, *mestiço* (mixed), and so on. In sum, my target subject group came to include all Brazilian nationals involved in or raised within the framework of transnational labor migration between Japan and Brazil over the last three decades.

BACKGROUND:
FROM JAPAN TO BRAZIL AND BACK

In order to understand the emergence of Brazilian migration to Japan beginning in the late twentieth century, it is important to return first to an earlier period of history. Between 1908 and 1940, some 140,000 Japanese emigrated to Brazil alone, and another 60,000 in the early postwar period (Roth 2002). Most were second-or third-born sons and daughters who would not inherit their family land or business in Japan. After the Meiji Restoration of 1868, which officially opened Japan to the outside world and ushered in a period of rapid modernization, population growth, and social dislocation, especially of rural Japanese, private emigration companies organized groups of people to be sent to Canada, the United States, and Hawaii (Daniels 1988). In the early 1900s, however, American and Canadian immigration policy grew increasingly exclusionary toward Asians (Fiset & Nomura 2005) and the flow of Japanese migration shifted to South American destinations, particularly Peru and Brazil. During this period, emigrants were encouraged by the Japanese government, together with private companies, to move to South America, Manchuria, and the Philippines in what can be classified as "state policy emigration," aimed at easing population pressures and social unrest at home, especially among the working classes of southwest Japan (Endoh 2009; Lesser 2013). In the case of Brazil, rates of Japanese emigration remained strong well into the 1960s, creating a large population of ethnic Japanese in the already diverse South American nation.

Most of the early Japanese emigrants to Brazil dreamed of striking it rich and returning home, an idea that parallels the goals of many Brazilians moving to Japan today. Despite their initial intent, however, the majority ended up staying in Brazil. Many of the first-generation immigrants in Brazil continued to teach their children and grandchildren Japanese, though second-generation (*nisei*) and especially third-generation (*sansei*) Nikkei-Brazilians are now often far more fluent in Portuguese than Japanese (if they speak Japanese at all). The fact that Nikkei-Brazilians originally left Japan primarily for economic reasons does not signify that they maintained a culturally or linguistically "Japanese" lifestyle in Brazil, regardless of how much they did or did not identify with their Japanese heritage. Still, because of shared origins and experiences of discrimination and displacement, these first-generation Japanese emigrants and their descendants in Brazil belong to what scholars broadly term a "diaspora," or a dispersed ethnic population (Adachi 2006; Cohen 1997; Safran 1991).

At the same time as the influx of Brazilian labor in Japan beginning in the 1990s aided in filling empty positions in Japanese industry, the revised immigration policy also affected the discourse and treatment of migrants in Japan. By giving preference to Nikkei migrants over other foreigners, the Japanese government proved that ethnicity, not skill or experience, was the determining factor in deeming which foreign laborers were desirable and hence eligible to enter and work in Japan. Still, despite the fact that they emerged as the only legally accepted group of foreign unskilled workers in Japan, Nikkei workers, as well as illegal migrants, occupied—and continue to occupy—a subordinate position in the domestic labor market (Chiavacci 2016; Roth 2002 & 2007; Sellek 1997).

From the beginning, Nikkei workers were marginalized within Japan's segmented labor market primarily as a result of the system of *haken gaisha*, or employment brokerage firms, whereby third-party companies acted—and still act—as a go-between linking Japanese factories and most foreign, unskilled workers (see, for example, Tanno 1999; Urano 2004). *Haken gaisha*, as they are known in Japanese, or *empreiteiras*, as they are known in Portuguese, generally take a percentage of temporarily contracted workers' earnings in exchange for placing them in factories, organizing and translating their contracts, and assisting them with, among other things, housing, work visas, and other bureaucratic affairs. As Joshua Roth (2002) found, they often allowed for a significant amount of discrimination and exploitation, and determined the limited nature of interactions encouraged between Japanese and Brazilian workers. Thus, fragile working conditions, as well as gaps in the housing, education, and social spheres resulting from the segmented labor market and *haken gaisha* system, rendered early Brazilian migrants to Japan relatively isolated from broader Japanese society. Because as a group they experienced dispersal and discrimination much like their ancestors did before them, and have therefore been displaced more than once, scholars such as Wolfram Manzenreiter (2017) refer to Brazilians in Japan as a "squared diaspora." Others, such as Angelo Ishi (2011), demonstrate how diasporic consciousness is formed on the ground among Brazilians in Japan via shared media, among other means.

METHODOLOGY

During more than two years of multisited ethnographic research spanning the years 2009–2013, I conducted participant-observation and interviews in Japanese and Portuguese among more than 100 Brazilian migrants and their children (ages eleven to eighty-five) in both Japan and Brazil. Based on this combination of participation/engagement, observations, and interviewing across a single transnational landscape, I drew profiles for comparison among the following: (1) Brazilians who migrated to Japan as adults and ended up living there long term, raising families and putting down roots in the process; (2) the children of Brazilian migrants who spent part or all of their lives in Japan, and located themselves somewhere between their parents' culture and that of their host society (also referred to as the 1.5 generation or "third culture" kids);[4] and (3) Brazilians who returned to Brazil either through a process of temporary sojourn in Japan or circular migration between the two countries.

Instead of settling into a single, "bounded" community, I aimed to "follow the people" (Marcus 1995), whether from one city to another in Japan, from Japan to Brazil, or from capital to countryside in Brazil. In Japan, I based myself in Okazaki City, Aichi Prefecture, where in 2011 Brazilians made up about 1 percent of the city's overall population and constituted its largest group of registered foreigners. I also spent two days of every week in Minokamo, Gifu, and one day a week in Toyohashi, Aichi, as well as making regular trips for events and interviews in other small cities in Aichi, Gifu, and Shizuoka. I chose to conduct fieldwork in this part of central Japan because of the large numbers of Brazilians living there,[5] and because of the contacts I made in the region early on in my research. In an attempt to be involved with my interlocutors on an ongoing or at least frequent basis, and to further contextualize my observations and interviews, I was a participant-observer in a Brazilian-run employment brokerage firm, as well as Brazilian schools and churches in Aichi and Gifu.

In Brazil, most people of Japanese descent are from the states of São Paulo, Paraná, and Mato Grosso do Sul (Sasaki 2009: 110), but these populations are far less concentrated than they are in the labor migration hubs of Japan. For example, my interlocutors—almost all of whom were from the three states mentioned earlier, with the greatest majority born in São Paulo State—did not necessarily live in the same neighborhoods or attend the same schools or churches in Brazil as they often did upon migrating to Japan. Thus, to "follow the people," I made regular—and often repeat—visits to the interior[6] of the states of São Paulo and Mato Grosso do Sul, where I stayed in the homes of labor migrants returned from Japan. In order to gain access to these individuals, I depended primarily on previously established connections, following up either with people I had met during fieldwork in Japan and who had since returned to Brazil, or snowballing my sample to extend to their family members and friends there. Finally, in order to further contextualize these interviews and the experience of return to Brazil, I attended regular workshops and events in São Paulo City, including at the Center of Information and Support to Overseas Workers (abbreviated in Portuguese as CIATE), the Nikkei Group's Tadaima ("Welcome Home") Project, and the Institute of Educational and Cultural Solidarity's Kaeru ("Return") Project.

SITUATING THE FIELD/FIELDWORKER

Intensified globalization, both as a condition of contemporary life and an object of social science theorizing, has reshaped the way anthropologists approach their field sites. Rather than focus on what might once have been imagined as bounded communities, many of us aim to construct our sites according to the interconnected fluxes and flows of globalization. My own fieldwork was multisited not only in terms of moving across national borders but also across sites within both Japan and Brazil. Though worlds apart from each other, in many ways the social and cultural landscapes of Aichi and São Paulo blurred throughout my fieldwork. The same mixed vocabulary (e.g., "*é sugoi, não é?*" or "It's great, isn't it?") of Japanese (underlined in this example) and Portuguese (not underlined) characterized my interviews in both places, and sometimes I found myself waking up in the morning unsure of where I actually was: on an island in East Asia or somewhere south of the planet's equator. Perhaps technology contributed in part to this sensation. After all, I was able to keep abreast of my interlocutors' lives in Japan as much as I was in Brazil through a daily scan of social media. I could also fly from Japan to Brazil in a matter of twenty-four hours, instead of the weeks it once took to complete this route by ship. At the same time, though, I do not wish to overemphasize the interconnectedness of this experience. Like my interlocutors who ran into points of contention and friction moving between Japan and Brazil, I too went through a series of difficult transitions, struggling at times to navigate the institutions, lifestyles, social relationships, and languages of two distant national settings.

Having found that previous studies of Brazilians in Japan tended to focus more on men, I aimed to include a greater number of women's voices in my work. Of my key interlocutors, roughly two-thirds were women. This is not to say, however, that I always or easily gained the trust of women in the field. The fact that I was, at the time I carried out the bulk of my fieldwork, an unmarried, childless woman in her late twenties living alone in Japan and Brazil led some interlocutors, at least initially, to mistrust my intentions and objectives. My position as an unattached, female researcher did not always fit nicely into the more widely accepted social roles of mother, wife, daughter, or labor migrant. Even to children, this could be perplexing. On the bus to a Brazilian school in Aichi one day, a seven-year-old boy cross-examined me: "Are you married? Do you have children?" Since my answers to this usual string of questions were negative, he finally asked, frustrated at not being able to figure out how I fit into the larger social world around him, "Well, do you have any aunts and uncles at least?"

As is often the case, it took time and perseverance to gain people's trust. It also took a lot of false starts, and hiccups along the way. Though I already had some Brazilian friends in Tōkyō, having lived and worked there for several years after college, I only began studying Portuguese formally in my first semester of graduate school, and I did not start my PhD research with any Brazilian acquaintances in Aichi or Gifu. I first met Brazilians working in this part of Japan by enrolling in a language school in Aichi during a summer of preliminary dissertation fieldwork in 2009, and by attending local events and organizations that catered to Brazilians and other foreign residents. Since I did not qualify for the government-subsidized evening Japanese classes targeting Nikkei workers at the language school I attended, I would occasionally hang out in the school parking lot in the dark, waiting to see if I heard Portuguese speakers on their way out of class before approaching them to talk. Doing so without coming across as creepy—and without putting myself in too vulnerable a position—was a challenge. Also, at this early stage of research, in 2009, my Portuguese was decent but by no means as fluent as it later became. My initial parking lot approach was nerve-wracking and awkward, but with time, it worked. I befriended a number of Brazilians who worked in local factories and fast-food restaurants, and from there I expanded my growing network of acquaintances.

Throughout fieldwork in both Japan and Brazil, being perceived as white, or *não descendente* (not of Japanese descent), I was quite obviously in the position of ethnic outsider among most of my interlocutors. Unlike Nikkei-Brazilians, I was not necessarily marked as other in Brazil based on my ethnic appearance alone (though of course I was in Japan). One of my Nikkei interlocutors articulated this difference in the following way: "Asians and Blacks are always singled out as different in Brazil. Not like you, you can say you're French, Italian, American. But not me, even though I don't walk like a Japanese, in Brazil no one will call us Brazilian, they'll always call us Japanese."

Because most Brazilians in Japan are, as a result of Japan's ethnicity-based immigration loophole, of at least partial Japanese descent, the fact that I was not occasionally led interlocutors to suspect my legal status and even my legitimacy as a researcher there. "If you're not even *hāfu* (half Japanese), then how are you here?" I was often asked. In other words, how could I (not to mention *why* would I), an unmarried, non-Nikkei woman (and therefore not eligible for a special work visa), possibly be in Japan, immersed in the world of Nikkei labor migrants?

The fact that I did not have to work an hourly wage in Japan also contributed to unequal and occasionally uncomfortable dynamics in day-to-day interactions. Hailing from a wealthy American university and funded throughout my research by generous Japanese and US government grants, I was often perceived as a highly educated "First Worlder" who did not have to *ralar* (work, struggle) to get by. When meeting me for the first time, interlocutors invariably asked how I made a living, or how I put food on the table. "You must be rich" and "How fancy!" they would say, even after I explained my student stipend. Whatever the truth about my income, the important difference was that I *chose* to be in Japan in order to live among Brazilian labor migrants and their families, while most of my interlocutors did so in the quest for a better life/lifestyle.[7]

Over time, though, I developed significant connections with key interlocutors, and perceptions of my outsider status did not necessarily preclude meaningful rapport. The fact that I could speak comfortably in Japanese and Portuguese (and eventually an interior of São Paulo accent, where so many Nikkei-Brazilian migrants are from), or a mix of the two, and that I was versed in both cultures, meant that I was not just a *gringa* or *gaijin* (foreigner); to a degree, and for a time, I was also a peer.[8]

More than nationality, ethnicity, class, gender, or legal status, in fact, religion appeared to be the greatest difference separating me from many of my interlocutors. As it turned out, and as will be discussed in detail in chapters 5 and 6, a growing number of Brazilians—and Brazilians in Japan, including roughly a quarter of my interlocutors—are socially conservative Evangelical Christians. Having been raised and educated in largely secular environments, I found myself at odds with some interlocutors' beliefs, especially when it came to homosexuality, non-Christians, and expected gender roles. Observing Evangelical church services almost always led to requests to participate more directly, either by converting or donating money. "Have you accepted Jesus into your heart yet?" was a standard question I confronted throughout fieldwork. The way I responded to this sort of question varied depending on whom I was speaking with, and how long I had been doing fieldwork. At first, and especially with people I did not know well, I tried to hedge. "I do not have any particular religion" or "I am still figuring it out" were standard answers I gave. This was often met with disappointment or skepticism, however. "Your name is Sarah, that's such a good Christian name," I was told on several different occasions. I could almost hear my father, who had intentionally given me a Hebrew first name to honor our family background, rolling in his grave. Although Sarah often indexes a Jewish name in Brazil, and especially in São Paulo where there is a large Jewish population, among many Evangelical Christians from Brazil it is considered a traditional, Biblical, and hence Christian name. After a while, although I was not raised religious by any means, I realized that starting the conversation off by saying I was Jewish was simply easier—and more acceptable to those who were devout—than fumbling through explanations of personal agnosticism. Claiming I was Jewish was true enough given my heritage, and because most of my interlocutors were not familiar with Judaism, they respected what seemed to them at least vaguely sacred and traditional. Nevertheless, though I always tried to understand and respect their faith, as long as I did not convert or admit to the same beliefs and values, I was necessarily something of a moral/spiritual outsider among the more religious individuals I worked with.

STRUCTURE AND CONTENT OF THE BOOK

Now that Brazilian labor migrants and their families have spent much of their adult lives in Japan or else grown up partly or entirely outside of Brazil, how have they come to express belonging across national borders? In answering this question, I demonstrate the unique constellations of constraints and possibilities that structures such as family, work, education, and religion place on individual lives as Brazilians navigate belonging in the context of transnational labor migration between Japan and Brazil. Throughout this book, I pay close attention to the experiences of gender, generation, and class, such that the question of how belonging operates is understood not only in terms of ethnic or national orientation but also in terms of these other salient—and until recently in *dekasegi* studies, relatively under-examined—dimensions. In this way, my work looks beyond ethnic and national identity concerns (Brubaker & Cooper 2000) to the unique structural, social, and subjective forces shaping people's lives,[9] as well as the particular constraints and possibilities brought about by differences in gender, generation, and class.

Chapters 1, 3, and 5 follow in detail the stories of three different families in their movement across borders and years. Chapter 1 examines the Silvas, a family residing partly in Japan and partly in Brazil; chapter 3 follows the Matsudas, a family settled in Japan to the point of naturalizing as Japanese citizens; and chapter 5 traces the Pereira family's return to Brazil (throughout this book, I use pseudonyms for all the names of people I worked with in order to protect their privacy). In the epilogue, I provide an update on these three families based on fieldwork I carried out in the summer of 2018. Chapters 2, 4, and 6, for their part, are organized according to three major institutional settings where the process of transnational living actually takes place: factories, schools, and churches, respectively. Together, these interlaced chapters serve, on the one hand, to document different possibilities along the horizon of back-and-forth migration, settlement, and return, as well as to complicate the very binary of migrant versus immigrant. Furthermore, by focusing on family, education, and religion, I demonstrate the various structures, besides work, through which transnational labor migrants and their children find both channels and barriers to belonging.

NOTES

1. In Japan, any foreign residents who have arrived since about the 1980s are referred to as "newcomers." Those who trace their arrival to earlier periods are known as "oldcomers."

2. Source: "Foreign Resident Statistics" [*Zairyū Gaikokujin Tōkei*], Japan's Ministry of Justice: http://www.moj.go.jp/housei/toukei/toukei_ichiran_touroku.html.

3. The original Japanese term *dekasegi* referred to people working away from home, usually as temporary or seasonal laborers. In recent decades, it has come to refer to anyone of Japanese descent—usually from South America—who moved to Japan to work in unskilled labor.

4. Sociologist Rubén Rumbaut (2012) is generally credited with coining the term "one-and-a-half" or "1.5" generation, distinguishing those who migrate as children from both the "first" generation who migrate as adults and the "second" generation who are born in a new host society to foreign parents. The term "third culture kids" (or TCKs), for its part, is attributed to the anthropologist/sociologist Ruth Useem (1973) in the context of her research among the children of mostly white, American expatriates in India. In their influential work on TCKs, Pollock & Van Reken expanded on Useem's original formulation to define a TCK as "a person who has spent a significant part of his or her developmental years outside the parents' culture. The TCK builds relationships to all of the cultures, while not having full ownership in any" (2009 [2001]: 13).

5. In 2011, when I conducted the longest sustained stretch of fieldwork in Japan, the five prefectures with the highest population of Brazilian residents out of a total population of 210,032 were, in order: (1) Aichi (54,458); (2) Shizuoka (33,547); (3) Mie (14,986); (4) Gifu (13,327); and (5) Gunma (12,909). In 2016, these were still the prefectures with the largest numbers of Brazilians in Japan. Data is drawn from Japan's Ministry of Justice website.

6. In Brazil, state capitals are considered distinct from the rest of Brazilian states. This "rest" of a state is usually referred to as the "interior." In states like São Paulo, where the Brazil portion of my research mostly took place and where many

Nikkei-Brazilians are from, the interior includes both large cities and rural areas. Even so, the word "interior" often implies the idea of rurality, small-town life, and/or a lack of cosmopolitanism.

7. Tim Cresswell (2010) makes an important differentiation between being compelled to move versus choosing to move to a different country. However, being compelled to move is not always only a matter of searching for food, shelter, and safety. As anthropologist Michael Jackson (2013) points out, mobility must "be understood existentially as well as phylogenetically. It is a metaphor for freedom as much as a means for accessing life-giving resources" (229).

8. In other words, through cultural and linguistic know-how, I achieved "partial insider status" (Tsuda 2003: 14) among *dekasegi* and their families, even though I did not belong ethnically or nationally to either Japan or Brazil.

9. This approach draws on Kelly (1993), who examines the transformations that have standardized and differentiated modern Japanese society through an analytical triptych that includes the ideological process, institutional patternings, and everyday routines of individuals.

Chapter 1

The Silvas

Life between Japan and Brazil

Around the world, people are often conceived of as either migrants (temporary) or immigrants (permanent), as though their alliances and affiliations must fall into one localized space or another. Most of my interlocutors, however, fell somewhere in between, or "both-and-and," as Michael Kearney (1995) suggests. They may not have imagined staying in Japan forever, but at the same time, many spent decades of their lives there, all the while keeping ties to family members and friends in Brazil. Still others returned to Brazil but maintained important ties to Japan.

In the same way that transnational Brazilian labor migrants are in and of various places/spaces—in other words, they are both migrants and immigrants at the same time—so too do they express multiple and shifting forms of belonging. These forms of belonging cannot be understood without examining the contexts of family, work, education, and religion in which they are embedded, and the ways in which individuals are both constrained and fulfilled by their position as transnational labor migrants. In order to explore the ways in which belonging is shaped by these settings, I use chapters 1, 3, and 5 to trace the lives of three families: one residing partly in Japan and partly in Brazil (with back-and-forth movement between the two countries over the years), another residing long term in Japan to the point of naturalizing to Japanese citizenship, and yet another that returned—more or less indefinitely—to Brazil. While these three families came to represent the different general patterns of migration that I observed—back-and-forth, settled, and returned—their trajectories constantly changed tracks, and overlapped with other possible paths. In all three chapters, we see how people of different genders, generations, and class backgrounds experienced the limitations and opportunities of migration/immigration, and how the local contexts of family, work, education, and religion shaped what it meant to be Japanese, Brazilian, or both-and-and. It is my hope that, by providing something akin to the

19

emotionally attuned "descriptive detail, closely observed events, [and] complete life stories" (83) that anthropologist Michael Jackson (2013) calls for, my work might do at least some justice to the complex mix of motives that influence individual decisions, as well as the "double bind that every migrant experiences in some measure, and which speaks to us all, caught as we inevitably are between the circumstances that shape our lives and the lives we project and hope to create for ourselves" (ibid: 213).

THE SILVA FAMILY

This chapter traces the lives of Angela Silva and her three *sansei* (third-generation Nikkei) children—Carlos, Marcelo, and Jessica—who first went to Japan together in the early 1990s. The Silva family, like many early labor migrants to Japan, did not originally intend to spend more than a few years away from Brazil. Over two decades later, however, Angela and two of her adult children still lived in Japan, while her eldest son had since returned to Brazil. The transnational ties of this single family demonstrate the dynamic and ongoing nature of migration between Japan and Brazil, as well as the ways in which *dekasegi*—especially those who grew up or spent extensive amounts of time in both places—variably situated themselves *in* and *of* two cultures (figure 1.1).

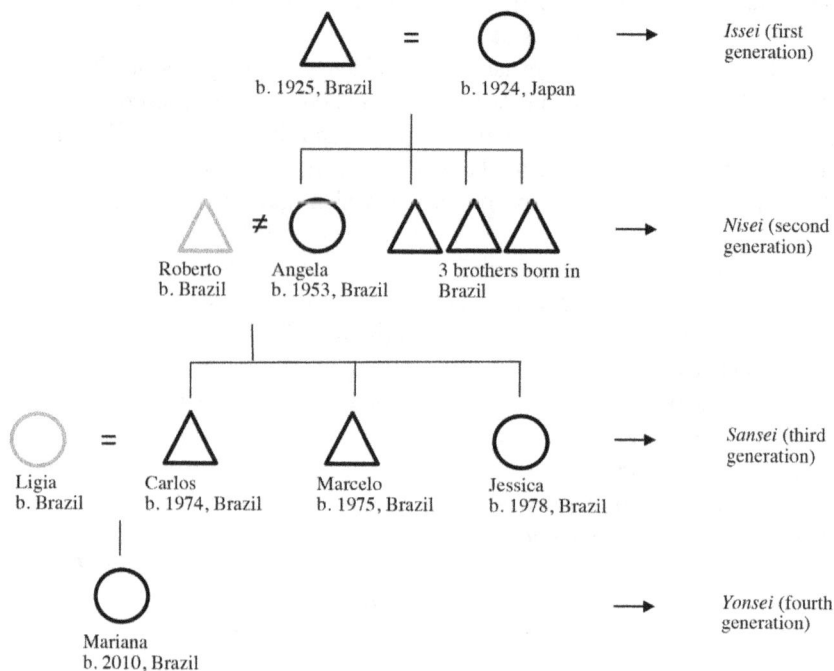

Figure 1.1   The Silva family tree.

For the ease of understanding, figure 1.1 provides an overview of four generations of the Silva family. Following the norms of classical anthropological kinship charts, I have marked females as circles and males as triangles. Angela's maternal and paternal grandparents, as well as her mother (born in 1924), emigrated from Japan to Brazil in the early twentieth century; her father was born in 1925 to Japanese immigrants already in Brazil. Angela, her three children, and her granddaughter were all born in Brazil post-Second World War. To illustrate the mixed ethnic backgrounds of children with only one Nikkei parent (as was the case of Carlos, Marcelo, and Jessica, as well as Carlos's daughter Mariana, all considered *mestiço*, or "mixed," in Brazil), individuals *not* of Japanese descent are marked in lighter grey.

JESSICA

Bridge between Cultures

I first met Jessica in Aichi in 2010, when she was thirty-two. Twenty years earlier, at the age of twelve, she had gone to Japan with her parents and two older brothers and had lived there ever since. Unlike the rest of her family, however, Jessica never went to work in a factory. Although she had already passed the fifth grade in Brazil, she was placed into a fourth grade class in Japan in order to make up for the fact that she did not speak Japanese. At the time, in 1991, Portuguese-language schools in Japan were not yet as available an option as they later became, and Brazilian children attending Japanese school often relied on their teachers' benevolence and extra help in order to adjust to the unfamiliar language and curriculum.

Embarrassed at being older and more physically developed than the other girls around her, Jessica refused to change in front of them during gym class. *Kokugo* (Japanese class, usually for native speakers) was also a struggle, as she could not complete the required assignments. Jessica was of visibly mixed heritage, and although she quickly grew fluent in Japanese, her physical appearance prevented her from fully blending in at school. "Kids used to call me *butajiru-jin*, which is a combination of 'pig' and 'Brazilian,'" she recalled, speaking with me in a mix of Japanese and Portuguese. "I was embarrassed to be Brazilian, and I really hated when my Mom spoke to me in Portuguese or kissed me on the cheeks in front of my classmates."

Every day after school Jessica waited at the factory for her parents and brothers to get off work. "I used to do my homework in the canteen, and a Japanese guy who was high up at the factory helped me with the homework that my parents couldn't understand. He even bought me one of those expensive *randoseru* book bags that everyone uses in elementary school here." With time, Jessica was able to catch up with her classmates, and in middle school she became increasingly involved in judo. Skilled in sports from an early age, she soon won a scholarship to a school with a strong women's judo team in Fukui Prefecture. There, throughout her high school years, she lived with a Buddhist temple-owning family far from her own family, immersed in Japanese language and the difficult daily training of her *dōjō*.

Despite pressure from her mother to continue on to university and further judo championships, Jessica opted for neither. Fluently bilingual in Japanese and Portuguese, after finishing high school she worked variously as a translator and interpreter at local international centers and for professional Brazilian soccer players in Japan, as well as at her mother's employment brokerage firm in Gifu. While she was once embarrassed by her Brazilian background, by the time I met her she appeared at ease in her role as a bicultural and bilingual mediator. She had many Japanese and foreign friends and was equally comfortable chatting with people in Japanese as she was in Portuguese. When we ate out at local restaurants together and perplexed wait staff invariably asked her why she spoke Japanese so well, Jessica offered the same stock phrase I heard her say time and again: *"Nihon wa nagaidesukara"* ("Because I've been in Japan for a long time").

With characteristic humor and pluck, Jessica narrated, usually in a mix of Japanese and Portuguese, her early process of adjustment to Japanese school, when she was still just a teenager, as an oscillation between silence (or silencing) and anger:

> At first when you come to Japan you want to die, you don't know anything. Then you start to understand a little and you want to kill everyone. First you want to die, then you want to kill. Then you enter middle school and you want to beat people up, because they're really annoying. Then you want to kill everyone again! And then you enter high school, you start to feel all shy and everything, you quiet down, you want to die all over again. In the second year, though, it's the same thing, you want to kill again, and in the third year you can kill because you're already powerful. You know everything at that point. But you're a foreigner, you'll always be a foreigner here. With this face!

Despite her initial frustration and embarrassment at school, judo later turned into a tool that Jessica used both to fight bullying and to find a place for herself in Japan where her parents and older brothers could not. Her introduction to training in Japan, however, was difficult. Although she had practiced the sport in Brazil since the age of four, she was afraid at first to try judo in Japan:

> The person who encouraged me to work toward my black belt was my Mom, because if it were up to me, I wouldn't have gone for it. I didn't even speak Japanese. I thought, how am I going to manage? But after I got my black belt at 14, I gained a little more confidence. Kids at school were afraid of me because

I would hit them back. When I entered, there was a lot of *sempai-kōhai* [older-younger student] stuff. So when I started my first year [in judo], girls in the third year used to mess with me. They gave me their kimonos to wash. And I didn't understand that too much. So I said I wouldn't wash their clothes, and one girl grabbed me, pushed me, and I hit her in the face. Her nose bled, so I was expelled for a week. During judo class we both had to clean the school. But then that put an end to this business of girls in their first year washing the kimonos of girls in their third year, acting like their little maids. Until that point the teachers didn't know, everyone was afraid to tell them, but they asked me why I hit the other girl and I told them. And so they discovered that there was *ijime* [bullying] in the school. I didn't even know what bullying was at the time.[1] It's a good thing I practiced judo, otherwise I'd have been screwed. They respected me because in my second year [of middle school] I'd already won a prefectural championship, a first for our school.

Judo thus became a source of confidence for Jessica, as well as a means of understanding—and ultimately fighting against—certain unfamiliar customs, such as the hazing that so often happened to younger students in Japanese schools. However, the bullying Jessica faced at school was not only a matter of typical *sempai-kōhai* dynamics; it was also the result of her being marked as an outsider:

Since I was Brazilian, they used to tell me that Brazilians are nothing, that they're just thieves. You started to feel like shit. But you got back up. Because you were Brazilian. I wasn't going to let them get away with that. My passport is Brazilian, I'm not Japanese. [Look at] my face, I'm Brazilian. I was a little embarrassed about that but there was no way to deny it, I'm Brazilian. So then you win and they're like, oh, Brazilians are amazing . . . [I was the] first foreigner to win a Japanese judo championship, I think it was in Hokkaidō. It was the first time, you know. In high school it was the first time they sent a foreigner to the *kokutai* [national championship]. And they didn't want to accept me because my nationality was Brazilian. It was a mess. I went the second year, but that first year, I think it was in Kyōto, they wouldn't let me because you had to be Japanese. People who make it there go on to the Olympics. So the judges had to get together and discuss whether or not they would let me compete.

As a teenager, winning judo matches represented more than just athletic achievement; it was also a means of proving Jessica's worth as a foreigner. Although she talked tough about her experiences in Japanese school, asserting her Brazilian identity was not always such an obvious option. Initially embarrassed at being Brazilian in Japan, Jessica also described a phase, around fourteen- to fifteen-years-old, when she was thoroughly confused about her own identity: "I didn't know if I was Japanese and I didn't know if I was Brazilian, either. I didn't speak either Japanese or Portuguese perfectly. I thought, what the Hell is this? What language do I speak? Where am I from?"

When I asked what had changed since then, Jessica pointed to the pivotal experience of working as an interpreter at an international center immediately following high school. There, she had to attend primarily to Brazilians, helping them with matters ranging from visa concerns and unfair treatment at work to personal problems such as domestic violence and children dropping out of school. For the first time, at age nineteen, Jessica found herself truly exposed to the realities of Brazilian migrant labor workers in Japan—a world that her family belonged to, but that she herself had largely been cut off from due to her schooling and living away from Gifu for so many years. At the same time, working at the international center in Fukui, Jessica grew to know people from many other countries and cultures and, as she put it herself, no longer felt she had to choose one or the other, Japanese *or* Brazilian. Her exposure to people from a variety of backgrounds led her to see that it was in fact *normal* (her word choice in Portuguese) to be different.

Looking back at her mother's decision to place her in public Japanese school, Jessica was grateful. She felt certain that if she had not learned Japanese well, she would never have achieved all that she did, and that if she had started working in a factory as a teenager, as her brothers did, she would still be in one today. Thus, the linguistic and cultural capital she acquired in Japanese school far outweighed the bullying she initially experienced. At the same time, she felt that the advantage of acquiring this kind of capital had in fact stemmed from the limits—in this case, being forced to attend Japanese school—imposed upon her when she was a child: "A lot of Brazilians don't want to put their kids in Japanese school because they're afraid they'll suffer. Suffer? Sure, they'll suffer! At least at first they will, just like I did. But there was no other option for me."

In the more than twenty years she lived in Japan, Jessica had only returned twice to Brazil, the first time for a few weeks when she turned eighteen and the second time to attend her eldest brother's wedding. When we discussed the possibility of her living in Brazil one day, she told me she felt open to the idea, though she was somewhat hesitant because of the terrible news she watched on Brazilian cable TV every day. Like many people I spoke with throughout my fieldwork, Jessica felt much safer in Japan than in Brazil, even if the dangers associated with Brazil were more often a product of media exposure than firsthand experience. In fact, for Jessica, life in Brazil was for the most part a distant memory, comprised of the years she remembered *desde que ela se entendeu por gente* (from the time she understood herself to be a person) until the age of twelve, when she moved to Japan.

In an interview several years later in April 2013 in her apartment in Aichi, Jessica told me it was possible that her whole family might return to Brazil one day and that she would stay in Japan. She was accustomed to the rhythm of life in Japan, she said, and to the kind of lifestyle her job and income permitted. Without a university degree, she felt life in Brazil would be difficult, as it often was for Brazilians returning after years of earning a relatively stable and comfortable income in Japan, regardless of their educational background: "Going back to Brazil without anything, you have to pay rent, you don't survive very long. The most you can stay is one year. And you end up spending all the money you worked years to save. Lots of people come back [to Japan] after one year. And they aren't OK. They're broke. They don't have anything."[2]

Keenly aware of the income and corresponding lifestyle differentials between Japan and Brazil, Jessica was also clear in how she felt about potentially working in Brazil in the future. She believed she would return to Brazil one day only if she could work with a company linking Japan and Brazil, and that she would not be comfortable basing herself entirely or only in Brazil: "I would have to spend a little time there, and then come back [to Japan] a bit. To be, like, a bridge. To work with Japanese people in Brazil and then come to Japan from time to time. Because if not I don't think I could stay. I don't think I could get used to [Brazil]."

Thus, in the same way that Jessica was reticent to choose between being either Japanese or Brazilian in her identity, she also preferred a job that did not deal exclusively with either Japan or Brazil but ideally both at once. Tellingly, Jessica narrated her ethnicity to me in the same way, laughing over the limitations of the five *cor/raça* (color/race) categories of the Brazilian National Census, which in 2010 were *branca* (white), *parda* (brown), *preta* (black), *amarela* (yellow), and *indígena* (indigenous):[3]

Jessica: I think I would be *amarela* [yellow], right? Because I'm not white. I'm mixed. Isn't there a mixed option, a *mestiça*[4] option? Or could I just fill in both white and *amarela*? How about light *amarela*?

Sarah: So for the purposes of these categories, if your Dad were considered *branco* [white], and your Mom *amarela* [yellow], why do you consider yourself *amarela* over *branca*?

Jessica: I think because I came to Japan, too, and because in Brazil people called me *japa*. In school [in Brazil] my nickname was *japinha* [little Japanese girl], *olho rasgado* [slanty eyes, lit. torn eyes]. My eyes weren't slanted at all, but people are crazy. I grew up being called *japinha, japinha, japinha*, so maybe that's why I consider myself *amarela*.

Sarah: How about here in Japan?

Jessica: Here I am a *gaijin*. A foreigner.

Sarah: How about *hāfu* [lit. half, the term often used in Japan to designate people with only one ethnically Japanese parent]?

Jessica: No. What would third generation be? *Sansei*. Here we're not *japa*. Here we're foreigners. Only foreigners. Brazilian.

Despite self-identifying as ethnically and culturally mixed, or what people increasingly refer to as "double" rather than "half" in Japan, Jessica was keenly aware of—and often saw herself through—the categories imposed on her from the outside, both in Japan and Brazil. On the official, national scale in Brazil, for example, the census still does not allow for a "mixed" option in answer to the question of color/race. And, while she might be considered mestiça *within* Nikkei communities (by virtue of having only one Nikkei parent), as a child in Brazil, Jessica was still regarded by the majority around her as, simply, *japinha*—little Japanese girl. Because her Japanese ethnic background—in other words, what made her stand out as a visible minority in Brazil—was so often highlighted to her in how she was called and categorized, Jessica came to see herself as more *amarela*, or yellow, than *branca*, or white. It made sense, however, that she did not see herself as *hāfu* because, as Stephen Murphy-Shigematsu (2012) points out, in Japan this term refers to someone who is half Japanese and half another nationality, usually Western and/or English-speaking. Furthermore, as Tamaki Watarai (2014) shows, Brazilians of mixed descent are rarely considered *hāfu* unless they are labeled as such for the purposes of the modeling industry. Jessica was neither half Japanese in terms of citizenship nor did her Brazilian half fit into what is imagined in Japan to constitute the cosmopolitan, Global North.

On the other hand, but analogously, in Japan, Jessica viewed herself as a *gaijin* (foreigner) or Brazilian rather than half Japanese, or *hāfu*, or even *japa*, because that was how majority Japanese saw her. In other words, she was singled out for her Japanese-ness in Brazil, and her Brazilian-ness in Japan, despite identifying as *both*. When I asked her if she thought she would still be considered a foreigner in Japan were she to naturalize to Japanese citizenship one day, she responded:

Yes. First because they look at me and already call me a *gaijin*. Physical appearance. If I naturalize, I will still be Brazilian, a *gaijin*. Why would I naturalize if they are still going to look at me and I don't look Japanese? I always liked to be different. I never wanted to be the same as them [majority Japanese]. At school everything I learned I wanted to do it the same as them, but also a little differently. It was the same, but I turned it into something else. . . . Like in judo. Judo is Japanese. But whenever I practiced it, I took their techniques and transformed them into my own thing. So they used to say that my judo was Brazilian, that it was my own individual style. Something about my maneuver was different. I had my style. I put together the two things and mixed them. I took advantage of what I had. Ever since I was young, I didn't want to be the same as other people. I never thought about being Japanese. You're born in Brazil, you're going to be Brazilian until you die, there's no way around it. Even being born, growing up here [in Japan], if it so happens that your parents are Brazilian, you're always going to be Brazilian.

Thus, no matter how well Jessica spoke Japanese and embodied Japanese cultural scripts and etiquette, she was markedly different from the majority around her because of her ethnic appearance.[5] While she could easily pass as Japanese over the telephone, in person Jessica was reminded of her difference by how people responded to her: Where are you from? How do you speak Japanese so well? What is your nationality? In this way, the linguistic and cultural capital she gained early on in Japan could not easily be translated into full membership and inclusion among majority Japanese, no matter how long she stayed there. Nonetheless, even in her practice of judo, Jessica exercised a kind of agency and flexibility by mixing Japanese and Brazilian elements, as she did later on in the workplace, too.[6] Though she faced limitations in being accepted as fully Japanese, still she practiced her own form of private, flexible belonging. In other words, she negotiated social and cultural belonging by being *both* Japanese and Brazilian in her language use, work habits, and bodily habitus in sport. In this way, she used the "ability to negotiate across barriers—language, cultural, spiritual, racial, and physical—[as] an asset" (Iyall Smith & Leavy 2008: 5), even in the face of social and structural barriers.

MARCELO

Resolutely Resigned

Jessica's older brothers, Marcelo and Carlos, were fifteen and sixteen when they arrived in Japan in 1991. The first times I spoke with Marcelo, who was thirty-five when I met him, he appeared aloof and reserved. He lived together with his mother Angela in Gifu and left early every morning for his shift at a nearby silicon processing factory. In the evenings I regularly spent with the family between 2011 and 2013, Marcelo would usually browse the Internet while his mother and Jessica kept up with the most recent Brazilian soap operas on TV.

"He's lost in not being able to find his way between Japan and Brazil," Angela told me. "Marcelo makes a living but he's not really *living*, you know." Of her three children, Angela worried most about Marcelo's future.

Despite his more than two decades living in Japan (with a few brief periods working or trying to finish his high school diploma in Brazil over the years), Marcelo had not learned much Japanese, and continued to work at the same type of job he began as a teenager.

Marcelo felt he stood out visibly in Japan, as well as in Brazil. When I spoke with him about Brazil's ethnic census categories, however, he had a different interpretation of his ethnicity than his sister. Whereas Jessica considered *amarela* (yellow) to be the most applicable available category for herself (*mestiça* or, as she put it, "light yellow" not being an option), Marcelo was more hesitant to view himself as *amarelo* (yellow) or Japanese, preferring *pardo* (a term encompassing various shades of brown) for its connotations of ethnic mixture: "Color? I'm *pardo*, right. *Amarelo*. But I'm not *amarelo* because *amarelo* is Asian. *Pardo*? Because I'm mixed. I have an Indigenous side because all Brazilians have a bit of that in them. Asian, *amarelo*—I'm a little bit of *amarelo*. Actually, when I was little and the teacher made me put [down my ethnicity], I was *amarelo*. But I'm not *amarelo*! I'm not Japanese. Asian Japanese are *amarelo*."

Like Jessica, Marcelo had distinct memories of the ethnic category he was placed into as a child in Brazil—a category he did not feel comfortable with. But perhaps because he identified less with Japanese culture than his sister did, he associated *amarelo* exclusively with Japanese *from Japan*, in other words not people of Japanese descent like himself.

Marcelo was, in fact, far less attached to his life in Japan than Jessica was. In the car to Nagoya on the way to renew his Brazilian passport one day, Marcelo confided in me that he only planned to stay in Japan for five or so more years:

> Japan for me is a prison, but a prison that allows me to make money. I have my routine here. I eat, sleep, work, but I don't have people to call or hang out with. A lot of my friends have gone back to Brazil already. I may not have an education, but I have income and I have goals to pursue with that income. I want to return to Brazil to buy and rent apartments to students. Business can fail any time, money can disappear in front of your eyes, but property—that is something certain to invest in.

Before he went to work in a silicon processing factory, Marcelo spent four years at an automobile suspension factory. He had one picture from the time, stored in a pile of personal mementos in his bedroom. When he showed me the photograph, suddenly I saw him as he had appeared two decades before, a teenager newly arrived from Brazil, dressed in a factory uniform and staring straight, somewhat sullenly into the camera: "I was fifteen going on sixteen then. There's just this one photo. At the factory where I worked there were four or five women who inspected pieces for defects. They liked me and, one day, I was sitting down during a break and they took this photo of me. But it's the only one I have from that time."

I asked Marcelo what he remembered about his family's decision to come to Japan, just a few years before the photograph was taken. At the time, his father had run a business into the ground and already showed signs of a serious drinking problem:

> Life with my Mom and Dad was crazy. I had already given up on studying. I'm kind of like a kamikaze. I was getting really high grades. Only high grades. Until the middle of the year. After that I gave up on going to class. Never again. I left the house but didn't go to school. At the end of the year my Mom found out I had been held back, that I wasn't going to school anymore. She said to me, "Since you don't want to study anymore, let's go to Japan." I said right away, "Let's go." I wanted to come. The way I saw Brazil at that time and with everything going on in my head . . . I came to Japan and didn't even know what it was all about here. I didn't know I would make money. I just wanted to get out of Brazil. I wanted to take a different path, go to a different place. I started working as soon as I got here, using a false document, as if I were 18. The labor brokerage firm set that kind of thing up, you know. It was like that for most [of the young] people who came. We worked as if we were 18. Except that we weren't paid well. I think I was paid 600 yen/hour [roughly half what Marcelo made at the time of this interview].

Marcelo, his older brother Carlos, and one of their cousins all worked illegally, and for a low wage, as minors in Japan. But for Marcelo, he remembered the experience more in terms of what he could buy and access than how he was exploited. After the family paid back the cost of the airplane tickets to Japan (the labor brokerage firm that sent them charged 370,000 yen—about US$3,700 per person just for the ticket, when in reality it probably cost the brokers less than half that amount), Marcelo and Carlos went out and bought a remote-control car. With their second paycheck, the teenage brothers bought a stereo system. "I had never seen CDs in my entire life. The first ones I bought here were one by Michael Jackson and another by Cyndi Lauper," Marcelo told me, transporting us back to the musical and consumer trends of the early 1990s.

Like many Brazilians moving to Japan for the first time in the 1990s, Marcelo was struck by the cold, cramped, and often isolating conditions of their new home. Before moving to Gifu, the family spent their first nine months in an apartment near the Chubu International Airport, also in central Japan:

> And the cold! We didn't have a space heater or an AC unit, we didn't have anything when we first got here. My Mom got Garoto [a Brazilian brand of]

chocolate bars as gifts and we couldn't even cut them with a knife. It was like a fridge inside our home. We just had that kind of table with a futon and heater underneath [a *kotatsu*]. We used to cram under that table, all of us together. We'd get back from work. The small TV set was yammering away in Japanese and I used to say, turn that thing off or I'll go crazy! There wasn't Internet, there wasn't anything. It didn't exist. Not like today. Now, if you want to see Globo [Brazil's national news channel] live you can just go online and watch it. In the summertime we used to hang out outside, we lived right near the sea and we would sit on the rocks talking and listening to the sound of the water until 11 at night, then we'd go home and sleep to get up the next day and go to work again. When we got here, there were only five Brazilians registered in the local City Hall.

In his early twenties, Marcelo used to enjoy nights out in Nagoya drinking with his Brazilian relatives and friends. The sociality that he spoke of in his early years in Japan stood in contrast, however, to his life two decades later. By the time I met him, Marcelo rarely wavered from his daily factory-to-home routine:

It was healthier back then, you know. I have a lot of headaches today, my back hurts, and I know it's because of the computer. On the one hand, I stopped missing Brazil so much. Because you don't miss it, you watch it [on TV, or online], you're just not there. But there are times when you feel tired. I can tell I'm mentally tired. That I need to shut it all off. This last holiday [Golden Week] I shut it all off. I lay there, I was quiet. Not like before, when we would go downstairs, and probably a neighbor would too, and we'd hang around talking, talking about Brazil, talking about life, about what we wanted, our goals. Today no one talks about that anymore. No one has any more goals for anything.

Indeed, Marcelo appeared to spend a lot of time at home, removed from social contact beyond his immediate family. In all his years in Japan, he had avoided getting seriously romantically involved with anyone locally, and spoke regretfully of his long-distance relationships that never seemed to pan out: "You end up losing those relationships because you're leading different lives. You wake up in the middle of the night and think about a person who is far away, and then you realize you're not really living your life when you spend it all missing someone on the other side of the world." When I asked him why he avoided dating Brazilians in Japan, he said that there was no way to get to know women in day-to-day life. Inside the factory where he worked, there were mostly only men; outside, the only thing left to do was to go out at night with women, and Marcelo was averse to dating someone he met drinking and partying in Japan.

At eighteen, Marcelo had been seriously involved with someone in Brazil, and he still considered it to be the most significant romantic relationship of his adult life. At the time, he was back in Brazil to finish his high school diploma. As he saw it, however, his status as a labor migrant in Japan, without a proper education, ruined the relationship's future:

> Brazil is all about education. Without an education you aren't worth a thing. Like one time the father of a girl I was hooking up with got all up in my face. "You aren't worth a damn," he said. And what can I say to that? I have to take it, right? Same thing happened with my girlfriend when I was eighteen. She was fifteen, and imagine, a *dekasegi* from Japan, living in Japan, a laborer. . . . It's tough, parents want [their daughter] to marry a guy with a name, a guy with an education, a guy with money. I get there, and who am I? I'm just a guy who works in Japan. Parents are going to find a way to send me packing. And that's what always happened.

In my conversations with him (always only in Portuguese), Marcelo repeatedly pointed out that without a university education not only would he have trouble meeting a plausible marriage partner, it would also prove very difficult to lead a comfortable life in Brazil. With his background, he would earn at most 1,000 reais a month, he thought, which in 2011 translated roughly to US$500 but was still almost double the Brazilian national minimum wage of 545 reais.[7] As he put it, however, earning 1,000 reais a month to spend twenty-five out of thirty days working a crummy job in Brazil was simply not worth it compared to the salary he earned in Japan. How do you go from 10,000 reais (roughly US$5,000) a month to 1,000 (US$500), he asked, and one could easily see his point.

Thus, Marcelo, like Jessica, was reluctant to return to Brazil in part because of the comfortable lifestyle and income he had grown accustomed to in Japan. In fact, he felt keenly the stigma of being a *dekasegi*, especially when he returned to Brazil. The trade-off of what he achieved for himself in Japan, he felt, was that he would never find a suitable person to marry, because no one in Brazil respected or accepted his way of life:

> Who's going to want to live the live I lead? I'm a nomad. When I'm in Brazil girls tell me to stay, but how, I ask? I earn my bread in Japan. There's no way for me to stay. Of course, if there were a way for me to stay [in Brazil] I would, but it's tough. People in Brazil discriminate a lot against those who are in Japan. Those of us who are here, they say we're *bóias-frias* [peons].[8] They say, look, [he] came from Japan, made money there, in a little while he's going to spend it all and will have to go back.

Marcelo was well aware that, despite being considered a "peon," the income he earned in Japan was not something he could easily turn away from after so many years. At the same time, however, although he enjoyed the lifestyle his income permitted, he also felt trapped and dissatisfied with his day-to-day life in Japan:

> To me this here is Hell. Here you work, you make money, you have a good car, you buy things. You buy whatever you want. You eat whatever you want. You wear whatever you want. You want Chanel, you want Prada, you want Gucci, you go buy it at the end of the month. You work and you buy. In Brazil you can't even dream of buying these things. So for me it's Hell. Why? Because Hell gives you everything. But at the same time it knocks you down. Here you can see that everyone has money, money, money, everything is money. But if you fall headfirst in this world you're going to sink. That's what happens with most Brazilians here. You live in a good place, you have a big house, you have everything, and yet you have nothing. You don't have money or a life, because what kind of life is this here? And at the same time, when these [economic] crises happen, where are the Brazilians then? They go back [to Brazil] without a penny to their name. They spend how many years here and don't have a penny in the end? This here is Hell because at the same time that it gave something to you, it also took something away. It gives, and it takes away.

Clearly, for Marcelo, the years he spent in Japan had brought him economic capital but little else of value.[9] Even money had come and gone over the years. In the mid-1990s, for example, he had joined his cousins and uncle in a plan to build an expensive restaurant chain in Brazil. In the end, his relatives swindled Marcelo's family and the business failed, so that they had to spend years in Japan recouping the money they lost. Then, in the early 2000s, Marcelo bought an expensive imported car in São Paulo—a beautiful red Mitsubishi convertible he once took me for a harrowingly fast spin in during a visit to Brazil in 2012—leaving it in his brother's garage and sending money on a regular basis to pay for upkeep and new parts. While money had come and gone, and the years had stretched on, Marcelo was well aware that he was not much better off than he had been when he arrived in Japan as a teenager. His social and cultural capital in Brazil were the same as when he was fifteen and, in part for this very reason, he felt reluctant to return to the country he called home. More than anything, he longed for a safe haven, a place he could really return to once all was said and done: "What I need in Brazil and never had is a safe haven. And we here in Japan, me, my brother, my mother, after my parents separated, we never had that. Never. And so we kind of got stuck here too. Because like [my brother] Carlos says, we don't have anywhere to run to! We have to stay."

When I suggested that Japan was, by default, a kind of safe haven for Marcelo and his family, he replied:

> No, not here in Japan, I'm saying in Brazil. In my country. But yeah, of course, Japan has always been a safe haven, so much so that I'm still here today. That's why I haven't left. I went to Brazil and got burnt, I lost everything [referring to the failure of the family business venture there]. Where did I end up? I came back to Japan. But I want to do the opposite. I want my safe haven to be in Brazil, I don't want to stay here. I'm not Japanese, I'm Brazilian, I want to go back to Brazil. Stay in Japan for the rest of my life, no! No, because here it's not like Brazil. As a foreigner in Brazil, you're accepted. Here many people don't like foreigners. Especially here in the countryside. In the capital [cities] it might be different, people with money, an open mind, who travel a lot. Here it's the countryside. People look at you badly.

Unlike Jessica, then, who could not ever imagine living full time in Brazil, Marcelo dreamed of the day he could return there. He spoke at length about various business ideas, but in the years I saw him he had yet to invest in another venture. Instead, he sent regular remittances to his older brother in Brazil to help pay for his medical school and living expenses: "I help [Carlos] today because tomorrow he's going to help me. I could take my money and go to Brazil right now, spend time there without having to work. But I won't go because I still need to help my brother. If he's alright, I'll be alright. And I'm not going to go because my Mom is still here. I can't just leave her on her own."

To Marcelo, then, Japan appeared to be a kind of holding place, or non-place in which he had spent over half of his life, and where he had to stay until his family sorted out a safe haven for themselves in Brazil. His independence in Japan was limited by the fact that he spoke little Japanese and still lived with his mother. To a certain degree, he resented the fact that his sister was sent to school in Japan while he and his brother had to work almost as soon as they arrived. However, when I asked him about the possibility of furthering his studies now, as his older brother had decided to do in Brazil, Marcelo was resolutely resigned against it:

> Can I go to university like my brother there? I can. But I don't have the heart, I don't have the motivation. You have to be motivated to get to that point. I'm not anymore. It's like I'm just really tired. Give me a place to sleep inside a car, a place to take a bath, and I'll sleep in a car, I'll live in a car! It's not that I'm trying to rebel or something, it's not even that, because I don't even have the heart for that anymore. The way I'm living life is fine for me. . . . The same thing every day. Life just keeps on going, without any expectations or anything. I'm here now, but who knows what'll happen to me tomorrow.

Clearly, then, Marcelo experienced even less flexibility than Jessica, espe-cially in the context of Japan. On the one hand, he earned a salary that allowed him a comfortable lifestyle unlike anything he could expect in Brazil. At the same time, however, it led him to feel trapped, both in his personal life and his sense of future opportunities. Thus, no matter how much money he saved or sent to his brother, he experienced social and occupational immobility in both Japan and Brazil because of his limited education and linguistic capital, his attachment to a lifestyle possible only in Japan, and his sense of family obliga-tion (i.e., not moving away until his mother chose to, or his brother finished medical school). Unlike his sister, then, he lacked what one might call hope, or "the confidence that we have the capacity to move and to act, albeit within limits" (Jackson 2013:69). In his case, "to be subdued by circumstances one cannot change, acted upon yet powerless to act, may be bearable if there is the hope or promise of some reward, a return on one's suffering. If, despite one's patience, no amelioration in the situation is forthcoming, it is all too easy to believe that one's life has been unfairly taken away and that one is therefore owed a new lease of life in lieu of the life that has been lost" (ibid: 212).

Marcelo's anger and sense of resignation could, in short, be read as a response to the "collateral damage" (Jackson 2013: 80) of his initial migra-tion to Japan. While at first the move represented a way out of difficult fam-ily and financial circumstances in Brazil, and was financially and socially rewarding, with time Marcelo came to see his life in Japan as professionally and personally futile. This gradual change in perspective over time serves as a reminder of the importance of the "life course" approach to migration studies, demonstrating how "a move takes on different connotations and implications as people age, take on new relationships, obligations and aspirations [and how] the potentialities, objectives, motivations and/or plans associated with mobility are therefore constantly being disrupted and revised over the course of people's lives" (Amit 2014: 400).

CARLOS

Hope for the Family and Future

I first met Carlos in August 2011, when he was back for a brief visit to Japan to see his family, resecure his permanent residency, and buy a suitcase full of clothes and Hello Kitty dolls for his infant daughter Mariana. Carlos was Angela's first-born son and had the same bright, affable smile as his mother. After seventeen years or so working in factory-related jobs in Japan, he returned to Brazil, where he finished his high school diploma and, in 2010, entered medical school in a private university[10] in São Paulo State. Accord-ing to his mother, Carlos took it harder than her other children when, in the

1980s, the family was evicted from their beautiful gated home[11] in Minas Gerais (a state adjacent to São Paulo) due to her husband Roberto's financial struggles. Carlos remembered very clearly, at the age of fourteen, being the first to see the eviction notice. Later that day, when he realized how much trouble his family was in, he attempted to hang himself from the post of his bed:

> If it hadn't been for my Dad's drinking problems, probably only my mother would have come to Japan to make money for us. But with everything going badly we had to relocate the whole family. My Dad was unemployed, my Mom was working a ton, and it was a huge step back for us. Because before then we had had a good life, we had a certain status, but then my Dad went and lost everything and we couldn't get it back. In the late 1980s, after we were kicked out of our apartment, we spent about two years living in the back of a maid's house. My Mom didn't want to split the family up, she was trying to see if my Dad could set himself straight again. Because, imagine, we had a whole life there [in the state of Minas Gerais]. I competed in swimming events, and I remember I was embarrassed, I had to walk for miles because I couldn't afford to take the bus anymore. I had to choose between taking a bus to school or to the swim meets, I couldn't afford both. I went to school in the mornings and worked as an errand boy for an IT office in the afternoons, from age fourteen to sixteen. They only paid me half the minimum wage, but it helped my family out.

After about two years of Carlos working as an office boy, however, the time came for the Silvas to go to Japan. Carlos was sixteen at the time. An aunt called and suggested to Angela that they go, since the family was having a tough time and Roberto was still unemployed. At first, Angela suggested moving alone, but then her husband wanted to go too, and they decided to take the children with them. Like so many other early *dekasegi*, they went first for an interview at a labor brokerage firm in Brazil, which then financed their way to Japan.

In the beginning in Japan, Carlos remembered earning 700 yen an hour, then 800, and then 900 (which, he said, was the salary women made) but nothing close to the 1300 his father made. Since Carlos and his brother Marcelo were minors, they were paid less, even though they performed the same work as their parents. At first, the idea was to stay for only two years, but when they saw that they could continue in this way, they decided to stay on to save more money. Carlos's father controlled the money the family earned, and soon his drinking and spending led to family fights. After nine months living in Tokonami, near the Chubu Airport of central Japan, he moved everyone to Gifu. Soon after, two of Angela's brothers arrived to work in factories, and stayed with her before finding a place of their own. For a while, then, their two-bedroom apartment housed eight people: Angela, her husband, three children, two brothers, and one of her nephews who, at age fourteen, had decided to come along as well, more for the adventure than anything else.

Indeed, thinking back on their arrival in Japan, Carlos remembered both the fear and the excitement they all felt, and how nostalgic it appeared to him over twenty years later:

> When I go back to Tokonami I feel this nostalgia. Wow, here's where I saw my first *jidōhanbaiki* [automatic vending machine] to get a drink. Our first idea of what Japan was. Because we arrived at night, you see. And so during the day it was like, wow, we're in a different country, because until then the furthest we'd gone was Paraguay. I hadn't left Brazil before. It was an adventure for us. Because we'd always been under our parents' wings. Even though I was 16 I was with my parents, but for them it was a shot in the dark because they didn't know if it would turn out to be slave labor, or who was going to help us get settled. It could have been like what happens with those coyotes in Mexico.

Carlos had always wanted to continue school but moving to Japan changed that. "I had to quit high school and start working in a factory here alongside my family. We never thought we would stay in Japan as long as we did. But time kept passing, you know. When you work in a factory, it's like you're a horse with blinders on. You can't see beyond it." Carlos spent a total of nearly eighteen years in Japan before returning to Brazil to begin medical school in his late thirties. Although he had tried to learn Japanese on his own over the years, he did not have much reason to use it anymore, and preferred to speak with me in Portuguese.

Although he spoke of the importance of living life without regrets, Carlos admitted that he would have preferred to go directly to university in Brazil instead of moving to Japan as a teenager. He considered the years he spent in Japan to be those of a *bóia-fria*, or peon. As he put it, "If you lost the years you could have been studying, it should be worth it, you should have worked for something bigger, better. But if you spend your youth working and end up back in Brazil without any money, which happens to so many Brazilians who come back from Japan, then it's all just an illusion, it's not worth it."

By the time I conducted fieldwork, it was increasingly difficult for labor brokerage firms to hire minors and avoid paying insurance and proper severance for their workers. Because of unions and NGOs helping foreign workers throughout Japan and, in general, the influence of media and now years of experience, Brazilians were more aware of the advantages of paying into *shakai hoken* and *kokumin kenkō hoken* (national life and health insurance).[12] Still, many Brazilian factory workers I met in Japan continued to feel as Carlos did when he still worked there, that they were not treated the same as Japanese (or, at the least, regular) employees, and that they had to struggle to be recognized as anything other than temporary, faceless labor. Speaking of the factory where he once worked, and where Marcelo continued to work when I met him, Carlos said:

> I used to say to my boss, "Look, I'm not a robot. I have a heart." And the day I said that to him he started to look at me differently, not the general manager, but the sub-section chief. We won that space. Every six months there's a company bonus, but we didn't get it, ever, because we were hired by a labor brokerage firm, not directly by the factory. But one day I said, "We work more than anyone else here and don't get anything for it? I think we should get the bonus." And so they started to give it to us, and still today they give it to Marcelo, 30,000 yen [~US$300]. We participated in staff meetings, got a special *bentō* [boxed lunch], while before we didn't get anything like that. As small as it was, it already made us happy, to be able to participate and eat together [with the rest of the workers], because we were part of the team. But it took a long time for them to realize that, it took years.

The important thing for Carlos, then, was to feel acknowledged at work, and to a certain degree, he was able to achieve that while still in Japan. In fact, he found it difficult to leave his position at the factory, because of the good salary. What he made there, and what Marcelo continued to make after his older brother left, ranged between 400 and 500,000 yen/month. For many Brazilians in Japan, following the economic crisis of 2008, it became increasingly difficult to earn more than 250 to 300,000 yen/month. Despite the good salary and having achieved a certain amount of acknowledgment at the factory, however, Carlos struggled to answer my question of whether his time in Japan had been advantageous overall. Sometimes, he said, he found himself thinking that if he had gone to medical school when he was seventeen instead of thirty-seven, today he would be earning enough to support his family and no one would have to be working in Japan. As for Brazilians in Japan in general, he reflected:

> To what extent was it good for them? Some who returned to Brazil have been able to start up a business. There were those people who went to Japan focused on making money and took advantage of the money to be able to open something in Brazil. But most of the Brazilians who went to Japan ended up lost. Because they're there, they don't have the money to come back, and they lost all this time that they could have been studying or building a career. And now they're getting older and it's tough to get back into the job market here. So it's like a lost generation, both here and there. A lot of people who have been in Japan since they were twenty, who got there at twenty, twenty-five, those people are forty, forty-five now. It's even difficult for them to find stable work in Japan now, let alone Brazil.

In other words, Carlos's understanding of being lost had little to do with what Takeyuki Tsuda (2003) calls ethnic "identity diffusion," and more to do with the struggles many transnational migrants faced as a result of local, structural limits in professional and personal advancement. Over time, and as *dekasegi* aged and struggled to achieve greater cultural or social capital, the more immobile they felt, whether they stayed in Japan or returned to Brazil. As for Carlos, the return to Brazil was also not a simple or straightforward process. His wife Ligia, who he married in 2000 and who lived with him for five years in Japan before he started medical school, played a major role in encouraging him to leave factory life in order to pursue a university education. Carlos left Japan at the end of 2008 and throughout 2009 completed a *cursinho* (preparatory course) for university entrance exams, as well as the ENEM (a non-mandatory, standardized national exam that has become increasingly important in the Brazilian university admissions process since 2009). The first entrance exams Carlos attempted, he failed. Even before that, though, he often felt discouraged in his first few years back in Brazil:

> When I arrived in Brazil I felt really down. Because I was so used to making money. I couldn't see anything else. I only focused on how much I needed to earn. I read books on economics, finance, I wanted to know how to make money grow. But there comes a moment when you get back to Brazil and you're not earning anything anymore. I would think to myself, today I lost the chance to make 200 dollars. If I were in Japan today I'd make 15 to 18,000 yen. I would have to work from 8 a.m. to 8 p.m., dead tired, but I'd have earned money. That was all that mattered. It was like total neurosis. I needed to make money, and that's all that mattered. Today that's not part of my life anymore.

After the second entrance exam, Carlos succeeded in entering medical school. At first, he was not sure whether to tell classmates about his background working in factories in Japan. Because of his age, too, he felt a certain amount of prejudice on the part of younger students. Many of them did not understand what he was doing studying in his thirties. Some asked if he already had a previous degree. "I don't have a degree because I lived in Japan, I worked," he would answer. Since he entered a private university, though, many of his classmates were from privileged enough backgrounds that their families could afford to pay the expensive tuition fees: "They don't know what suffering is. So when they see me now with a car, a good life, it's like it all fell from the sky. I live the same life they do because I'm in university with them and all, but the difference is I don't live off my parents' money."

Carlos displayed a sense of camaraderie with people who had been through the same *dekasegi* experience as himself. When he took me on a tour of

Presidente Prudente, the city where he lived and studied in the interior of São Paulo, he showed me a photocopy shop he always frequented, once owned by Brazilians returned from Japan: "I try to help people in the same situation as myself, even if indirectly. When I saw that they had come from Japan and were just starting out, I felt a kind of empathy for them, and started bringing my friends to make their copies there too. It's a way of helping them so that they can stay here, so that they don't lose their money and find themselves forced to go to Japan again."

Carlos felt worried that he himself might end up spending too much in Brazil, and considered the desire for consumption and status to be a real challenge for people returned from working in Japan:

Many people experience high living standards [in Japan], they have a good cell phone, a good computer, good clothes—because in Japan it doesn't cost very much. People go to malls and stuff is cheap, compared to Brazil. Here, clothes are all so expensive. But people want to try to keep up the status they had in Japan. And when they do that, well, it's an endless pit. They start spending a lot. . . . I'm afraid of doing the same thing because I spend a lot of my time around people with money, and here are all these social events I'm expected to attend—birthdays, weddings, *churrascos* [Brazilian BBQs]—and it adds up. It's another level. I don't live at that level anymore, I don't make money anymore. I'm lucky to have the Mom I have because if anything happens, I know she'll help me, but we have to pay our bills and know when to put on the breaks a little. If not, money's going to disappear and before you know it, I'll have to pack my bags and go back to Japan.

In fact, many people Carlos knew had returned to Japan after a brief stint back in Brazil. Like his brother Marcelo, they bought expensive consumer goods such as cars once in Brazil, only to discover that in the long term they could not maintain the same level of material comfort they had experienced on a factory salary in Japan. According to Carlos, returned *dekasegi* were often judged for spending money indiscriminately in Brazil, only to have to return to Japan again to keep up their middle-class lifestyle. As he put it, "If you talk to one of these elite Nikkei here and tell them you were in Japan, some will say to you, 'Ah, I didn't have to go there.' Because you know, those who went to Japan it's because they didn't make a decent living in Brazil." In other words, Japanese-Brazilians who went to work in Japan were sometimes considered a different class of Nikkei, despite the prevailing assumption in Brazil that most of them were middle to upper middle class.

Because he joined Presidente Prudente's Nikkei Association's soccer team, Carlos did indeed have contact with people from the local Nikkei community, elite or not. The second time I visited him in his home, he brought me to a game, explaining that *gaijin* (foreigners) could not participate in the association's tournaments. When I inquired about his wife Ligia, who was not Nikkei, he said that since she had married a *descendente* (lit. a descendant), they would probably make an exception and allow her to play volleyball but not soccer. "Why the discrimination?" he asked. "Because if they didn't do that, all kinds of Brazilians would be able to play at the association, pros and amateurs alike, and the *colônia* [lit. colony][13] would lose its identity. It would end up just a drop of Japanese and the rest of the players would be Brazilian."

In contrast to Ligia, Carlos's *yonsei*, or fourth generation, daughter Mariana, born in 2010 in Brazil, would be allowed to participate in all association events in the future because of her Japanese heritage. Ligia, who felt members of the Nikkei community treated her better once they discovered she was the wife of a *descendente*, imagined her daughter would grow up well aware of her Nikkei status in Brazil: "Even though she doesn't have a Japanese face, as soon as she's able to tell people she has roots, blood, the Nikkei will treat her differently, they'll treat her like she's one of their own."

Carlos's sense of his own Nikkei-ness dated back to childhood visits to his mother's parents in the interior of São Paulo State:

> When we went to our grandpa's he always talked in Japanese, played with us, and our grandma too. We used to fool around with the TV, for example, it was on Channel 8, Globo, and we'd switch it to 3, but it was Globo too and she'd say "No, no, no, bad!" We'd laugh a lot. She spoke Japanese. But of course all this stuff about heritage we had an idea about because we spent more time around the Japanese side of our family than our Dad's. We'd visit the Japanese side, my uncles and all, my aunts who made *mochi* [glutinous rice cakes]. We had that, not that we spoke Japanese though.

In contrast to growing up with a sense of Nikkei-ness, as well as, as an adult, efforts to connect to the Nikkei community in Presidente Prudente, Carlos described his experience in Japan in much the same way that Takeyuki Tsuda's (2003) interlocutors did:

> There we felt more Brazilian because the Japanese didn't treat us as Japanese. Doesn't matter how much Japanese you learn. I always felt like a foreigner. There were days when I thought, wow, I'm going to live in Japan forever, because it's a good country, you get used to it. And the Japanese tolerate you. They *tolerate* you. Only that. But here in Brazil you see that there's nothing better than living in your own country.

So, interestingly, while in Brazil Carlos capitalized on his Japanese heritage (his social capital, or group membership) to join Nikkei association events and the like, he felt his position as a Brazilian *dekasegi* in Japan was a form of negative capital in a country that did not view him in terms of positive ethnic stereotypes. In fact, during the period his non-Nikkei wife lived with him in Japan, people often thought she was American or Italian, and, as a result, Carlos believed they were treated better—in this way, passing as "First World" or "Western" instead of Brazilian.

Still, when they returned to Brazil, Carlos felt that it was his Nikkei status that was viewed positively, while his experience as a *dekasegi* was not. "The question of profession is really difficult for those of us who worked in Japan. What do you say? Profession: *dekasegi*? No. Then what, machine operator? That really makes you feel low. In Japan we're all just peons. My Japanese is horrible too because I worked as a peon and I don't know that correct, polite Japanese people learn in school." In other words, many labor migrants like Carlos found that it was precisely their position as *dekasegi* that led to discrimination in both Japan and Brazil, on the part of Nikkei, non-Nikkei, and Japanese alike. Nikkei-ness could be used as a form of cultural or social capital in Brazil but only so long as it was separate from some of the connotations of being a *dekasegi*; similarly, in Japan, where Nikkei-ness did not hold the same positive weight as it did in Brazil, Brazilians were often viewed, first and foremost, as *dekasegi*, and consequently as little more than lower-class, disposable laborers, if not a threat to Japanese social order and homogeneity. Moreover, because the nature of their work made it difficult to achieve greater linguistic capital (not just Japanese but polite and formal Japanese), Brazilians were even more limited in their mobility in Japan.

When I visited Carlos in 2012, he drove me to the plot of land his family had recently purchased in a gated community in Presidente Prudente in order to build a house for the day his mother and siblings might return from Japan. To Carlos and his family, the future house represented something fixed, and concrete. Indeed, he often spoke of it as a *porto seguro*, or safe haven, along the lines of what Marcelo had mentioned as well:

We've become like gypsies. That's something that we feel a lot. In Japan we never do anything because we say, no, no, this is not our home, here we're working a lot but we'll have things in Brazil. So I just want my Mom and Marcelo to have something that's theirs, for Marcelo to have a room that he knows is his, that if he comes back it's his room, it's his. The world can fall apart there but if he comes back, he'll be coming back to his house, his room. Same for my Mom, and for Jessica, so that she knows she'll have a place to come back to. Over there they don't have that. It's a symbol of roots. For her to know that she can put everything in one spot and no one will take it away. With land, a thief can enter, sleep, and in the morning give the land back to you. It's something secure, that no one can steal. No one carries land away on their back.

Besides physical property, Carlos felt certain that his medical degree would help the entire family in their eventual return from Japan. No one would ever be able to take his education (cultural capital) from him, he often said, unlike money (economic capital), which could disappear from one day to the next. Even the skills he learned working in Japan were not transferable to Brazil. He would have to invest in education, he believed, in order to help his mother and siblings: "I'm helping my family's morale, too, in the sense that now they can say, hey look, there's a doctor in our family. Because think about it, none of us went on to study. Even Jessica, who had the opportunity to do so, preferred not to study. Now I'm getting my degree and this way I'm going to give my family a new perspective. One day, we'll be able to be normal people again."

And so, Carlos used his savings from years working in Japan in order to pay for private medical school, as well as to maintain a comfortable quality of life for his wife and daughter. Even with the additional financial help of his mother and siblings in Japan, he had to borrow money from the government to finance his degree. Still, he seemed unconcerned about debt, confident that in the end he would have something stable and concrete to offer his family. Thus, aware of the limitations he would face were he to remain a *dekasegi*, Carlos opted for what he considered a secure route of education and professionalization in Brazil in order to increase both his own and his family's social status and mobility across national borders.

ANGELA

Mother, Boss, and the Glue That Binds

Every time I saw her, Angela's salt-and-pepper hair was tied in a tight, practical bun. One day, sitting at her kitchen table, she sliced into the tough flesh of a cantaloupe and sighed, speaking primarily in Portuguese—with a sprinkling of Japanese words—as she usually did with me, "Life doesn't always turn out the way you want it to." Glancing around her small but bright fifth-floor apartment in Gifu, where she lived with Marcelo, I thought about the many changes that had occurred in her life since, over twenty years earlier, she arrived with her husband and three teenage children from Brazil.

Angela spoke nostalgically about her youth in the interior of São Paulo State. Her father was the child of Japanese emigrants to Brazil and her mother, born in Japan in 1924, migrated to São Paulo as a young girl. Angela was raised with the comforts of a successful farm-owning family of the 1950s and 1960s: hand-sewn organza dresses, sunset evenings with family out on the front porch, visits to the traveling amusement fair that came all the way from Italy, country dances, and her own car as a teenager. She remembered helping with the farm's finances—listening to the price of cotton on the radio to figure out if her father should buy or sell that day—and driving a truck around the family property as migrant workers from the northeast of Brazil arrived in time for the season's harvest. Her father paid for the two oldest sons—Angela's brothers—to study agronomy, but one dropped out and the other did not continue because their father decided to put him in charge of the farm instead. Angela remembered her father telling the children that they did not need to study because the family already owned so much farmland, and because he himself had been successful without having studied.[14] Her mother, however, believed an education was more secure, that no one would be able to take it from them. Still, her words went unheeded and although Angela completed several years of university, neither her nor her brothers ever obtained a degree.

"Everything changed when I married a *gaijin* [foreigner]. My father was very opposed to my marrying a man who wasn't Nikkei."[15] Despite her family's disapproval, Angela married Roberto at nineteen, unaware of his love of drinking and philandering. Her father promptly wrote her out of his will and she moved off the family farm. Her brothers took over the family farm and eventually ran it into the ground. In the first years of their marriage, Roberto successfully managed a small business. He insisted that they live in an upscale apartment building and send their children to expensive private school and an elite swimming club. He was very proud of his once illustrious family and used to tease Angela for not being of European ancestry. "What do you mean I'm not pure? You're the mutt with all your mix of Portuguese and Italian and whatever other races. I'm the one with 100 percent Japanese blood," Angela recalled shouting at him in one of their many fights.

With time, Roberto's drinking problem grew increasingly severe and his business eventually failed. It was around this time that the family decided to take advantage of Angela's status as a *nisei* (second-generation Nikkei) and Japan's newly amended immigration policy to leave Brazil. "When we first got here, that was back in 1991, everything was so exciting. It was really emotional to arrive in Japan. We felt we were doing something new, like we were on an adventure. I'm proud to have come with my generation to Japan." After the initial excitement of discovering her parents' homeland for the first time, Angela quickly grew frustrated with life in Japan. Like many Nikkei-Brazilians who arrived in Japan in the early 1990s, she was disappointed to be treated as a foreigner, and struggled with her new status as a blue-collar worker. Passing me a slice of cantaloupe, she noticed her rough, tanned hands and laughed, "My fingers used to be so fine. Now they're the hands of a laborer."

Besides adjusting to a drop in social status, Angela was also disappointed with how she was treated in Japan, compared to what her mother had taught her, growing up in Brazil, of Japanese culture:

> I even got into a fight at the factory here once, I nearly broke the table where I was sitting, I was so mad. You see, I had defended Japanese people so much in Brazil, wouldn't let anyone speak poorly of them because we were *descendente* ourselves, descended from Japanese, but then I got here and I was shocked at how they treated us, especially inside the factory. As though we were inferior. We were in the *shokudō* [dining hall] one day and a Japanese woman started handing out food to all the other Japanese employees but skipping over us Brazilians. At that moment everything my Mom had told me about Japan came crashing down, and I was outraged. The *buchō* [manager] came in to see why I was so angry and I told him that my mother had taught me that Japanese people always share their food with others, that if there's not enough to share with everyone then no one eats at all, and here we were, *descendente* and all, and they were skipping over us, humiliating us. So I decided to show how we're actually superior to them—at least that! To make up for their disrespect. The next day I came in with Brazilian chocolate bars for *everyone*, I gave them to every single person in the room. Boy did that show them!

As this episode illustrates, when in Brazil, Angela had felt the need to defend Japanese against discriminatory or essentializing remarks. Once in Japan, however, she felt both disappointed in and excluded from the Japanese culture she had previously thought she belonged to. In other words, while at one time the emulation of another, powerful and prestigious, ethnic identity—that of Japanese—offered a model, rather than an anti-model for the Self (Harrison 2003: 357), Angela soon discovered that her understanding of "difference-as-superiority" (Ibid) in Brazil did not correspond to the ethnoracial hierarchies of Japan. In this new context, Nikkei-ness represented not a source of pride or superiority. Instead, it was associated with the censored and disowned aspect of the poor, often more rural (read: backward) Japanese who had originally emigrated to the so-called Third World over the last century.

Having been raised under relatively affluent conditions by first-generation Japanese emigrants to Brazil, Angela was used to thinking of herself on equal footing as Japanese, and at times even superior to the Brazilian migrant laborers—usually from poorer parts of the northeast—employed on her family's farm. Working in a factory in Japan was the first time she experienced a sense of inferiority based on her ethnic background, or "difference-as-inferiority" (Harrison 2003). It was also the first time her Japanese-ness was called into question: "The biggest disappointment for me was when I got here and they started calling me foreigner, *gaijin*. Because I'm not mixed, my father was descended from Japanese, my mother was from Japan, she was even born here. How could I be a *gaijin*?"

Although she no longer worked in a factory when I met her, Angela had spent her first years in Japan earning a living "on the line." After her marriage broke up and Roberto went back to Brazil, she had no choice but to support herself and her children on her own: "The only reason I moved forward was because of the three lives that depended on me. I couldn't look backwards or I would trip and fall, and then my three kids would fall too." After years working in a factory, Angela gradually moved on to a position at a Japanese-run brokerage firm. Later, she opened her own small employment brokerage firm, which she had managed for over ten years by the time I met her. She was responsible for placing primarily Brazilian, Peruvian, and Filipino workers—most of them women in their forties and fifties—in local factories and taking care of their visa documentation, medical problems, and other bureaucratic and personal affairs.

As a foreigner, opening the firm in Japan was not a straightforward process. When the Japanese owner of the employment brokerage firm where she worked first on the line and then as a translator and assistant went bankrupt, he asked Angela to use her name to open a new company and transfer his debts. As the new owner of the firm, Angela found herself deeply involved in work, struggling to keep it afloat as her former boss fell deeper into debt and eventually died, leaving all of the responsibility and check balancing to her. Having witnessed the mismanagement and then loss of her family's farm in Brazil, followed by her husband's bankruptcy and then sons' misguided business endeavor in São Paulo, Angela was determined not to run into debt herself. As much as she longed to retire to Brazil, she felt she was still not at liberty to leave, because of her responsibility both as a boss and as a mother:

> Circumstances put you in this position—adversity, life. But today if I could just have a small piece of land in Brazil, a little bit of peace and quiet, I would trade this all in. If only there were someone I knew who could take over the firm for me. Because I know that if I were to stop now, my kids would lose their stability. They depend on me, and they'll be at a loss if I stop working now. I'm doing this work because I didn't find any other alternative, and because I took on the consequences of my husband's foolishness.

Angela felt that she had had fewer opportunities than her children because of her decision to marry and start a family at a young age. Until then, she had not worried about a thing, and was free to do as she pleased. With children and an irresponsible husband, however, she had more than just herself to worry about. The dreams she had at nineteen were no longer the dreams she had at sixty. Today, she was much more concerned about her adult children's

future than her own. Although she regretted not having sent her children back
to Brazil after a few years in Japan to continue their studies, she felt that without her their life would have been too *desestruturada* (unstructured/unstable).

Still, it was clear that Angela was lonely in Japan. Even though she made
enough money at the employment brokerage firm to lead a comfortable life
and support her three grown children in whatever ways they needed—Carlos
with medical school expenses, Marcelo with a roof over his head and someone
to nurture him, and Jessica with a sense of family and home in Japan—still
she missed the social capital and positive status of her elite Nikkei childhood:

> You know, you get to a new world and you have to adapt, but you find that
> it's not really *your* world. I wish I had more knowledgeable people around me
> that I could learn from, like I did when my Dad still had his farm and many
> of his friends were local politicians, academics. . . . But I don't find anyone
> like that here. All people talk about is the factory, you don't learn anything
> from that, you don't get anywhere. So I feel I've regressed in Japan, regressed
> a lot. There's nothing better in life than sitting down with a group of friends
> and being able to speak the same language with them—not Japanese or Por-
> tuguese I don't mean, but the language that you speak and they understand,
> and can teach you things in return. That's what I miss most in Japan, that kind
> of friend.

In other words, Angela's sense that she was an outsider, or a *gaijin*, in
Japan, was compounded by her feeling out of place in terms of class status
and symbolic capital. Shared ethnicity and language were not enough to make
her feel at home with other Brazilians in Japan. The language she missed was
in fact the register of an entire social world—that of elite, educated Brazilians.[16] Working at an employment brokerage firm in Japan, Angela found
that she could not relate to most of the people around her: "I miss the level
of people I interacted with in Brazil. Here I've come to live among people
of a very different level. Unfortunately, it was the only way I found to make
money, by coming here."

Angela had not planned on staying as long as she did in Japan. There were,
of course, times when she could have packed up her savings and returned to
Brazil, but something invariably happened to hold her back. Besides the time
she and her sons lost their money in a misguided business venture in Brazil,
she also felt responsible for keeping the employment brokerage firm in Gifu
afloat and, later, for supporting her eldest son in his medical studies. What
is more, like her children, she was used to the comfortable income level and
lifestyle she had achieved in Japan, and was hard-pressed to give it up: "It's
that greed that kept us here too, always wanting more, wanting something
better. We kept saying we'll stay just a little bit longer, just a little bit. Well

just a little bit longer, just a little bit longer, and before you know it, you're old!"

After more than twenty years in Japan, Angela still did not feel secure in her work or her place in Japanese society. She spoke enough Japanese to get by but often relied on Jessica to translate for her or negotiate directly with Japanese factory owners, lawyers, doctors, and so on. The success of her employment brokerage firm depended on her being able to place foreign workers in factories—the factories paid her the workers' salaries, which she in turn paid to the workers after taking a certain percentage cut for herself. In the years I knew her, Angela was responsible for fifty to sixty workers, but there was always the fear that factories would close, downsize, or merge, something that happened frequently following the economic crisis of 2008–2009: "I could end up with just four workers tomorrow, and my salary depends on them. I'm always prepared for the worst. And for the Brazilians who work in factories here, what kind of future do they have? They get old in the factories and then they hit fifty and no one wants their labor anymore. And then what'll happen to them?" Thus, Angela was aware that, even as a small business owner who did not have to rely on her physical strength and health in a factory, working in the foreign brokered labor sector of Japan was made precarious by—besides limited social and linguistic capital—market vicissitudes and the declining opportunities of age.

As for her own future, when I asked her about the possibility of staying in Japan, Angela shook her head emphatically. "Japan offers us money but not security. That's why I'm saving money to build a house in Brazil. It'll be my refuge. One day I'll retire and hopefully all my children will live there with me." As she said this, she thumbed through an interior design magazine, showing me the kind of swimming pool and patios she imagined building for herself and her family in Brazil one day. "Money can disappear at any moment. If there's one thing I want to leave behind for my kids, though, it's a house. A place they can call their home," she said, echoing both Carlos and Marcelo's wishes.

Besides saving to build a house in Brazil, Angela also felt that Carlos's medical school education was the greatest investment she could make:

The best form of capital is education. It's something *dekasegi* didn't value enough. Even if money is well invested, it's never certain. The only certainty is studying for a real profession. So I'm happy that Carlos will graduate and be an anchor for us all. Even if I die tomorrow, I know that Carlos will give structure to my other children's lives. He's opening a future for them right now, giving them light at the end of the tunnel to look forward to.

In this way, Angela used the language of capital to describe that which she felt was most valuable to her and her family's future mobility: education, or cultural capital.[17] Only if Carlos were to succeed in medical school in Brazil could she imagine it being possible to move beyond the limitations of life among *dekasegi* in Japan. Thus, while family—working, fighting for family—was part of what had kept her in Japan for so many years, family, too (particularly Carlos's eventual position and status as doctor in Brazil), shaped what she saw as greater future flexibility in Brazil.

CONCLUSION

The Silva family's trajectory over the last several decades followed a path familiar to many early *dekasegi* to Japan. After running into financial trouble, Angela and her husband opted to work for a few years in Japan, and to bring their children with them. Migrating to Japan via an employment brokerage agency, their excitement at pursuing a new adventure soon faded as they discovered the difficulties of adapting to grueling factory conditions and a largely unfamiliar culture and language. Then, as Angela's children grew up in Japan and the family became increasingly accustomed to a materially comfortable lifestyle, the decision to move back to Brazil felt further and further off.

While these experiences were common among *dekasegi*, each member of the Silva family experienced and dealt differently with the same constraints and opportunities of being a transnational labor migrant. After many years in Japan, Carlos returned to Brazil to further his studies, while Marcelo bided his time waiting to go back with his mother. Marcelo had already attempted opening a business in Brazil, but after that did not work out, he returned to Japan to continue working in a factory, an experience of circular, or back-and-forth migration also common to so many *dekasegi*. Jessica, for her part, had little memory of Brazil and continued to view Japan as her primary home for the foreseeable future, although she expressed her ethnicity and belonging in mixed, or flexible ways.

Despite their varied attachments to Japan and Brazil, and the different ways in which they saw themselves as Japanese and/or Brazilian, the context of family—including both the pressures and the possibilities inherent to family—shaped the Silvas's experiences as much as, if not more than, ethnicity. Angela, for example, continued on in Japan not because she felt at home there or needed to save more money for herself, but because she wanted to secure enough of a future for her and her children. Building a house in Brazil large enough for the entire family and supporting Carlos through medical school were her two primary goals. As long as she stayed in Japan, Marcelo, too, felt he could not leave her alone. Part of his salary also went toward supporting his older brother. In doing so, he would be able to rely on Carlos's social and cultural capital once he moved back to Brazil, even if he himself never secured a well-paid job again.

While it was clear enough that Angela and her son Marcelo would eventually return to Brazil, and continued to work in Japan primarily to help one another out, her youngest daughter Jessica, having attended Japanese school and moved beyond the usual set of opportunities available to *dekasegi* (i.e., brokered manual labor), had less reason than her mother and brothers to want to leave Japan. Her Japanese and Portuguese abilities, as well as her ability to comfortably navigate Japan, placed her in a more flexible position there than the other members of her family. Still, without the right connections or higher education in Brazil, she was afraid she would face downward occupational mobility were she to return with her family.

Despite the fact that Jessica felt at ease in Japan in ways the rest of her family did not, she saw herself as a partial outsider, and one who would never be fully accepted there. Still, she was successful in being both Japanese and Brazilian at the same time. Even though she would never be able to pass as fully Japanese, she could engage in a kind of linguistic and cultural (including bodily) code-switching that allowed her entry into occupational and social worlds that her mother and brothers did not have access to in Japan.

As this chapter has demonstrated, Angela and her children experienced transnational living according to the various constraints and opportunities of family structures. The Silvas migrated, in the first place, as a family, even though this meant cutting short the typical trajectory through Brazilian education that Carlos, Marcelo, and Jessica might otherwise have followed. Then, they stayed in Japan for as long as they did in part to continue supporting one another, first when Carlos and Marcelo's business venture went awry and they lost most of their savings, and later as Carlos pursued a medical degree in Brazil.

In the end, the transnational ties of the Silva family demonstrate the complex ways in which different generations of Nikkei-Brazilians often situated themselves *in* and *of* both Japan and Brazil. Besides ethnic identity and national affiliation, family considerations, as well as concerns about social mobility and material comforts, led people to settle, migrate back-and-forth, and return migrate to their country of origin. In the next chapter, I will more closely address these questions by examining the broader contexts of work, social class, and (im)mobility among Brazilian labor migrants and their families.

NOTES

1. According to Naito & Gielen (2005), the Japanese term for bullying (*ijime*) is "rather frequently used in everyday speech both for certain school situations and for other forms of 'mobbing' in work situations or elsewhere" (175). It also points to "more indirect styles of aggression [including] strategies designed to isolate a person socially . . . and in general, the not so gentle arts of social manipulation and intimidation" (ibid: 176). Since the 1980s in Japan, the term has "been elaborated and more sharply defined in order to focus on a group of problematic behaviors distinguished from other types of school violence" (ibid). It has come to be recognized as a major social problem over the last several decades, causing absenteeism and even suicides among school children. According to Tamaki Mino (2008), it is the product of Japan's regimented education system, which places a heavy emphasis on conformity, and whereby students and even some teachers initiate or participate in *ijime* in order to discipline nonconformists and guarantee collective identity. Many of my Brazilian interlocutors experienced *ijime* in Japanese school, either because of their appearance and/or limited Japanese language abilities, or because they stood out in other ways. Some, like Jessica, fought back. Others suffered more quietly, dropped out, or switched to a different school.

2. This is similar to what Nicole Constable (1999) found when she noted that Filipina migrant workers "who 'dress up' and feel 'like their own boss' in Hong Kong may experience a sense of diminished class identity when they return to the Philippines as one-day millionaires" (214).

3. Brazil's census agency, the Instituto Brasileiro de Geografia e Estatística (IBGE), collects official race/color statistics. It has always included a "mixed-race" or "brown" category, corresponding with Brazil's self-definition over the course of the twentieth century as, essentially, a "mixed" nation. The Census has included the white, brown, black, and *amarela* (yellow) categories since 1940 (with the exception of the 1970 census when the question of race was not included), and in 1991 it added the fifth category of Indigenous (Loveman et al. 2012). In comparison, on the 2010 US Census, Americans could answer the race question by choosing among white, black, American Indian/Alaska Native, several Asian options, Pacific Islander options, and "some other race." As of the 2000 Census, they could also opt to select one or more races. In fact, according to a *New York Times* article (Saulny 2011), many young Americans of mixed race are now rejecting traditional color lines in favor of a more fluid sense of identity.

4. While discourses surrounding different *mestiço* types are widely connected to the meanings attributed to whiteness and blackness in Brazil (see, for example, Pinho 2009), among Brazilians of Japanese descent, *mestiço* refers to a particular kind of "mixture"—that of Brazilian (already imagined to be a generic mix of white/black/ Indigenous) with Japanese.

5. This has much in common with Sara Friedman (2015)'s work with Mainland Chinese migrants in Taiwan. Her interlocutor Xiao Hong, for example, was originally from Mainland China, but eventually naturalized to Taiwanese citizenship. Though she was "happy to benefit from the privileges of juridical citizenship, especially

with regard to cross-border mobility, . . . she had no illusions that she would ever be accepted by locals as Taiwanese" (189).

6. Beyond agency and flexibility, Jessica's actions might also be interpreted as a kind of resistance. As Nina Glick Schiller (1999) notes, migrants often "express resistance in small, everyday ways that usually do not directly challenge or even recognize the basic premises of the systems that surround them and dictate the terms of their existence" (11).

7. In Brazil, university graduates make up only 11 percent of the working-age population and earn, on average, 2.5 times as much as those without degrees, and five times as much as the majority who never finished secondary school (*The Economist*, September 15, 2012). What is more, wages in Brazil are lower than in Japan not only in terms of absolute value, but also comparative consumption possibilities. As Suzana Maia (2012) points out, "goods and values that are taken for granted in the United States [and elsewhere in the Global North] represent luxuries that most Brazilians must strive hard to earn" (7). For example, in Brazil a Honda is an expensive foreign import car, whereas in Japan it can be bought relatively cheaply. Thus, Brazilians working as unskilled laborers in Japan could purchase a culturally fancy car, whereas in Brazil—without higher education or more than minimum-wage work—they could not easily do so.

8. In Portuguese, the word *bóia-fria* is a colloquial term used to designate someone from the countryside who works temporarily as a hired hand. In this way, it resembles the original meaning of the term *dekasegi*. The word *bóia* is slang for food, and *fria* means cold, referring to the food that laborers would bring with them from home. By the time they ate it at lunch, it was no longer warm.

9. Although Marcelo could hardly be described as (materially) poor, according to James Foster et al.'s (2013) definition of poverty—that is to say, "the absence of acceptable choices across a broad range of important life decisions [resulting in] a severe lack of freedom to be or do what one wants" (1)—he was in fact impoverished.

10. In Brazil, universities are private (either for-profit or charitable, usually Catholic), or public (government-sponsored). While admittance to university is based on *vestibular* entrance exams, public universities (which account for roughly 10 percent of all universities or colleges of further education) tend to be the most competitive and prestigious, and lead to better-paying jobs. Most of the students admitted to public universities can afford private high school and/or preparatory courses and are, therefore, richer than the average Brazilian (though they pay nothing to attend public university). Private, for-profit universities, on the other hand, while easier to gain admittance to, are generally less prestigious, and charge expensive tuition fees (McCowan 2004). Still, medicine is significantly competitive in the private sector as well (Schwartzman 2004), and is considered a secure and prestigious career route whether students are admitted to private or public programs.

11. Gated communities, though a global phenomenon, take on specific meanings in countries plagued by violent crime (Landman & Schönteich 2002). In Brazil, where rates of murder and inequality are among the highest in the world, Teresa Caldeira (2001) refers to such enclosed areas as "fortified enclaves" that include office complexes, shopping centers, and residential communities. Closed condominiums,

like the one the Silvas previously lived in, tend to have "total security"—fences and walls, twenty-four-hour guards, and video monitoring and alarms—and are also an important symbol of social status and wealth.

12. By the time most Brazilians arrived in Japan in the late 1980s and early 1990s, national health insurance had already been made available (from 1986 onward) to foreigners following a long struggle for access by second- and third-generation resident Koreans (see Roth 2002). However, as Yasushi Iguchi (2007) showed years later, according to surveys, still only about 10 percent of Nikkei workers were enrolled by their employers in health and pension insurances, and only 20 to 30 percent paid into the national pension system.

13. Originally, the term *colônia* referred specifically to "rural agricultural enclave communities established on land set aside with the assistance of the Japanese government" (Tsuda 2003:56), though in today's common usage it also includes any large concentration of Nikkei-Brazilians living in smaller cities and towns in Brazil (often near or on the sites of the original *colônias*). As Mieko Nishida (2017) further points out, "Until the present day, many immigrants, as well as São Paulo's Japanese-language newspapers, have continued to use the word *colônia* to refer to a collective of Japanese-speaking Japanese Brazilian organizations and associations, while others have insisted since the 1980s that *colônia* is an inappropriate and outdated term" (13).

14. Although many early Japanese emigrants to Brazil were farmers who suffered harsh conditions working on plantations throughout Brazil, eventually, many became small proprietors in Japanese *colônias*. In contrast, today 90 percent of Nikkei-Brazilians live in cities, with only 10 percent left in rural areas (see Tsuda 2003: 56–57).

15. This kind of reticence toward inter-ethnic marriages was not uncommon among first- and second-generation Nikkei-Brazilians, and regularly figured in the family histories I inquired about.

16. Though he does not ascribe it to social class, Joshua Roth (2002) notes a similar sense of dissatisfaction on the part of one of his interlocutors who had few Brazilian friends in Japan and "complained that most Brazilians talked only about work, money, and girls" (98).

17. Although Angela was rare among my interlocutors in her use of the term "capital" to refer to symbolic resources such as education, her view on the link between education and social mobility was echoed among many *dekasegi*, and is explored in greater detail in chapters 2 and 4.

Chapter 2

Working-Class Jobs, Middle-Class Desires

Foreigners or not, the lifestyle in Japan is really good.
Garbage collectors can shop in the same stores as bankers.

—unemployed Brazilian
factory worker in Japan

While most early labor migrants to Japan dreamed of earning quick money and returning to Brazil within a few years, many of them ended up staying in Japan long after they had saved enough to buy property, pay for their child's university education, or set up a small business back home. Others found themselves migrating back-and-forth between Japan and Brazil, aiming to maintain the same middle-class lifestyle and consumer habits they had grown used to while working in factories in Japan.[1] For those Brazilians living long term, or repeat migrating to Japan, then, working-class jobs provided them with middle-class comforts and possibilities. Their children, too, many of whom grew up in Japan, became used to a lifestyle their families might not have been able to easily provide for them in Brazil and that, without higher education and the right social and cultural capital, they themselves would be hard-pressed to obtain.

At the same time as migration to Japan allowed many Brazilians to achieve or maintain middle-class consumption habits, for those who did not learn enough Japanese or otherwise find work outside the segmented labor system through which most labor migrants were channeled, they came to constitute a sort of underclass in Japan. Even in the case of Brazilians who learned Japanese language and customs, and/or moved beyond the segmented labor system, for the most part they still belonged to the *hiseikikoyō* (irregular) workforce of Japan, that is, those with low-status temporary,

53

part-time, short-term, or contract jobs.[2] In other words, the achievement of positive cultural capital (including linguistic), while it may have spelled greater inclusion among majority Japanese, did not necessarily translate to upward social mobility in terms of education or employment, either locally (in Japan), in migrants or migrants' parents' home society (Brazil), or internationally.

Since the 2000s, as Brazil's middle class began to rise significantly, inequality and *kakusa shakai* (disparity society) have simultaneously become increasingly significant problems in Japan. It is estimated that one-third of all workers in Japan today form part of the irregularly employed precariat (Allison 2013: 19), and an increasing number of young people find themselves in poorly remunerated, dead-end jobs (Kariya 2010). As Anne Allison (2013) points out, those most at risk of becoming irregular workers are youth, women, those with less academic credentials, foreign migrants, and, increasingly, men in their fifties. Thus, although Brazilian labor migrants in Japan—many of whom, besides being foreign, are young, female, aging, and with limited academic credentials—maintain middle-class standards of living and consumption habits according to Brazilian values, norms, and aspirations, they still form part of the overall precariat in Japan. Furthermore, because they spend so many years working in unskilled labor in Japan, migrating back to Brazil without further skills or academic credentials often spells downward mobility there, at least in terms of earning potential, material comforts, and status/prestige.

In the last chapter, we saw how different members of the Silva family variously experienced (im)mobility in Japan and Brazil. In this chapter, I examine more broadly how, for Brazilian labor migrants and their children, migrating to Japan via a brokered labor system represented both significant opportunities and constraints in terms of purchasing power, class status, and (im)mobility in Japan and upon their return to Brazil. Specifically, I examine the role of an employment brokerage firm—particularly in light of a factory fight—both in mediating problems for its workers and keeping them "in their place" as members of the irregularly employed precariat in Japan. I also explore how, for many migrants, working in Japan has come to represent the achievement or maintenance of middle-class subjectivity[3] and consumption, even while it limits or reduces their long-term social mobility, whether in Japan, Brazil, or further afield. Finally, I highlight gender in the discussion, showing how mobility can mean different things for women and men, given that they often face different social positionings to begin with. In these ways, I pay heed to James Ferguson's (2006) intervention in discussions of globalization that we need to center our work "less on transnational flows and images of unfettered connection than on the social relations that selectively constitute global society" (23).

BROKERED LIVES IN JAPAN

On a sunny summer Sunday in 2011, forty or so foreign workers gathered at the park adjoining an electronics factory outside Okazaki, Aichi, for a *churrasco* (Brazilian BBQ) that lasted all day. Two acquaintances of mine from Brazil, Miriam and Julio, were celebrating their recent marriage at City Hall, and it was also the birthday of twin sisters from São Paulo, Katarina and Kelly. The BBQ took place under a large sprawling Japanese red pine tree, a symbol in Japan of long life, which was fitting given the celebration of a marriage and a birthday, as well as the presence of three visibly pregnant women and a handful of young children. People played soccer and softball, and children rode their bicycles around the park, while others played cards on a tarp stretched out in the shade, and the rest of us ate our leisurely fill of skewered meat, Brazilian vinaigrette, and *onigiri* (Japanese rice balls).

Most of the people present at the BBQ were Nikkei-Brazilian, aged roughly between twenty and forty, and all worked as brokered laborers at the large grey-box factory visible through the trees behind us. Some had been in Japan for just a few years; others had grown up there. Besides Brazilians, there were also several young Japanese factory workers present, as well as two Nikkei-Peruvians, and two Nikkei-Paraguayans who spoke with each other in a mix of Paraguayan Guarani and Spanish. People generally communicated with one another either in Japanese or Portuguese, Portunhol (a mix of Portuguese and Spanish), or a mix of Japanese and Portuguese. As we cleaned up the park and prepared to leave around 7 p.m., just as the sun was setting behind the pines, another acquaintance of mine, Tati, glanced at the sky and shrugged, "Well, most of us will be here again tomorrow morning for work. I have to wake up at 3:30 a.m. to make it for my shift."

For the most part, over the past several decades, Brazilians in Japan have continued to work in unskilled labor, whether they arrived as adults or grew up there as the children of *dekasegi*. When they first arrived in the late 1980s and early 1990s, they were almost always sent through employment broker-age firms, or *haken gaisha*, which took a percentage of their wages in return for setting them up with plane tickets, job contracts, and a place to live. This brokered system of work was well documented in early studies of Brazilians in Japan (see, for example, Roth 2002 and Tsuda 2003), and continued to be a salient part of the *dekasegi* experience over two decades later. By the mid-2000s, although many Brazilian workers no longer relied on *haken gaisha* for airplane tickets or an apartment—instead, they often relied on friends or family already working in Japan, or else their own experience and knowledge as repeat migrants[4]—they still sought contracted work through employment brokerage firms. This was in part due to the difficulty of finding a job on one's own without being sufficiently proficient in Japanese. Still, as Takeyuki Tsuda (2009) pointed out, it was also due to the fact that as long as Brazilians "remain dependent on the labor-broker system for jobs, they continue to be confined to the informal and marginal sector of the Japanese working class, and very few have been given permanent jobs with the possibility of regular promotion" (222). One of the main reasons Brazilians in Japan remain segregated is, as Joshua Roth (2002) has so effectively demonstrated, due to this segmented labor system.

Throughout my fieldwork in Japan, I observed up-close the activities of an employment brokerage firm in a city in Gifu that, in 2011, counted nearly 9 percent of its total population as registered foreigners and 5 percent Brazilian. Although most of the largest employment brokerage firms there were Japanese-owned, a number of the smaller ones were operated by former Brazilian factory workers engaged in a kind of "middleman minority" work (Blalock 1967; Bonacich 1982).

The employment brokerage firm I visited every week was first opened by a Japanese man but later run by a Brazilian woman and her family. Located under a noisy bypass, it stood unremarkably on a congested street between a sheet-metal warehouse and a gravel parking lot. On the same street, within just a few minutes' walk, were the more familiar establishments of everyday, small-city life in Japan: family restaurants, a green-grocer, and a tatami repair shop. Further down the street, and perhaps less familiar to many of the city's Japanese residents, was a second, brightly lit employment brokerage firm, this one with a welcome sign blinking phosphorescently in Portuguese. Nearby was a brand new Brazilian Evangelical church marked on the outside by a large sign and cross and, across from it, an inexpensive Chinese restaurant adorned in bright red and golden lanterns where we would occasionally stop in for a plate of cold spring rolls after work.

The employment brokerage office itself was divided into two rooms. Walking in through the main entrance one would find a table and four chairs set up for people to sit at and fill out contracts or employment requests. Directly ahead of this area was a front reception desk, and behind that a set of six grey metal desks where one Japanese administrative assistant—Itō-san—had worked regularly from 9 a.m. to 4:30 p.m. every day for the last six years. In 2011, a nearby factory paid the employment brokerage firm 1,280 yen per hour per contracted worker, regardless of whether it was for regular work or overtime. The brokerage firm then paid 850 yen to each foreign worker per hour, or 1,070 yen for each overtime hour, making the profit margin to the brokerage firm approximately 430 yen an hour for regular hours or 210 yen an hour for overtime hours.[5] Before the economic crisis of 2008–2009, the firm was responsible for approximately 100 foreign workers. By 2011, however, the number had decreased to close to sixty, most of them Brazilian but also including a handful of workers from the Philippines and Peru. Half of the firm's foreign workers were contracted to a tofu factory, three or four to a car parts factory, another fifteen to twenty to an iron parts factory, and the remaining two to a textile factory.

A typical day at the employment brokerage firm involved driving employees to and from the factories, translating and having employees sign temporary contracts, organizing schedules and salaries, interviewing potential employees, and meeting with factory or division bosses to discuss contracts and worker relations. At times, it was also necessary to bring employees to the hospital or local immigration office, resolve disputes between employees, or check in on them at home when something serious such as domestic abuse, depression, or blackmail was suspected. The darkest moments, without a doubt, were the times I witnessed employees after they had been fired or injured on the job—or, in one case, detained in prison and awaiting deportation to Brazil. Usually, though, the employees' concerns were more trivial—someone was holding up the line at work, or else forgot to take off her nail polish, and needed us to swing by the factory with acetone before she got in trouble with her section leader for wearing it.

One incident in particular, though unusual in terms of day-to-day activities at the office, is worth detailing insofar as it illustrates the complicated and delicate triangular relations that continued to characterize Japanese factories, foreign contracted workers, and the employment brokerage firms connecting them. The fight described here between an elderly Brazilian factory worker and his Japanese coworker offers a glimpse into the social drama (Turner 1974) of brokered work relations, as well as the continued underclass status of many Brazilian laborers in Japan.

FACTORY FIGHT

On an otherwise average November day in 2011, a Japanese factory employee in Gifu punched a sixty-three-year-old contracted Brazilian worker—Miki—in the face. No one but the two involved witnessed the fight. Miki, who had been in Japan off-and-on for exactly twenty years, wore a hearing aid, spoke only limited Japanese, and could not read or write Portuguese beyond the elementary school level.[6] He went home after the fight and, hours later, dropped by the employment brokerage firm that had hired him. Still in his factory uniform, with a bruised nose and blood drying darkly on his olive-colored shirt, he stood for photos in case we needed to show them to the police later, and then went quietly home.

Later that same afternoon Miki showed up at the office again, this time with his wife who, brandishing a bag of used bloody tissue, and outraged that her husband's nose had not stopped bleeding, announced: "If the Japanese guy lies and says my husband started this fight when he didn't, we'll bring this to the police! Language difficulties are no excuse not to deal with this properly!" Sueli, the owner of the employment brokerage firm, then left with Miki to take X-rays of his nose, which we later learned had not been broken. Itō-san, the office's Japanese administrative assistant, appeared confident that if the Japanese worker had started the fight, he would be the one responsible for paying all of Miki's medical expenses.

As Sueli, Sueli's daughter, Itō-san, and I continued to discuss the case later that afternoon, Miki's son, also a contracted factory worker, suddenly came bursting into the office with his wife, shouting in Portuguese and hitting the walls with his fist: "I want to know who punched my Dad! I want to know why the police are not involved, not doing anything. I'm going to get all my friends from the gym to come and get this guy. My Dad busts his ass getting a shitty pay in a shitty factory and then a fucking Japanese guy punches him in the face and nothing happens! This would never happen to a Japanese worker, they'd call the police right away!" Lowering his voice somewhat but still trembling with anger, he continued: "My father is simple, and a layman. He didn't know to file a police report. That's up to [the employment brokerage firm] to do. He has a headache and his nose is still bleeding. There's been an injury and justice must be paid."

In her defense, Sueli explained that she only found out about the fight hours after it happened, and still had no idea how it had really unfolded. "Miki left the factory without saying anything to his bosses there. We still haven't heard the other side of the story," she explained. Itō-san agreed, saying that a representative from the brokerage firm and one from the factory would have to meet with each other and the two involved in the fight in order to hear the whole story out, before deciding whether to call the police or not. As she explained later to me in private, speaking only in Japanese (she did not understand any Portuguese), "*kōjō kakawaritakunai*," or "the factory does not want to get involved." Itō-san seemed to feel that we should only call the police if a major injury had occurred, and that this fight could now lead to problems in the business relationship between the employment brokerage firm and the factory. "It could mean a Japanese *seishain* [regular, as opposed to contracted employee] gets fired and then the yakuza [mafia] get involved," she worried.[7]

Following a meeting between Sueli's daughter and one of the bosses at the factory, it was established that Miki had repeatedly dropped empty boxes on the Japanese worker's foot over the preceding weeks. Because Miki had failed to apologize properly, this led the other man to lose his temper, at which point they entered into a tussle and Miki was punched. Sueli decided to call the brokerage firm's lawyer to take care of the case, and that evening a feeling of tension mounted as we four women—Sueli, her daughter, Itō-san, and I—waited inside the office until an unfamiliar car parked just outside in the dark with tinted windows and several men smoking inside finally drove away. We never found out who the men were. Once the car was gone, however, we breathed a sigh of relief and called it a night.

The next morning, the brokerage firm's Japanese lawyer showed up at the office, followed by Miki and his wife, their daughter-in-law, and their young grandson. As they sat around discussing the case, Miki's daughter-in-law spoke up:

> The Japanese worker is probably jealous thinking Miki is taking his job because he's been asked to start work earlier recently. That's the trouble on any assembly line, the competition that goes on between two workers because the factory wants the fastest and most productive workers. But two workers are never equal in production or speed, so there's necessarily competition between them. Also, the two of them can't speak to each other because of the language barrier.

While what she said certainly spoke to the underlying causes of the trouble,[8] the primary issue at hand now was whether or not the brokerage firm should have immediately brought the fight to the police's attention. Sueli's daughter maintained that the firm could not say anything to the police without knowing what happened and negotiating with the factory first: "This cannot be covered by our firm's *rōsai* [accident insurance] because the family has reported it as aggression. If Miki had simply said it was a work-related accident, insurance would pay for it." Nevertheless, Miki and his family felt, without a doubt, that it was a case of aggression, of Japanese against Brazilian, native against foreigner, and that, consequently, it had to be justly accounted for. To complicate matters further, Miki also ran the risk of being fired at the factory because, according to his contract with the employment brokerage firm, he was not supposed to cause any trouble while at work. Sueli explained to him: "I have a contract with the factory, and you have a contract with me, Miki, so I have to make an agreement with the factory. I can't act just on behalf of you." In this way, she made it clear that the role of the employment brokerage firm was not necessarily or first and foremost to defend its contracted employees but rather to mediate between them and the factory, and to ensure smooth, continued business relations.

At this, Sueli's Japanese lawyer interjected, saying that the fight itself was caused by the built-up frustration of foreigners always feeling *damasareteiru* (fooled) in Japan, as though people were necessarily taking advantage of them because they did not understand the Japanese language. "Japanese or

Brazilian, it doesn't matter," he went on to say, speaking in Japanese. "People want money when they can get it, and this case might bring money if it goes to court. It's human nature after all, it's got nothing to do with nationality. Everyone wants to defend their family, too." Here he recognized that the case had escalated not due to cultural differences (e.g., resorting to the police versus apologizing and striking an unofficial agreement) but because of universal human nature as well as the specific, unequal power relations caused by Japan's system of brokered foreign labor. This echoes Joshua Roth's (2002) argument that it was not cultural difference but rather the marginalization of Nikkei-Brazilian workers in the segmented employment system that led to exacerbated relations between them and their Japanese managers. As he demonstrated, accidents on the job provided a particularly dramatic context in which to examine how membership was negotiated between workers and their managers, and how marginalization at work led many Nikkei-Brazilian workers to pursue justice and acknowledgment in a different form.

Exactly one week after the fight, Miki returned to the employment brokerage office with his family and a Portuguese-speaking lawyer friend who, although trained in Brazil, was not technically allowed to practice law in Japan (and, therefore, was on unequal footing compared to the Japanese lawyer Sueli hired). He offered his informed advice free of charge, speaking at length about how the local Gifu government had promised that they would no longer treat Brazilians as *dekasegi* but as proper citizens. "Japan is changing, we live here, have kids, kids who go to school here. It's not like the Edō period[9] when foreigners couldn't get in. What Miki wants is not just financial compensation, but justice too. The police should be involved," he maintained. Clearly, the issue was not only about money but also about Brazilians proving their worth as residents—"proper citizens" of Japanese society—who could not so easily be taken advantage of.

In the end, however, the employment brokerage firm and the factory agreed to pay for Miki's medical expenses on behalf of the Japanese worker who punched him, provided that Miki agree to sign a document apologizing for the fight and stating that he would not sue anyone involved. The Japanese worker who punched Miki was unable to pay out of his own pocket, and the employment brokerage firm was willing to pay part of the fees to ensure that the factory would continue doing business with them. And so, later that month, I watched as the employment brokerage firm's lawyer prepared a legal document in Japanese, which Sueli's daughter then translated to Portuguese, stating that Miki was sorry for having caused trouble at the factory, and that while he appreciated the offer to continue working there, he preferred to seek work elsewhere. In truth, he did not wish to work any longer with the man who had punched him, and so he chose to quit. Miki walked away from the firm with 150,000 yen (less than US$2,000) in medical expenses paid but no other obvious job opportunities in sight. His wife, worried that no factory would hire her hard-of-hearing husband at his age, and concerned that they were broke and too old to seek work in Brazil now, wondered what would become of them.[10] As was also the case for many of Joshua Roth's (2002) interlocutors, money was not the main issue at stake for Miki and his family. Rather, Miki's "dignity had been compromised by [his] managers' lack of remorse" (ibid: 89), both those at the factory and the employment brokerage firm.

As this account demonstrates, what was essentially a minor fight between two factory workers escalated into something much more significant, because of the underlying tensions that were due not only to the relations between "natives" and newcomers but also to the segmented labor system through which foreign unskilled workers were necessarily funneled in Japan. The blow-up between Miki and his Japanese coworker revealed the essential fault lines of such a segregated labor system: mistrust on the part of foreign workers of employment brokerage firms trying to collaborate with Japanese factories, the business concerns at stake between the two, and the employment brokerage firms' fears that, should one of their contracted workers get into trouble at a factory, it could jeopardize all of their foreign workers' contracts, due to the inherently precarious nature of the system.

The fight also pointed to resentment and a broader belief on the part of Brazilian workers that they "just couldn't win" against the Japanese and were being taken advantage of both by the factory and the employment brokerage firm that employed them because of their continued position at the bottom of the labor ladder and their limited knowledge of Japanese. While it would have been possible for Miki and his coworker to meet and apologize to one another, and to the factory, the fact that it was a Japanese man who punched a Brazilian exacerbated Miki's sense of injustice to the point that he and his family preferred to bring the case to a higher authority: the police. However, because the lawyer they hired was not actually allowed to practice law in Japan, and because their knowledge of Japanese was significantly limited, it would have been difficult to make a convincing case to the police or court over what was, ultimately, a relatively small-scale fight. In the end, it was simply easier to smooth over the trouble with an official apology and payment, a practice commonly found in workplaces in Japan (e.g., Roberts 1994; Wagatsuma & Rosett 1986).

As the anecdote of the factory fight also shows, two and a half decades after Brazilians first began working in Japan, brokered labor there remained far from glamorous. Examples of grueling schedules and injuries including repetitive stress syndrome are well documented in early studies of Brazilian labor migrants in Japan (Linger 2001; Roth 2002; Tsuda 2003). During the course of my fieldwork, most Brazilians of working age in Japan—unless there was a halt to production due to market fluctuations—continued to work long, tedious hours, often under physically demanding conditions. Generally, they were still hired through employment brokerage firms on temporary, renewable contracts of one to three months, whether they had been in Japan for two years or for twenty. One interlocutor, for example, a *sansei* Brazilian in his forties and father of three, who had been in Japan for over twenty years, told me (speaking mostly in Japanese) that he worked ten-and-a-half-hour factory shifts for days on end, and that when he left the house at 8 a.m. in the morning, his wife would just be returning from her night shift, such that they barely ever saw one other: "There are days when I think, man, I'm so tired of this life. All we ever do is go to work, home, then back to work again. On the weekends, we might be able to do a bit of shopping, but there's really little time for family." While this sentiment might easily be echoed by many a mainstream *kigyō senshi* (corporate warrior) of contemporary white-collar Japan (see, for example, Hidaka 2006; Okura Gagné 2010), or else members of the Japanese working poor, Brazilians in Japan, in addition to working long hours usually under precarious and/or harsh conditions, were rendered even more structurally vulnerable by virtue of being ethnic and/or cultural outsiders, non-citizens, often socially isolated, and almost always brokered.

Also, following the global financial crisis of 2008–2009, hourly factory wages decreased in Japan, as did the number of overtime hours, making it difficult to earn a large sum in a short amount of time, or to save as much as before. For someone like Miki, a foreign worker already in his sixties and with limited education and Japanese abilities, job prospects were even scarcer. Miki already accepted "women's pay" for his work at the factory—that is, he earned a lower salary than most Brazilian men in Japan because he took on "easy" work (i.e., not especially heavy or dangerous) usually considered more suitable for women. This is what his son alluded to, then, when he claimed that his father earned "shitty pay in a shitty factory."

Whether or not they suffered a cut in wages or overtime shifts, long hours "on the line" often meant migrant workers had few opportunities for leisure and socialization. What is more, the tiring repetitiveness of work, coupled with feelings of isolation and loneliness, and the difficulty of moving beyond unskilled labor in Japan, led many Brazilian laborers to feel acutely depressed, as was the case of Marcelo Silva in the last chapter. A *sansei* interlocutor in his mid-thirties, Eduardo, who spoke mostly only Portuguese, related in vivid terms the psychological numbness that resulted from performing the same tedious work day in and day out, with little time off, and almost no sense of social connectedness. He told me how, on the plane to Japan for the first time in 1996, he met two other young men sent via the same employment brokerage firm as he was. The three of them decided to live together in Japan, working long, hard hours with the goal of later paying off debts in Brazil:

> One night, I woke up around 3 a.m., and realized my roommates weren't in the apartment. I looked out the window and that's when I saw them, on the baseball field nearby, naked, and running around in the snow like a bunch of crazy people. I shouted at them, "What the Hell are you guys doing?!" and they called out for me to join them. So I went out to the field, in the dark, and that's when one of them explained to me, his skin red from the cold: "It doesn't hurt here in the snow, see. We can't feel that awful pain here," and I realized he was referring to the loneliness of being in Japan. A day later, one of them disappeared, and two weeks later, the other asked his father to send money from Brazil so he could go home. I'm the only one who stayed, and today I'm a samurai.[11] I kill myself working for my family.

By the time I met him, it was Eduardo's second time living in Japan, now with a wife and young daughter to support, and he felt a clear sense of purpose working (even sacrificing himself) for his family, as did the Silvas of chapter 1. In earlier years, though, when he was alone in Japan and had no social structure around him, he felt the same kind of dark disconnectedness he witnessed his roommates suffering from. "Only God and I know what I went through then," he told me, blinking away tears. Thus, while migrating to Japan presented people with opportunities to save money and achieve or maintain a certain kind of material lifestyle, grueling brokered work also took its toll on migrants' physical and psychological wellbeing. When interlocutors spoke of feeling connected to work, it was usually through being able to help others (on the line or in schools, for example). Only in rare cases did they feel valued, for example, if they had stayed at the same factory for a long time and were recognized in some small way as more than simply temporary, replaceable workers.

GENDER AND ETHNICITY ON THE LINE

For Brazilian labor migrants in Japan, work was mediated not only by immigration policy and visas, employment brokerage firms, and temporary contracts but also by gender and ethnicity. As illustrated in the case of Miki, who received a "woman's salary" at the tofu factory where he worked, women migrants often earned less than men, even if they performed the same duties as them. At some factories, where the work was considered "light" labor (e.g., putting cameras together), women and men tended to earn the same salary. But in most other unskilled labor in Japan, women still earned less per hour than men. As Keiko Yamanaka (1997) pointed out, Nikkei-Brazilian women were regularly paid 20 to 30 percent less than men for the same jobs, so that during the period of top pay in the 1990s, women in manufacturing averaged US$2,000 a month, whereas men earned an average of US$3,000.

By the time I conducted the bulk of my fieldwork in 2011–2012, wage differentials based on sex were still as evident as they had been ten to twenty years earlier. They were even openly advertised in Portuguese-language magazines and newspapers in Japan, and women interlocutors often told me of their lower earnings compared to men. One *sansei* woman in her late thirties, for example, said that in all of the factories she had worked in Japan, women earned 900 to 950 yen/hour, while men earned 1,200. "Even when I did the same work as men, I earned less than them, and sometimes I saw men doing easier jobs but still earning more than women," she recounted in a mix of Japanese and Portuguese. Another *sansei* interlocutor of about the same age told me that at one factory where she worked, she earned 900 yen while men earned 1,300 per hour, even though they performed exactly the same duties.

Paying women and men different wages for the same work is in fact illegal according to Japan's 1985 Equal Employment Opportunity Law (EEOL). As Anne Aronsson (2015) shows, however, "even though the EEOL ensures that women and men should earn equal wages for equitable work, women still earn much less" (5) in Japan. By paying higher wages for jobs deemed more difficult and labor intensive than others (referred to colloquially as "men's work" as opposed to "women's work"), in practice, it was still possible for employers to carry out this kind of informal gender discrimination among foreign workers. Also, even when women were paid less for the *same* work as men, they were still hired under the assumption that they would perform less physically demanding work than men and, in this way, were effectively discriminated against. This was not only the case at Japanese companies or organizations. At one of the Brazilian-run schools I visited in Japan, for example, I found that there too, women were generally paid by the hour, while men were paid a fixed monthly salary, based on a yearly contract. Thus, women teachers ended up making less per month, and were placed in a more precarious position than men. "It's because men are assumed to be the main breadwinners, I guess, in terms of supporting a family. It's really annoying, though, because our work is the same, we carry out the same duties," one elementary school teacher confided to me.

Gender discrimination also took the form of policing women's appearance at work, in ways that men were usually not subject to. One interlocutor, who was not Nikkei but had been married to a Nikkei-Brazilian man, was told on two different occasions that she could not be hired at a factory in Japan because of her natural hair color: "The *tantōsha* [person in charge] at this one place told me he wouldn't even interview me because I'm blond, only if I dyed my hair dark. He said I couldn't draw attention to myself and away from the machines." In this case, discrimination based on gender and ethnicity overlapped, in the sense that the woman was considered too "alluring" because of her natural hair color. Here, Foucault's (1995 [1975]) notion of disciplining the body took on a specifically gendered form, as women were seen as threatening to men and "thus in perpetual need of containment and control and subjected (condemned) to particular disciplinary techniques" (King 2004: 30)—in this case, artificial hair darkening. While it might be argued that the employee in question was asked to dye her hair so as not to "stick out" more generally (and not necessarily ethnically), still it was clear that the combination of her being a woman and of fair hair color was considered doubly threatening to the men in charge.

Ethnic-based discrimination was, for its part, frequently alluded to during informal conversations and interviews about work and hiring processes in Japan. It has also been documented more broadly via a recent government survey on discrimination and human rights issues in Japan. The results of this survey, which were published in 2017, demonstrated that one in four foreign residents who had sought a job said they were denied employment because they were a foreigner; of those denied employment, about 95 percent of them spoke Japanese conversationally, professionally, or fluently.[12] Although Takeyuki Tsuda (2003) predicted that Nikkei-Brazilians in Japan, once they adopted Japanese language and habits, would grow to be exclusively a cultural minority, I contend that, because Nikkei-Brazilians are increasingly of mixed descent (*mestiço*), and are by and large still foreign citizens, they will continue to stand out as a visible or marked ethnic minority in Japan. Like Paul Green (2010), I found many of my interlocutors, especially the third and fourth generation, to be of mixed descent. When asked, most of them remembered being singled out or discriminated against at least once, if not many times, based on their appearance, either at school, or during the process of looking for work in Japan.

One interlocutor told me how, because she went by her non-Nikkei father's last name, when she applied for jobs, employers invariably asked, "But what generation are you? Why don't you have a Japanese name?" "I've had to apologize several times during interviews for not having a Japanese name," she told me. In other cases, discrimination was based more blatantly on the way people looked, even when prospective employees could speak Japanese fluently. Tiago (who went by his second name Hideki among Japanese friends), for example, was Nikkei and Afro-Brazilian, and was much more comfortable speaking Japanese than Portuguese. He arrived in Japan at the age of four, and was educated in Japanese school until he was fifteen. When

I met him, he was in his mid-twenties and was working part time in a car manufacturing company and part time at an *izakaya* (Japanese-style pub) in Aichi. Although as a child Tiago had wished he were fully Japanese, as an adult he felt proud of his difference, and aware of the ways in which he could contradict people's preconceived ideas about race: "When people see a Black guy coming, they get surprised. But I use that as a tool [*buki ni suru*]. Because I'm Black, I stand out, so I use that as an advantage. I always work hard [*ganbaru*] and do things right so that they see I don't just stand out, I stand out in a positive way." Still, on several different occasions, Tiago remembered showing up for interviews at employment brokerage firms that hired only Japanese workers and, as soon as he stepped in the room, was told, "Sorry, we don't accept *gaijin* [foreigners] here." Again, linguistic and cultural capital did not easily translate to social mobility and acceptance due to the "ethnoracial moral order" (Ong 1999: 25) of Japan, which privileges Japanese and whites/Westerners over others.

CHASING MIDDLE-CLASS SUBJECTIVITY

Given that most Brazilian migrants continued, into their third decade in Japan, to work in brokered, unskilled labor—not only dirty, difficult, and dangerous but also physically and psychologically draining, with limited chances at moving up within or outside the factory—why did so many opt to stay, or to return to Japan time and time again? For many, the answer lay in the comforts and freedoms of a middle-class lifestyle, for oneself or one's family, rather than any kind of ethnic or cultural identification per se. In other words, people's decision to stay long term in or repeat-migrate to Japan was not due, for example, to greater assimilation or integration over time. Rather, it had at least in part to do with achieving and/or maintaining a middle-class subjectivity that, in itself, signaled belonging to the Global North and all it represented in terms of purchasing power, personal safety, and material comforts.

When I spoke with interlocutors about why they stayed in Japan long term, or else decided to repeat-migrate there, the most common responses were, "life is easy in Japan," and "we got too comfortable" (*acomodado*). Clearly, though, they did not mean it was easy or comfortable in terms of finding social support, navigating unfamiliar customs and language, or working around the clock at repetitive, dead-end manufacturing jobs. As one interlocutor in her mid-twenties put it: "Life in Japan is easy because it's easy to *have* things. Even when the country is in crisis, if you work a little you can soon buy a TV, a camera. . . . But in Brazil, you have to think twice before buying things."

Indeed, despite Brazil's rapid economic growth and the stabilization of the national currency in the first decade of the twenty-first century, prices of consumer goods and property remain high, while salaries and wages are still relatively low. One *sansei* interlocutor in his early thirties, who had graduated from law school in Brazil and worked in factories in Japan for five years, said that he could not really see himself returning to Brazil: "I don't know where I'll live in the future but Brazil is the Third World. People in the Third World have to work miracles just to survive. Japan is good because it's the First World." In other words, despite having completed a university education in law, he felt he could not achieve the same "First World" lifestyle in Brazil that he could in Japan, and preferred to stay in blue-collar work in order to secure middle-class comforts and security.[13] If possible, he imagined moving to Australia or another third space beyond Japan and Brazil. Thus, his current life decisions and future aspirations had less to do with a sense of belonging (or lack thereof) in either country, and more with imagined opportunities around the world. Still, the fact that he was a relatively young man, single, and without dependents or much pressure from his family in Brazil, meant that he could move more freely after these opportunities than, say, Angela Silva (chapter 1) and her children.

Interestingly, even Brazilians who had never lived in Brazil or else had very little memory of it still believed they were better off in Japan because of easier access to consumer goods such as cars, name-brand clothing, and electronics. Students at a private Brazilian school in Aichi, for example, who grew up almost entirely in Japan, reiterated in Portuguese the same sentiments I so often heard from interlocutors who had migrated to Japan as adults:

Danielle (age 16): Besides family, and maybe food, there's nothing much else to say about Brazil. . . . Here in Japan, the lifestyle's better.

Sabrina (age 17): Yeah, it's that here, we've got more things, we have the means to buy things we just couldn't in Brazil.

Pamela (age 17): Japan is a place you don't want to leave because it's so comfortable.

In fact, the principal of the school these students attended believed that it was exactly this "easiness" (*facilidade*) that kept them from moving on with their studies. Once she started working at a factory in Japan, for example, a sixteen- or seventeen-year-old could make as much as her mother or father did, except that often she still lived with her family and did not have to pay rent or utilities: "So the kids start saving all this money, but then they say, wait, this life is good, this life is easy, I'm going to buy a car, new clothes, I'm going to move in with my girlfriend. And it goes from there. Most get swallowed up by the system, and how easy it is," he explained to me in Portuguese.

Another interlocutor in his early twenties, who started working in a car parts factory immediately upon graduating from high school in Japan, echoed these thoughts, relating how the greatest difficulty of being young in Japan is precisely how *easy* it is: "Because if you work at a factory, you get a good salary. Besides living comfortably, you can also buy all these things that in Brazil, you'd kill to have. But then time passes and you're still doing the same thing, you haven't moved up or studied or specialized in anything." Another interlocutor in her early forties, who raised her children in Japan and intended to stay there indefinitely, believed that parents were partly to blame for allowing their children to work in factories: "Teenagers can work, sure, they can earn a salary. Any little bit of money will seem exciting to them. But what about their future?" she wanted to know.

Nevertheless, earning good wages and having easy access to consumer goods allowed many people to feel secure and independent in ways they might not as easily in Brazil. It also allowed them a sense of belonging to both middle-class Brazil and, more broadly, a global economy of desire. Even for those who told me they could no longer save much money in Japan, due to the economic crisis of 2008–2009 and reduced wages/hours, still many preferred to stay there instead of return empty-handed to Brazil. "Here, even if we don't save money anymore, we live well, we eat well, and that gives us a sense of security we didn't easily have in Brazil," one factory worker in her forties told me. Another interlocutor in her early twenties was proud she could go to an American rap concert hours away by train in Ōsaka, something she believed she would not be able to afford in Brazil. "I have no money saved, but I live well here, I have a normal life," she explained. Thus, like the Filipina migrant workers in Hong Kong described in Nicole Constable's (1999) work, through the process of transnational labor migration, Brazilians in Japan found themselves exposed to "new material desires and different class identities" (224) and aspirations.

Many interlocutors told me how in their free time they were able to visit popular tourist destinations such as Universal Studios Japan and Tōkyō Disneyland, climb Mt. Fuji, ski and snowboard, eat out at nice restaurants, shop for name-brand clothes (which, in Brazil, as primarily imported goods would be even more expensive and inaccessible), and travel to other countries in Asia.[14] "That's why no one wants to leave Japan, because we can buy whatever we want here. And you can buy everything upfront, you don't walk away owing money," one interlocutor related.[15] Still, for others, symbols of middle-class status extended beyond consumer goods to include the cleanliness, safety, and organization they associated with

Japan. Similarly, in her study of middle-class Brazilians in Lisbon, Angela Torresan (2012) finds that "concomitant with their own personal and professional frustrations, [many immigrants were looking for an alternative to] the increasing poverty, violence, and physical insecurity, and the ubiquitous political corruption" (122) of Brazil. Among my interlocutors, access to decent public medical care, as well as relatively generous government assistance for unemployed workers and single parents, were also cited as reasons Japan was considered easier and more secure than Brazil. Efficient government services were, then, yet another symbol of "a country without intense social inequality, where [immigrants were] entitled to a sense of citizenship and personal safety" (ibid: 126) found so lacking in Brazil.

In sum, migrating to Japan allowed many Brazilians, while continuing to work in precarious, unskilled labor, the chance to achieve or maintain a certain middle-class lifestyle of comfort, safety, and leisure that was either difficult or impossible for them to imagine attaining in Brazil. In the next section, I examine issues of class more closely, and demonstrate how many migrants and their children, though they achieved a desired middle-class lifestyle, were still largely limited in their long-term social mobility, whether in Japan, Brazil, or beyond.

SOCIAL (IM)MOBILITY

Despite the fact that many Brazilians achieved significant economic capital as brokered labor migrants in Japan, scholars have tended to focus on the downward social and cultural mobility of Brazilians once they migrated there. While this was certainly true for many, there may also have been a bias for or overemphasis on Nikkei-Brazilians' white-collar or middle-class status to begin with. The idea of what constitutes middle class is itself fraught with contradictions, and shifts over time and across cultural contexts. Still, there has been a general notion—both among laypeople and academics familiar with Brazil—that Brazilians of Japanese descent are largely middle class and well educated compared to the broader Brazilian population.

Certainly, since urbanizing in the 1950s and 1960s, Nikkei-Brazilians have experienced considerable social mobility *as a whole*, in the context of Brazil. This does not mean, however, that *dekasegi*, or those Brazilians who have migrated to Japan, are necessarily middle class, nor that they achieved high educational and occupational status before leaving Brazil. In fact, of Brazilians who migrated to Japan to work, many of the people

I spoke with felt looked down upon by more "elite" members of Nikkei communities, who tended to distinguish between those who "made it" in Brazil and those who did not, and had little choice but to go to Japan for work. As Mieko Nishida (2017) notes in her analysis of self-published autobiographies and memoirs written primarily by Nikkei-Brazilian men, "there are no writings on 'ordinary' men, who did not make money or a name for themselves and therefore have been buried in the past as *shippaishas* (losers)" (6). This attitude was further reflected in comments I heard from Nikkei-Brazilians who never worked in unskilled labor in Japan. One *nisei* lawyer I grew to know in São Paulo, for example, worked for ten years in the 1990s for an employment brokerage firm based in Brazil, and was very critical of *dekasegi*: "The Brazilians who go to Japan are the ones who didn't succeed here. They went because they had nothing, or were nothing here, or because even if they did have a decent job or business here, something went wrong and they decided to try things out in Japan. But if they were nothing here, they'll be nothing in Japan," he said to me in Japanese, and with open disdain.

As it happened, at the employment brokerage firm where I worked in Gifu, I had access to surveys filled out by hundreds of foreign workers who had passed through the office to apply for jobs over the years. From these surveys (spanning the years 2006–2012), I was able to tabulate age, gender, city/ country of birth, visa status, marital status, and—importantly for my purposes—the reported educational background of over 500 *dekasegi*. In many cases, the surveys also included the number of family members/dependents in Japan (as well as dependents in Brazil) and previous occupational experience in Brazil.

In terms of education levels, applicants could respond that they had *at least some* elementary school, middle school, high school, or higher education (including postsecondary certifications and diplomas, and distance degrees), but this did not mean that they had necessarily graduated from said schools, only that it was the highest level of education they had attempted or begun. As seen from the tables here, education levels were similar for women and men. Of the 264 women and 258 men (total $n = 522$) that I tabulated, with ages ranging from fifteen to sixty-four (the bulk between twenty and fifty), a little over half had gone as far as (but no further than) high school, 21 percent only as far as middle school, and 6.5 percent only as far as elementary school. As for higher education, a full fifth of respondents claimed they had some postsecondary experience, a figure that corresponds, in fact, with data from Brazil's 2010 National Census, in which 19 percent of people over the age of twenty-five in the *amarela* (lit. yellow, referring to anyone who identifies as Asian) category reported having *completed* some kind of postsecondary education[16] (figures 2.1 and 2.2).

Women (n=264)

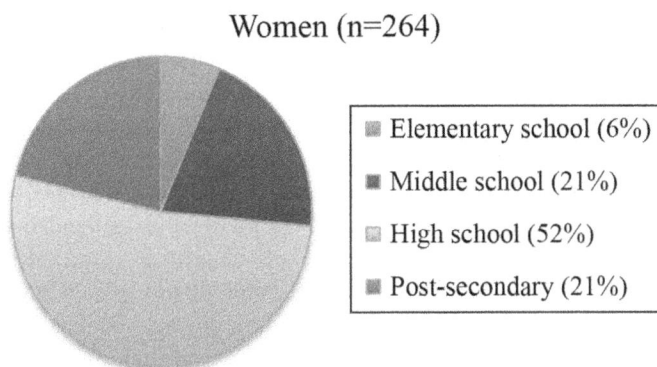

Figure 2.1 Self-reported education levels of *dekasegi* women in Japan (2006–2012).

Men (n=258)

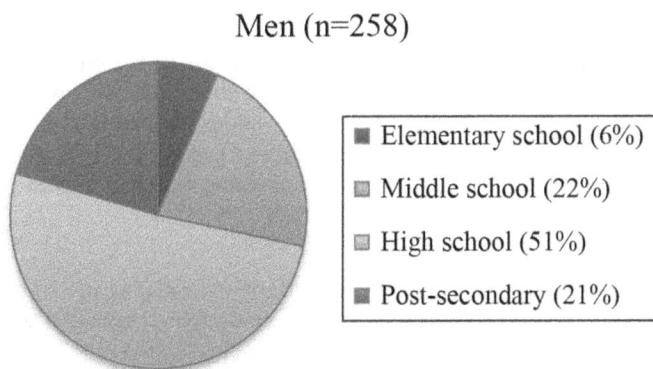

Figure 2.2 Self-reported education levels of *dekasegi* men in Japan (2006–2012).

Even if they had attempted postsecondary education, either in Brazil or via distance degrees in Japan, however, most interlocutors considered themselves or their families to be "lower middle class" before moving to Japan. In fact, of the minority of interlocutors I met who had completed university before leaving Brazil, they felt they had to hide their educational background from other Brazilians in Japan so as not to incite jealousy or suspicion. Still, most Nikkei-Brazilians, including those who went to work as labor migrants in Japan, had received more education than the average Brazilian. On the other hand, compared to figures for Japan, where in 2010 over half the population age twenty-five to thirty-four had attained tertiary education, they were less educated than the average Japanese.

Whether or not Brazilian labor migrants and their families experienced actual *downward* class mobility moving from Brazil to Japan is, therefore, a contentious issue. What is clear is that once in Japan, many Brazilians felt an

acute sense of *immobility* due to their position as brokered laborers in a segmented employment system, often without additional skills or qualifications
to bring back to Brazil should they choose to return migrate. In other words,
no matter what class, occupational, or educational background they came
from in Brazil, even after years working in Japan, many *dekasegi* encountered
significant difficulties moving *up* in terms of occupational status, either within
the Japanese labor market, or once they returned to the Brazilian labor market.

Lack of proficiency in Japanese was one of the primary obstacles to Brazilians finding work outside of the brokered employment system in Japan. As
many interlocutors observed, the fact that they did not speak or understand
enough Japanese meant they lost out on many opportunities in Japan. Even
if they applied to jobs on their own, they were often rejected because of language difficulties. In the case of one interlocutor who was turned away from
a job for this reason, she said:

> But I think that's my fault because I didn't really make an effort to learn Japa-
> nese. Since we come here and only work with Brazilians, we have Brazilian
> *tantōsha* [people in charge], and that makes things harder for us because we
> don't have to learn, we don't use Japanese. If I had worked in a factory just
> with Japanese people I would have learned, I would have had to. You get used
> to having someone do things for you.

As a matter of fact, many Brazilians in Japan worked next to other Brazilians, depended on their employment brokerage firms' translators, and had
little time or motivation to study Japanese because of the long, demanding
work hours. Still, for some, the issue was not just language but outright
discrimination. As demonstrated in the example of Tiago earlier, being of
visibly mixed descent meant that no matter how fluent one's Japanese was,
discrimination based on appearance was often a reality. Another interlocutor,
equally as fluent in Japanese as Tiago was, and more than sufficiently qualified for the job he was interviewing for, remembered the time he was denied
a further interview because, having showed his foreign identification card, he
was told outright, "*Brasileiro é kankei nai contratar*" ("Hiring a Brazilian is
out of the question").[17]

This kind of snap rejection of job applicants based on their ethnic appearance or foreign documentation came up in a number of conversations I had
with interlocutors, but language difficulties remained the primary barrier
cited. Education, of course, was another related issue, as explained in Portuguese by an interlocutor in her early sixties:

> We'll never be accepted in Japan. But a person who went to university, no mat-
> ter how poor, will be treated better here. People who didn't make money before

and now here they do, they grow, but not culturally, only financially. Then they act like they're high class. But they're not. We're not anyone here. These *dekasegi sem estudo* [uneducated *dekasegi*] are never going to gain respect here.[18]

As she pointed out, then, economic capital did not translate into social and cultural capital in Japan. What is more, the longer people spent working in factories in Japan, the more difficult it was to move up socially and culturally once they returned to Brazil. An interlocutor in his mid-thirties, for example, explained how Brazilians, because they generally did not gain education or professionalization in Japan, were simply replaceable labor with little future prospects: "People don't learn anything in factories in Japan. Anyone can do this kind of job and be replaced in a minute. Being able to screw things together or inspect cameras for defects isn't a profession, and it's not going to solve anything once we go back to Brazil." In other words, skills learned as manual laborers in Japan were rarely transferable to white-collar workplaces in Brazil.

In fact, many interlocutors cited lack of professionalization and/or education as one of the primary barriers to their mobility, either in Japan or Brazil. One *nisei* interlocutor, who came to Japan as a teenager, said he would not return to Brazil until he completed a long-distance university degree: "We've been here for twenty years in Japan and we're still in the same situation we were before. No one got a professional degree, no one learned anything, so going back to Brazil would be like starting at zero again." Even for those who wished to return to Brazil, then, lack of education meant that it would be difficult to find work that would allow them to maintain the same middle-class comforts they had achieved in Japan. Also, for those who did have higher education prior to moving to Japan, years outside the job market in Brazil made it difficult to return.

In the previous chapter, Marcelo, Angela's middle son, was a clear example of someone who, by spending years working in Japan, was able to achieve significant material comfort and security. At the same time as he accrued economic capital, however, he had little opportunity to move beyond unskilled labor in Japan. Moreover, because he had not acquired skills or knowledge in Japan that he could transfer to Brazil, Marcelo felt trapped in his position as a factory worker in Japan. Moving back to Brazil would necessarily mean downward mobility and was, therefore, a barrier to his leaving.

Yet another barrier to mobility had to do with age. Marcelo, though he felt too old to go back to school in Brazil, was still only in his late thirties. He had more opportunities, for example, than Miki, the man in his sixties we witnessed in a factory fight earlier in this chapter. Miki, like many *dekasegi* in their fifties or sixties, worried about returning to Brazil, not only because they lacked education and/or professional skills but also because of their age. Also, if they stayed in Japan, older workers were still largely limited to manual labor that they no longer had the same strength or energy to perform. What is more, factories often did not want to hire workers above thirty-five to forty. As one interlocutor in her fifties explained:

> If you're in your forties, it's okay, but once you get older you can't even get work here, can't even get an interview. I can see with my own health that I'm getting older now. I came here in my thirties, short and thin, but when I got to my fifties I thought, I can't keep doing this for very long. It's okay to want to die here but what about when you can't work anymore in Japan because of your age?

It was true that, decades after they first arrived in Japan, many Brazilians remained in brokered, temporary manual labor jobs, with limited access to further qualifications or the broader Japanese workforce. In many ways, this rendered them, as Takeyuki Tsuda (2003) pointed out, a kind of social underclass in Japan. What has tended to be overlooked, however, in studies of *dekasegi*, is the middle-class subjectivity that many migrants achieved through migrating to Japan. Furthermore, it is important to examine the social and financial independence that women migrants often experienced once they were far from home. This kind of mobility—though not necessarily upward class mobility—was especially meaningful to women who previously found themselves financially dependent on husbands or families or who, before moving to Japan, were generally expected to stay at home and take care of family members rather than work full time. For single mothers with little outside help, education, or job qualifications in Brazil, working in Japan also represented a stable means of supporting their children as well as themselves. The following cases offer a window into some of these women's lives, and the opportunities they gained by migrating to Japan.

DEBORA

Supporting Her Son from Afar

When Debora, *sansei*, in her early thirties, and divorced at the time of our interviews, found out she was pregnant at fifteen, she decided to carry her pregnancy to term while finishing high school in Brazil. Then, at the age of eighteen, she moved to Japan together with her non-Nikkei husband at the time, leaving her mother to care for her young son in São Paulo. As a child, Debora's father had worked for many years in factories in Japan, but by the time she went there, her parents had divorced and she was the only one of her immediate family to do so. The eldest of three children, Debora's younger brother and sister attended university while she moved back-and-forth between working in a factory in Japan and visiting her family in Brazil.

Since her ex-husband did not pay child support, Debora was largely responsible for supporting her son. When she moved to Japan, her mother, the daughter of Japanese emigrants to Brazil, warned her, "That's not your country, that's not your homeland." Worried that Debora would never come back, she tried to prevent her from moving to Japan. In the end, though, Debora went, certain she would earn more money there and that it would be better for her son to stay behind in Brazil surrounded by family and friends who had the time and means to take care of him.

The longest stretch Debora spent at a time in Japan was four years. Though she could not see her son during these times, she sent regular remittances to Brazil to support him. Over Skype, he would often ask her, "When can I come to Japan?" Worried that he would have trouble adjusting and that she would have no time for him, Debora had to repeat what she had said for years: "One day, love, one day."

In 2012, when I visited Debora's mother's apartment in Liberdade, the neighborhood of São Paulo where many Japanese emigrants and their descendants concentrated in the mid-twentieth century, her son Alexandre, twelve at the time, was just coming home from school. "Be careful, he's like gum, he'll stick to you like glue if he finds out you're a friend of his Mom's," Debora's mother warned me in Portuguese. According to her, Alexandre used to do well in school so long as he felt his mother was coming back for him. After her last visit a few years earlier, however, when it became clear that she would not be back again for another long stretch of time, he took a turn for the worse, acting up at school and wetting his bed at night. Debora's mother explained to me how Alexandre had also become a compulsive eater and talker in recent years and how, when left alone, he often spent his time shredding paper and picking apart the carpet.[19]

With me, however, Alexandre did not betray his heartbreak. Instead, he proudly showed me toy after toy that his mother had sent from Japan. Although Debora had paid for him to attend private school until recently, she decided to pull him out and put him into public school after he was held back a year. "Do you have anything from Japan to give me?" he asked hopefully as soon as we sat down for lunch. He inspected with pleasure the green tea Kit-Kat bar I gave him, turning it over and over again in his hands, as though the unfamiliar Japanese characters and glossy packaging might hold the key to bringing his mother home again.

But the chances of Debora returning to Brazil again soon were slim. Despite the pressure she faced—especially intense by virtue of her gender—to return to live with her son, she enjoyed the financial and personal independence she had in Japan, and felt it was the best, and only feasible

way, to properly support Alexandre.[20] As her father had done when she
was a child and left her in Brazil with her mother, Debora too was working as the chief provider of the family. Having spent a good part of her
adolescence tending to her infant son, Japan also represented a space where
she could experience, for the first time, the freedom to live on her own, go
out at her own will, and spend the money she made however she saw fit.[21]
Certainly, it allowed her son the option of private school in Brazil, as well
as other material comforts she would not otherwise have been able to easily
provide him with.

DANNY AND JULIA

Unemployed Friends in Japan

I met Danny and Julia at a six-month nail cosmetology course in Nagoya
offered for free by the Japanese government to unemployed foreign residents
who had lost their jobs in the 2008–2009 economic crisis. Danny, a *sansei*
Brazilian of mixed descent in her mid-thirties, had been in Japan for four
years, and Julia (early forties), though not Nikkei herself, had lived in Japan
since 1995. I interviewed them together in Danny's government-subsidized
apartment in rural Gifu, the building's corridors cluttered with junk waiting
to be thrown away. At the time, Danny's daughter was only six months old,
and she nursed her off-and-on throughout our conversation.

Danny's mother had died when she was very young, and her father
was a lifelong alcoholic. The father of her child, also from Brazil, was
absent from the picture, and did not pay child support even though he had
a relatively stable factory job in another city in Japan. Danny had started
university in Brazil but ended up dropping out before she finished. After
completing the beauty course in Nagoya (she left her baby with a Brazilian neighbor during the day), she aimed to learn Japanese, take a massage
course in Thailand, work in a spa in Japan, and then return to Brazil with
these new skills under her belt. "I'm against mothers who have babies here
and keep working three hours of *zangyō* [overtime] every day. What's the
point of saving up all that money for your kids if you can't give them love
and attention?" she asked.

Julia, because she was not of Japanese descent, could not have applied on
her own for a Nikkei visa to Japan. In the early 1990s, however, she happened
to meet a Nikkei man at the office where she worked in Brazil, shortly after
her father died and, devastated, she sought a new direction in her life: "I asked
this guy, 'do you have an older brother? I'm going to marry him and go to
Japan.' It was just a joke, you know. And this guy said 'no, seriously, my
brother actually does want to go to Japan.' And it was a joke like that but then

it actually happened, it wasn't really planned. I thought I should get away, to forget things. And then I did, I came here."

Trained as a schoolteacher in Brazil, Julia worked first in factories, before she was hired at a *sunakku*, or small hostess club,[22] where she worked for twelve years before returning to a factory in 2010:

> I used to think that when I went back to Brazil, I'd have to study more to get qualified again. But then I realized that it was good to come to Japan, that I experienced things I would never have experienced otherwise in life if I had stayed in the interior of Brazil. I gained work experiences and met people here that I would never have been able to there. I got to know people I would never have imagined meeting. I got to travel, got to know people from other countries, from Europe, Africa, etc. It's a lot of culture I got to experience, way more than if I had stayed in that hole in Paraná that no one's ever heard of, imagine! If I had stayed in Brazil, I would have four kids already. I would be married and fat as a whale. And crazy. Because Italian women like where I come from have to have more than two kids. But I always wanted to be independent, alone, work for my own money. Even though that wasn't really accepted in the interior at the time.

Danny, though she was less mobile than Julia, now that she had to raise a child on her own, agreed that working in Japan opened new doors in her life as well. After just five months of saving money from working in a factory in Japan, she would be able to travel to Thailand for an intensive massage course. This kind of "international exchange" was usually only available to Brazilians from wealthy families, she explained, or to the brightest of the bright, who were gifted enough to win a coveted scholarship.

Although she struggled to make ends meet, Danny was grateful to live in subsidized housing and for the government assistance she received as a single mother in Japan. She was also pleased with the free beauty course she was enrolled in, explaining how it had allowed her to finally learn more Japanese: "I learned *hiragana* [the basic phonetic Japanese script] in three classes that I hadn't learned in three years of being here. As long as I have health I want to work. I don't want to depend on a man's money. If I want to buy clothes, I want to have my own money to buy it." What is more, she felt, the skills she learned in the course would allow her to work in a beauty salon in Brazil, although not necessarily for very good pay.

Despite being temporarily unemployed at the time, Danny and Julia both earned enough on unemployment insurance in Japan to continue supporting themselves without the help of anyone else. They were free to buy their own clothes and food, and to live on their own. Thus, besides learning nail cosmetology and Japanese language for free thanks to a government program aimed at unemployed Nikkei-Latin Americans, Danny and Julia were also able to remain financially and socially independent in Japan.

CLAUDIA AND HER DAUGHTERS,
AND HER DAUGHTERS' DAUGHTERS

When I was first introduced to her, Claudia was forty and had been coming and going to work in factories in Japan for the past twelve years. She herself was not Nikkei but her husband was *sansei*, and their three *yonsei* daughters—Paula, Lana, and Leticia—came to live with Claudia and her husband in Japan in 2004 when they were fifteen, twelve, and eleven, respectively. Everyone in the household preferred to speak primarily only in Portuguese.

Paula, Claudia's eldest daughter, was in her mid-twenties when we met. The mother of a baby girl, she lived with her boyfriend, and had never completed high school. She started working in a *bentō* (boxed lunch) factory in Japan almost as soon as she arrived at age fifteen. Lana, for her part, went to Japanese middle school for three years and then, when she was graduating, told her teachers that she wanted to work instead of continuing to high school because she planned to go back to Brazil one day and study. Her school introduced her to a car parts factory, where she worked until the age of seventeen, and then entered a *bentō* factory herself. After two years at the *bentō* factory, while working as a model on the side, Lana had a child at nineteen. She stayed at home for the first six months while her boyfriend supported her. Finally, Leticia, Claudia's youngest daughter, also went to Japanese public school and, like her sisters, began working full time in a factory after middle school.

Claudia herself had never had the chance to finish elementary school in Brazil. "Before I came to Japan I still had that idea that a woman had to stay at home and obey her husband," she explained. "Then I came here in my 30s and everything changed. I went back to Brazil and got my elementary school diploma." Once back in Japan again, Claudia continued to work in a factory, making her own money and buying things for herself that once she had to rely on her husband for.

When I asked her if she was glad she had brought her daughters to Japan, Claudia hesitated: "In a way yes, but in a way no, because they didn't continue with their studies. None of them went on to high school or university. And now they're adults, and two of them are mothers already. On the other hand, though, in Brazil we couldn't give them the things we wanted to and that was tough." Although moving to Japan did not translate into her daughters furthering their studies, it did allow Claudia the confidence and means to return to Brazil and finish her own basic education. It also permitted her to work instead of staying home and caring for her family, and to provide her daughters with material comforts she could not easily obtain in Brazil.

For Paula and Lana, both young mothers, working in Japan meant that they could earn their own wages and help support their families. For Lana, this was especially important when her boyfriend, who she met at the factory, was diagnosed at age twenty-two with neck cancer. While he stayed home with the baby, Lana worked overtime to pay for his expensive medical treatment (only 70 percent of which was covered by Japanese national health insurance). "I'm doing well here, I'm twenty years old and I have my own money, my house, my car, my kid. And I'm the only one working. We would never have all this in Brazil. So I think we'll stay in Japan because we have a better life than we'd have in Brazil, because we didn't study there, and to have a good job in Brazil, you need to have an education," she reflected, echoing the sentiment of so many other interlocutors.

KIKUE

Sewing Together a Better Life in Brazil

I met Kikue, a *nisei* woman in her sixties, in Brazil, years after she had returned from working thirteen years in Japan together with her husband, also Nikkei-Brazilian. She recalled—speaking with me primarily only in Japanese—how difficult it was in the early years of her marriage, when she lived in her mother-in-law's home at the age of sixteen and had just two large pots to cook in, one for rice and the other for the vegetables they planted in the interior of São Paulo: "We never had any meat, and we divided all our food among the thirty people or so with whom we lived." Kikue originally met her husband through the town's local *kaikan* (Japanese cultural association) and, as a teenager, went to the same Japanese-language school as him.

Once they married, life for Kikue was very strict, and she learned a great deal more Japanese because of her in-laws. She was always criticized by her husband's mother and grandmother for falling short in her duties as wife and daughter-in-law. Kikue had always sewn clothes and hoped to sell them outside of the home but her husband never let her. Instead, before leaving for Japan in the late 1980s, she sewed from home and made very little money from it, while her husband worked in food distribution.

"If we hadn't gone to Japan we would have continued in that life, and it would have been very hard to get out of it," she told me. By migrating to Japan, Kikue and her husband were able to buy a house in Brazil for themselves, and create a life outside of either of their families' homes. What is more, Kikue was able to buy several expensive sewing machines in Japan and, when I met her, she was sewing every day, selling pieces here and there. Although her husband believed it was "too dangerous" for her to open her own shop in Brazil, and preferred to have her work at home, Kikue had achieved a certain level of independence and mobility thanks to her work in Japan. Though she was still limited by her gender, age, and educational/occupational background, she found her post-*dekasegi* life in Brazil far more comfortable than before she had left. As Pardis Mahdavi (2016) shows in her work with foreign women migrants in the United Arab Emirates, class immobility in the host country does not always correspond to lower wages or lack of mobility back in the sending country. In the end, Kikue, like all of the women I have described here, found that her decisions to migrate, settle, and/or return were rooted in personal and financial constraints and possibilities rather than, say, experiences of either ethnic belonging or displacement.

CONCLUSION

In the context of a "new mobilities paradigm" and more holistic understanding of mobility in recent years, Tim Cresswell (2010) describes a politics of mobility as the ways in which mobilities are both productive of social relations and produced by them, and how they include relations between classes, genders, ethnicities, nationalities, and religious groups. He suggests six facets of mobility—motive force, speed, rhythm, route, experience, and friction—that serve to differentiate people and things into hierarchies of mobility. Have migrants been compelled to go to Japan or back to Brazil for socioeconomic reasons, for example, or did they choose to go somewhere as a tourist or researcher might? What were the routes and conduits along which *dekasegi* and their families moved across borders? Was stopping, like going, a choice, or was it forced?

As I have shown so far, Brazilian transnational labor migrants were, for the most part, compelled to move to Japan because they or the people they supported could not sustain a comfortable enough lifestyle in Brazil, or because they needed to save for increased mobility (professional, educational, material, aspirational) down the road. They were then compelled to return to Brazil because of precarious and/or harsh working conditions, limited professional/educational opportunities, mental and physical health concerns, and/or in order to care for family members and other dependents.

In terms of how mobility has been channeled for Nikkei-Brazilians, the primary conduit along which they continue to move to Japan is that of *ethnic legitimacy*. After all, only people of Japanese descent up to the third generation or their descendants qualify for the special visa that has allowed them to work in unskilled labor in Japan since the early 1990s. This places them in a unique position in the hierarchy of global mobility since, on the one hand, on the basis of Japanese heritage (not something one works or studies for but happens to be born with) they are more mobile than both non-Nikkei Brazilians and other foreign citizens wishing to work in unskilled labor in Japan, while on the other hand, they cannot rely on their ethnicity alone to move anywhere else outside of Brazil besides Japan. In this sense, they are less mobile than, say, someone with skills or a degree that are valued and sought after in various parts of the world, and who can choose to move at will. At the same time, they are also more mobile than Japanese citizens—residents of the post-3/11 disaster-hit Tōhoku region, for example—who, though they may wish to move outside of Japan for fear of radiation, earthquakes, and so on, do not necessarily have the connections or economic and cultural capital necessary to ensure legal residency abroad.

How Brazilian labor migrants stop moving, or migrating is of course connected to the same immigration policy that allows them to shuttle between Japan and Brazil in the first place. If Japan were to discontinue the special Nikkei visa loophole, for example, or to put new constraints on those Brazilians already in possession of temporary or permanent visas to Japan, migrants would be limited in their movement between the two countries. Legally speaking, then, what both constrains and enables Nikkei-Brazilians and their dependents in their movement around the world is their citizenship (in terms of nationality) and their Japanese ethnicity (insofar as it allows them a special visa to work in Japan).

The politics of mobility are not, however, only a matter of citizenship, visas, and immigration policy. People are forced to move, and to stay put, because of other considerations such as the lack of viable job and educational opportunities, or "frustrated freedoms" (Fischer 2014), family responsibilities, illness and disability, age, and gendered and religious beliefs about one's appropriate place in the world. One of the broader aims of this book is to demonstrate the ways in which transnational Brazilian labor migrants are both mobile and immobile in the context of Japanese and Brazilian national settings, as well as global geopolitical realities. To do so, it is necessary to examine more than their ethnic positioning but also how that very ethnicity is connected to gender, generation, and class, as well as the contexts of family, work, education, and religion.

Thus, in this chapter, I explored in greater depth issues of social (im)mobility among Brazilians involved in the *dekasegi* movement. Specifically, I demonstrated how migrating to Japan via a brokered labor system represented both significant constraints and opportunities in terms of job options, purchasing power, and social mobility. By examining an employment brokerage firm—particularly in light of a factory fight—I showed how the brokered labor system both mediated problems for its workers and restricted them as part of the irregularly employed precariat in Japan. I also explored how, for many migrants, language and education barriers, as well as gender, age, and ethnicity affected their chances at upward mobility in Japan. Moreover, their lack of educational credentials and professionalization in Japan led to reduced job opportunities and mobility should they choose to return to Brazil.

At the same time as it limited or reduced their long-term social mobility, however, migration to Japan allowed for the achievement or maintenance of middle-class subjectivities. For many, access to relatively high economic capital irrespective of educational/class background represented a significant factor in migrants' decision to stay in Japan. Moreover, as illustrated in this chapter, for many women—particularly those with limited education and/ or who served as the chief supporters of their families—working in Japan allowed them a level of social and financial independence they felt would otherwise have been difficult, if not impossible, to achieve in Brazil.

In conclusion, through the process of transnational migration, Brazilian laborers in Japan simultaneously experienced upward mobility (in terms of greater purchasing power, financial independence, and material comforts) *and* downward mobility (as members of the brokered precariat in Japan, with limited opportunities for educational or occupational advancement in either Japan or Brazil). In other words, increased economic capital did not necessarily translate into social or cultural capital either in Japan or Brazil. Still, despite the limitations involved, many migrants opted to stay in Japan because of the possibilities it presented in terms of a coveted and comfortable middle-class life/lifestyle. In this sense, living transnationally involved navigating not only different ethnic, cultural, and national identities but also different class subjectivities, with both Japanese and Brazilian class frameworks as the referent points. By migrating to Japan for work, Brazilians engaged in consumption habits and behaviors associated with the Brazilian middle class, while at the same time remaining in low-status positions according to local hierarchies of value in both Japan and Brazil. They were, therefore, embedded in "a wider social field that spans two or more nations" (Glick Schiller et al. 1992: 17) and includes different national imaginaries of class and status.

In the next chapter, I explore the case of a Brazilian family that decided to stay long term in Japan, going so far as to naturalize to Japanese citizenship. While middle-class desires certainly played a role in their decision, family concerns as well as generational differences—that is, age at time of migration, education, and varying degrees of ethnic and national belonging—were also important factors to consider.

NOTES

1. Maureen O'Dougherty (2002) considers "middle-class home ownership, consumption, education, and work as the means whereby middle-class people, materially and symbolically, attain and perform their class" (6). By arguing that consumption is central to middle-class self-definitions, she does "not assume that productive

activities, usually translated into occupational categories, are the sole foundation of class identity or political practice" (ibid: 11). Similarly, I consider consumption to be central to Brazilian labor migrants' sense of having achieved a middle-class lifestyle in Japan.

2. Even recently, as many as 80 to 85 percent of Nikkei workers in Japan were hired as contract or dispatch workers (Takenoshita 2010).

3. Following Sherry Ortner's (2005) definition: "By subjectivity I will mean the ensemble of modes of perception, affect, thought, desire, fear, and so forth that animate acting subjects. But I will always mean as well the cultural and social formations that shape, organize, and provoke those modes of affect, thought and so on" (31).

4. Here we see a clear example of what Stephen Castles et al. (2014) mean by migration network theory, or "how migrants create and maintain social ties with other migrants and with family and friends back home, and how this can lead to the emergence of social networks" (39).

5. Compare this roughly 30 percent profit to Joshua Roth's (2002) similar observation: "In the mid-1990s, manufacturing firms often paid brokers 1,800 yen (roughly US$18 at the time) per hour for male workers and 1,400 yen per hour for female workers. Brokers would generally keep about 30 percent of these receipts for themselves, setting male workers' wages at 1,300 yen per hour and female wages at 900 yen per hour" (66).

6. According to Anne Allison's definition (2013), then, Miki fulfilled many of the criteria for those most at risk of forming part of the Japanese precariat: he had limited academic credentials, was a foreign migrant, and was over the age of fifty. Additionally, he was hearing impaired.

7. This was not an entirely unfounded fear since, as Joshua Roth (2002) notes: "[T]he quasi-legal status of employment brokers for Nikkeijin invited the entry of local gangsters (*yakuza*)" (71).

8. Joshua Roth (2002) calls this underlying problem of intense competition among workers for the recognition of their supervisors "the ideology of competitive meritocracy" (59).

9. Japan's Edō period (1600–1868) was marked by an isolationist foreign relations policy known as *sakoku*. During this time, foreigners could not freely enter or leave Japan, though trade continued with the Chinese, Koreans, Dutch, the Indigenous Ainu, and peoples of the Ryūkyū Islands (now Okinawa). By referring to this period in history, the lawyer intended to contrast it with twenty-first-century Japan, where foreigners are now a regular and everyday part of society.

10. The fact that someone of Miki's age was still working in as physically demanding a job as his was not unusual among Brazilians in Japan. Based on data from 2005, Sachi Takaya et al. (2013) found that over 90 percent of Nikkei workers in Japan continued to work even after the age of sixty-five. Furthermore, as David Chiavacci (2016) has shown, although Brazilians in Japan have achieved reasonable income levels, they are still restricted to highly insecure employment and potentially subject to a high risk of old-age poverty.

11. Thanks to historian Jeffrey Lesser for noting that the use of words such as kamikaze (e.g., in chapter 1) and samurai among Nikkei-Brazilian male interlocutors

points to a sense of ethnic pride, which in these cases is specifically expressed via images of Japanese self-sacrifice and masculine strength.

12. See, for example, Minami Funakoshi's (2017) article in *Reuters*, as well as Daniel Hurst's article in *The Guardian* from the same year.

13. This reference to a First World/Third World dichotomy points to how, "on the one hand, middle-class Brazilians occupy a privileged position within [Brazil]. On the other hand, they occupy a subaltern position vis-à-vis values constructed in colonial or post-and neocolonial centers of political and economic power" (Maia 2012: 55).

14. Maureen O'Dougherty (2002) points to how trips to Disneyland/Disneyworld in the United States have become a highly desired rite among upper middle-class Brazilian teens, and a quasi-requisite for social validation (98). Similarly, imported goods (such as Japanese or American cars or brand-name clothes) represented the acquisition of First World modernity and symbolic positioning in that world. Together, "these global consumption practices are central to the realization of middle-class identity, both as a symbolic means of presenting and proving status outwardly, and as the material means of securing and leading a modern life at home" (112).

15. Here, the speaker is referring to the practice, common in Brazil (but not in Japan), of buying goods and services in installments (*parcelas*), rather than making a purchase via a single debit card/cash or credit transaction. This is done when buying anything from sneakers to refrigerators, and in practice means that customers can easily walk away with a commodity but still owe money on it.

16. Compare these numbers with the overall figures for Brazil, where, according to the 2010 Census, among people over the age of twenty-five, 49 percent had not completed elementary school, 15 percent completed elementary school but not middle/high school, 25 percent completed high school but not higher education, and 11 percent completed higher education (IBGE 2010).

17. This anecdote was related to me in a mix of Japanese (underlined in the quote) and Portuguese (not underlined), though presumably the interlocutor in question was turned away by a Japanese speaker who did not mix the two languages.

18. See Maureen O'Dougherty (2002) for the ways in which middle-class speakers in Brazil "constructed a morally superior position on the (quasi-sacred) supports of home ownership, educational investments, and cultured consumption (plus ownership of an old car), in contradistinction to those who had a new car and engaged in vulgar, superfluous, materialistic consumption, but did not have a 'decent home,' education, or culture" (49).

19. For further commentary on the mental health conditions associated with the children of *dekasegi* left behind in Brazil, see, for example, Urano & Yamamoto (2008).

20. As Stephen Castles et al. (2014) demonstrate more broadly, for some people, migration can and does serve as a means of escaping families back home.

21. Similarly, Angela Torresan (2012) points out that "leaving their parents' home, gaining independence from the family, being able to travel, having access to entertainment, [and] being able to consume quality goods" (126) were all important issues to the Brazilian immigrants she studied in Lisbon.

22. Hostess clubs are common throughout Japan and are broadly defined as spaces of after-work, socially exclusive drinking where male (and sometimes female) customers individually or collectively, volitionally or obligatorily, visit on weekdays after work to receive the "service" of paid drinks, attendance, and conversation by women (Okura Gagné 2010: 170). They are not, however, to be confused with spaces of prostitution or any kind of *fuzoku* (sex industry). While some hostess clubs expressly hire foreign hostesses (thereby branding themselves as exotic), most of the Brazilian women I met who worked as hostesses, including Julia, were hired at Japanese clubs. Since they did not enter the industry via employment brokerage firms, they either spoke enough Japanese to be hired directly, or otherwise had or made personal connections to the clubs and/or club owners.

Chapter 3

The Matsudas

Becoming Japanese

Although the majority of Brazilians originally intended to work in Japan for only a few years, many of them settled long term, so that by 2008 an estimated one-third of the Brazilian population in Japan had acquired permanent residency. By 2011, well over half of all Brazilians living in Japan were registered as permanent residents. At the outset of my fieldwork, I interpreted these numbers as a sign that Brazilians had grown to be a more permanent part of Japanese society, and that their continued presence challenged ideas of an ethnically homogenous Japan.

Certainly, Japan is not ethnically homogenous, and the vast academic literature on the topic has played an important role in problematizing this myth. As noted in the introduction to this book, Brazilian labor migrants are one of many documented groups, including the Ainu, Okinawans, and resident Koreans, Chinese, and Filipinos, serving to illustrate Japan's inner ethnic diversity. As I came to understand throughout the course of my research, however, the presence of long-term foreign residents in Japan did not necessarily index greater attachment to or identification with things Japanese (or vice versa). For many Brazilian labor migrants, permanent residency in Japan was in part a practical step toward safeguarding the right to live and work in Japan, while maintaining legal citizenship in Brazil. Going so far as to naturalize to Japanese citizenship, on the other hand, required a greater deal of commitment in terms of time and effort, and was something few Brazilians felt the need or desire to do.

Brazilian labor migrants acquired and maintained permanent residency in Japan, then, not because they necessarily felt more Japanese with time but because, as Aihwa Ong (1999) showed in her studies of the Hong Kong business elite, flexibility (in the sense of membership in multiple states)

88

Chapter 3

was a useful strategy in maximizing possibilities in the precarious global economy. Whether or not they were temporary or permanent residents of Japan, or went to the extreme of naturalizing, Brazilian labor migrants and their families variously negotiated the meanings of membership in both Japan and Brazil.

In the case of the family focused on in this chapter, the Matsudas, who in various ways passed as Japanese and in 2011 in fact became Japanese citizens, they too continued to live the reality of multiple national orientations and affiliations. This kind of transnational living (which refers to various and variable forms of membership and belonging, if not full legal citizen status, across national boundaries)[1] was deeply embedded in the context of family. While each individual's experience of being Japanese and/or Brazilian varied according to a complex field of forces, including personality, age at migration, educational trajectory, sense of social (im)mobility, and the work and life consociates with whom they regularly fraternized, their expression of ethnicity and belonging was also shaped by a host of family-based constraints and opportunities.

As will be shown throughout this chapter, the long-term residency and/or naturalization of Brazilians in Japan did not result in either complete differentiation (e.g., ethnic resistance) or complete cultural assimilation. Rather, members of a single family engaged in various forms and degrees of transnational living—in other words, a dynamic, relational, and shifting blend of ethnic, cultural, and national belonging. What is more, individual positionings continued to shift throughout the course of people's lives, shaped as they were by a complex host of factors such as national immigration policy, work, school, health, marriage, chance encounters, friends, family, and neighbors.

FAMILY BACKGROUND

The Matsudas—Marcia, her husband Elio, and their two *sansei* daughters, Sayuri and Tomoko—came to Japan in the early to mid-1990s. Takuya, the Matsudas's youngest son, was the only one born in Japan. By the time I met the family in 2010, they had already lived in their eighth-floor apartment in Aichi for ten years, and were considering naturalizing to Japanese citizenship. For ease of understanding, figure 3.1 shows four generations of the Matsuda family. Cross-hatching indicates which members of the family either once worked or still work as *dekasegi*, that is, as part of the contracted foreign labor force of Japan (figure 3.1).

Over dinner one evening, we passed around dishes of ham and olive pasta casserole, sausage, and passion fruit juice from the nearby Brazilian

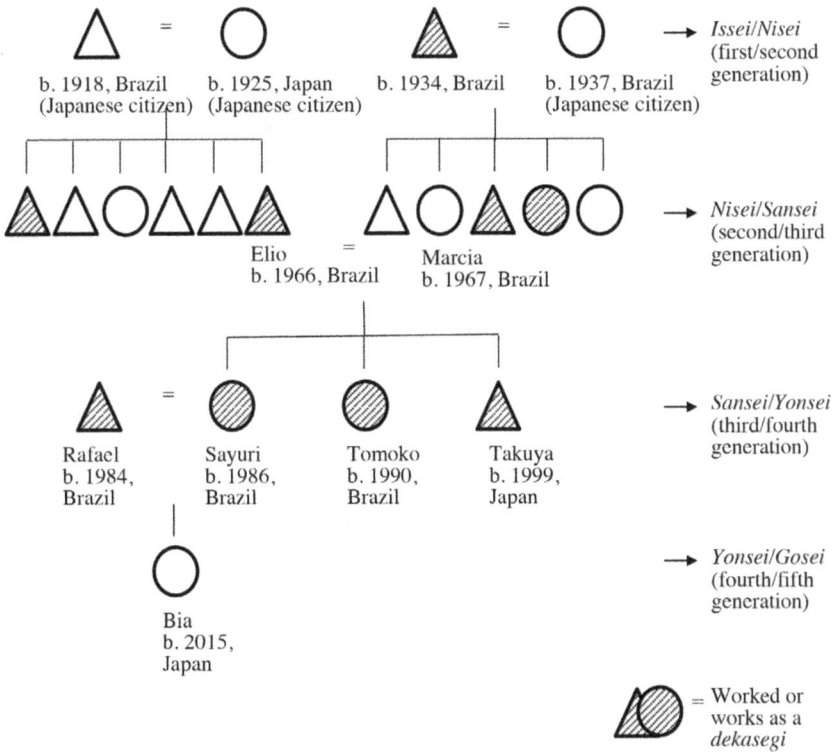

Figure 3.1 The Matsuda family tree.

supermarket, and the usual *arroz*, or rice. "*Arroz tte nani?*" Takuya asked in Japanese, wondering what the Portuguese word *arroz* meant. "*Gohan da yo,*" his eldest sister Sayuri informed him in Japanese. "It's rice." As the evening progressed, words in Japanese and Portuguese streaked across the table like differently colored fireworks. Marcia and Elio spoke to one other, and to me, in Portuguese. They spoke to their daughters in a mix of Japanese and Portuguese but to their son Takuya only in Japanese. Their eldest daughter Sayuri spoke in Japanese to her siblings and parents, and to her Brazilian boyfriend Rafael, though he responded only in Portuguese. I struggled to keep the two parts of my brain from fizzling into one, speaking to the young boy beside me in Japanese, and in Portuguese to Sayuri's boyfriend across from me. Figure 3.2 represents a partial linguistic map of the dinner table conversation that evening.

Marcia and Elio Matsuda were born in the late 1960s and raised in the same small city in the interior of São Paulo State, where there were many other people of Japanese descent. Both of them remembered making *mochi* (glutinous rice cakes) with their families at New Year's, and speaking basic

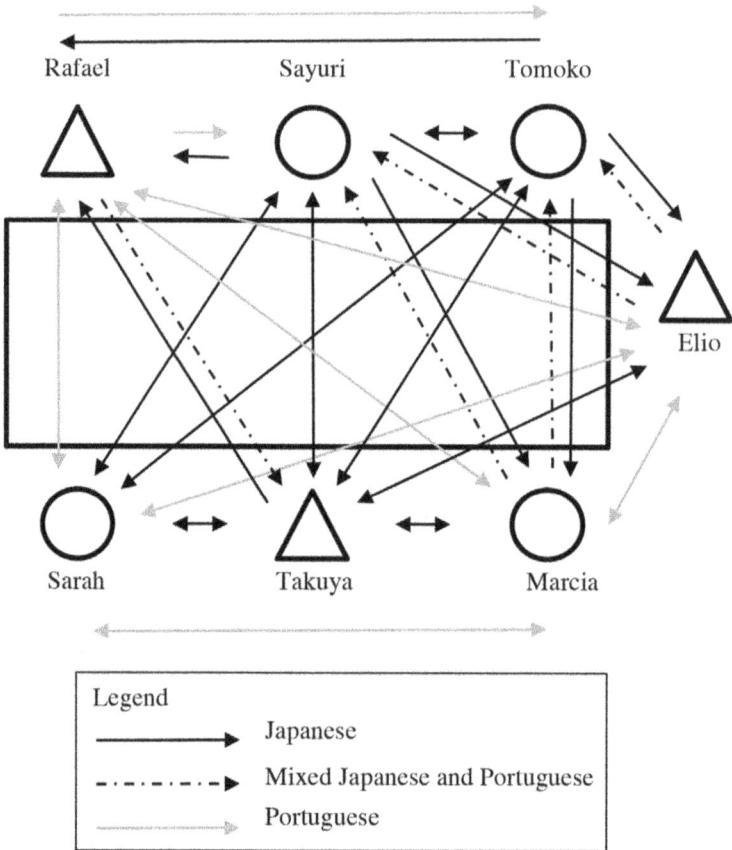

Figure 3.2   Dinner with the Matsuda family.

Japanese with their parents and grandparents. Elio's mother was born in Wakayama in 1925 and brought to Brazil as a baby. There she married Elio's father, who was born in Brazil in 1918 to immigrants from Saga, Japan. Elio's maternal grandfather had dreamed of returning to Japan one day, but he died within fifteen years of moving to Brazil, and never made the return journey.

During a visit to Japan in 2013, Elio's then eighty-five-year-old mother spoke to me in Japanese of how her family had suffered in Brazil, planting potatoes on land that would not yield. They migrated to Brazil because an uncle had gone first, because there was not enough food in Japan, and because everyone had believed that money would come easily to them there. Things improved a little once her family bought their own land, she told me, but she had to work hard for many years in the fields. She did not have much of a chance to study, although she did attend *nihon gakkō*, or Japanese school, as a child. She remembered clearly when, during the Second World War, once Brazil joined the side of the United States and other allied nations (Lesser 1999; Rivas 2011), Nikkei-Brazilians were not allowed to publicly gather in groups or speak Japanese. One day, Elio's mother told me, living far from everything, out in the countryside, she tried to take a bus to the dentist's, but the other children would not let her board because she was Japanese.

Unlike Elio, whose parents were both Japanese citizens and who considered himself *nisei* (second generation) throughout his life, his wife Marcia had always thought of herself as *sansei* (third generation), until the day her mother died and she discovered that, though her mother was born in Brazil, she had been registered on time as a baby to have dual nationality. For this reason, Marcia was able to obtain a *nisei* visa to Japan on the grounds that her mother had in fact been a Japanese citizen.

Marcia and Elio married when they were nineteen and twenty, respectively, and Marcia was already several months pregnant with their first daughter, Sayuri, who was born in Brazil in 1986. Tomoko, their second daughter, was born there in 1990. When the girls were little and they still lived in Brazil, Elio went to school at night to earn a university degree in business administration, working during the day in a blue-jeans factory in Sorocaba. Marcia studied to be an elementary school teacher and worked for a short time helping children at the *nihon gakkō* with their Portuguese before moving to Japan.

Elio came to Japan first, in 1992, toward the beginning of the "*dekasegi* boom." He stayed two years working in a factory, and was then joined by Marcia, her father, and their two young girls. Marcia's father had already been to Japan to work before, beginning in the late 1980s, and had stayed for six years. After suffering a heart attack, however, he was no longer able to work full time, and largely stayed at home caring for his young granddaughters while Marcia and Elio worked at the factory. The child of Japanese parents, Marcia's father spoke Japanese quite fluently, and so the girls began to learn more of the language from their grandfather. Marcia and Elio offered him a small *okozukai* (allowance) in compensation for staying at home and caring for their children. The Matsudas chose to live in a city near Nagoya because Marcia's brother and sister were already working there, thereby taking advantage of family networks to ease their transition. "We were lucky," Marcia recalled, "we were treated well at the factory because some of our relatives already worked there so we were seen in a positive light."

Although Elio and Marcia spent most of their years in Japan working in factories, the economic crisis of 2008–2009 changed their situation significantly. After thirteen years working at the same factory, Marcia entered a job at the local city hall in 2008 to help translate for and assist Brazilian residents who needed help sorting through taxes and other bureaucratic matters. Her job was offered on a year-to-year contract, and she hoped to keep it as long as they were willing to renew it. As for Elio, in 2011 he was asked to volunteer to leave his job at the factory in exchange for a compensatory bonus. Since then, he tried a variety of different part-time jobs, from massage therapy and translating for Hello Work (a Japanese government employment service center) to selling beauty and food products for multilevel marketing (also known as "pyramid scheme") companies.

THE 1.5 AND SECOND GENERATION

Growing up Japanese

The Matsudas moved to Japan with the intention of staying for only a few years, as was the case of their parents and grandparents before them when they first went to Brazil, as well as so many early labor migrants to Japan. When he first went to Japan to work in 1992, Elio had said that he would go back to Brazil but return again one day to Japan, because the salary was so high at the time. For this reason, Marcia decided after two years that it was time for the entire family to be together again. She did not wish to stay in Brazil any longer with her husband so far away, so she packed her bags and, in 1994, boarded a plane to Japan with her two daughters and her father. At the time, however, she had no idea how long they would stay in Japan, and expected to return to Brazil once they saved a certain amount of money. When they arrived, Tomoko was four years old, and Sayuri was seven going on eight. Sayuri was immediately placed in second grade in a Japanese elementary school, though she did not yet speak any Japanese. By the time we met, however, she preferred to speak only in Japanese:

Sarah: Do you remember when you arrived [in Japan]?

Sayuri: I remember I didn't know who my Dad was, so I checked by looking for his mole.

Elio laughed at this, though there were tears in his eyes as he explained how at the time his daughters had not seen him in two years—he had not returned to Brazil during this period—and they did not recognize him when they first arrived in Japan. His eldest daughter, confused about who he was, had searched for the prominent mole on his back that she remembered from their taking *ofuro* (baths) together before he left for Japan. Only when she found the familiar dark spot between his shoulders did she feel certain that he was her father. Tomoko, for her part, had no memory of her father having been with her in Brazil, because she was only two when he left to work in a factory in Japan.

When I met them, I noticed that both Sayuri and Tomoko introduced themselves by their Japanese names only, while Marcia and Elio used their Portuguese first names around me and other Brazilians, but their Japanese middle names with many neighbors, acquaintances, etc. Tomoko attended Japanese public school from nursery through high school, after which she worked first at a shopping mall bakery and then at a nearby Toyota subsidiary factory. The first time I met her she wore her hair tied in a bun high on top of her head, and her jean shorts and black leggings were very much the vogue in Japan that summer. Having been bullied as one of the only Brazilians in her class, Tomoko explained to me that she preferred to speak Japanese, and avoided telling her peers that she was originally from Brazil.

One year later, when I returned to Japan in 2011 and visited the local city hall where I lived to submit an application for a *gaikokujin tōrokushō* (obligatory alien registration card, which has since become the *zairyū kādo*, or resident's card), I was surprised to see a young woman behind the desk who looked very much like Tomoko. Dressed this time in a typical Japanese OL (Office Lady) outfit, it took me a minute to recognize her. Once I saw the *kanji* (ideograms) of her last name pinned to her blazer, however, I realized who it was. Tomoko seemed surprised to hear me speak in Japanese, and I switched to Portuguese, unsure at the time which language she felt more comfortable using. Although she appeared to understand what I was saying, she responded in Japanese only.

Later, I learned that Tomoko had been hired to work at City Hall on the basis of her being Brazilian and purportedly knowing Portuguese, in order to help Brazilian residents. In reality, however, she did not feel comfortable speaking Portuguese, and considered her previous job at the factory to be much easier. On one occasion, she was asked to translate at a workshop held in Japanese in a building complex that housed many Brazilian residents in the city where she lived. Besides having difficulty translating from Japanese to Portuguese, Tomoko also struggled to pronounce many words in Portuguese, and asked her mother for help with terms such as *permanência* (permanency), which she sounded out as *pre*-manencia (*pre*-manency). Two years later, in 2013, I found out that Tomoko was still living at home but had had to leave her job at City Hall because she had not learned enough Portuguese and her bosses eventually caught on. In my last visit with her that year, I learned that she had since begun working at a factory again, this time as a *seishain* (regular employee), and spent most of her salary paying off a car, her cell phone bills, and so on.

Sayuri, who was four years older than Tomoko, finished Japanese middle school at age fifteen and, against her parents' wishes, decided not to continue with her studies. At the time, Takuya, her younger brother, who was born in Japan in 1999 and was still an infant, was diagnosed with leukemia and hospitalized for many consecutive months while he underwent chemotherapy treatment. Marcia quit her job to take care of her son, and Sayuri, freshly out of middle school, decided to work at a beauty salon in order to help her family out financially. As she put it, speaking only in Japanese: "I saw both of my parents working, and then my brother was hospitalized, and my Mom had no choice but to be with him all the time. So it was too tough for my Dad to be the only one working. We had just bought our apartment too."

Growing up in Aichi, most of Sayuri's friends were Japanese and, like her sister, she went by her Japanese middle name rather than her Portuguese given name. Sayuri was badly teased when she first arrived at Japanese school, and her parents asked for her Portuguese name to be taken off the class roster so that she would not stand out as much from the other students. By middle school, and in contrast to Jessica of chapter 1, Sayuri was able to pass as fully Japanese, and many of her classmates only found out she was Brazilian when she turned twenty and her full name was revealed at their *seijin shiki* (coming-of-age ceremony).

Sayuri and Tomoko generally did not want their parents to come to see them at school because "their clothes were different and they stood out too much from other parents." Because he no longer worked and was relatively fluent in Japanese, their grandfather usually went instead to cheer for the girls at sports events or to meet their teachers. Although they still understood a fair amount of Portuguese, they grew up speaking mostly only Japanese. In their mother Marcia's estimation:

> The oldest [Sayuri] speaks Portuguese but she's shy about it. She doesn't want to speak it in front of us. Tomoko [the middle daughter] understands but when she tries to speak, she can't put sentences together. When we came to Japan, we had to speak Japanese everywhere we went. So we never worried about their Portuguese. Then, as the years went by and the kids grew up, we started to realize how important speaking Portuguese is. But it's hard even for us as parents to speak with them in Portuguese, it doesn't flow naturally, they're always asking us to repeat ourselves because they don't understand.

For Tomoko, working at City Hall was the first time she felt the need to speak Portuguese. Her older sister, Sayuri, only felt the urge to learn Portuguese once she was hired at an electronics factory at the age of eighteen and discovered she had difficulty communicating with many of the Brazilian employees around her. As it happened, she soon fell in love with one of her Brazilian *sansei* coworkers, an electrician who came to Japan at the age of nineteen and spoke only Portuguese when they met. Rafael was the youngest of five brothers from Santos, in São Paulo, and the only member of his family to be working in Japan. Since he spent most of his free time around Sayuri and her family, he had grown to understand a fair amount of Japanese. When he and Sayuri married in 2013, she took his Portuguese last name (only Rafael's mother was Nikkei, so his father's non-Japanese last name was the primary one according to Brazilian custom), though she continued to go by her Japanese middle name, and—once she naturalized to Japanese citizenship—legally disposed of her Portuguese given name.

Shortly after becoming a Japanese citizen in 2011, Sayuri was hired as a *seishain*, earning 1,500 yen/hour at the same factory near Toyota where Tomoko had found a job upon leaving City Hall. She and Rafael decided to move nearer to her work. Although Sayuri inquired about the possibility of her husband working there as well, her boss informed her that the company did not hire foreigners. "The work that foreigners do here is still the dirtiest, and the hardest," Marcia later told me. "Things are different for Rafael because he is *mestiço* [mixed], and people can tell right away he is a foreigner. He can't pass like our kids can." In fact, as Rafael later told me, he did not feel at home in Japan, even after working there for eight years, and hoped that Sayuri would return to Brazil with him to start a family in Santos.

Differently from his sisters, Takuya, Elio and Marcia's youngest child, was born in Japan, and given a Japanese name but no Portuguese one. He only ever studied at Japanese school, and had been to Brazil once, on a brief visit that was growing increasingly faint in his young memory. Takuya spoke of returning again one day to see the beautiful beaches and to taste the coffee he knew Brazil to be famous for, but it might as well have been Guam or the Philippines, so little bearing did it have on his own experience. For the most part, he spent his time doing what the majority of other teenage boys around him did: playing video games with friends, cramming for school exams, and, wherever possible, quietly ignoring his family.

When I saw the Matsuda family again in 2013, Takuya greeted me first with a bow of the head and then with a kiss on the cheek, eliciting a round of applause from his family. Marcia ruffled her son's hair and told me how proud she was of his "progress" as a Brazilian. In Brazil, friends often greet each other with one or several kisses, or else a handshake and/or hug, while in Japan, friends never greet each other with kisses. I knew that the Matsudas had become naturalized Japanese citizens since I last saw them the year before, so at first it surprised me to note Takuya's unprecedented performance of Brazilian-ness. In his second year of middle school by then, his voice cracking halfway through an *o-hisashiburi* (it's been a long time) greeting, he still did not recognize many words in Portuguese, and had since stopped taking Saturday morning Portuguese heritage language classes at the local

Brazilian Association. "I didn't like those classes anyway," he admitted, "My parents always made me go." In other words, though Marcia and Elio hoped Takuya would maintain a linguistic—if not ethnic or cultural—link to Brazil, he himself saw no real point to it.

THE PROCESS OF NATURALIZATION

Ever since I first met the Matsudas, Marcia and Elio had discussed the possibility of naturalizing to become Japanese citizens. "We arrived here when the girls were very young," Marcia explained to me during our first afternoon together. "We sent them to public Japanese school, hoping that it would make life easier for them to speak Japanese. Now they don't even speak Portuguese, and they aren't affectionate with us. Without meaning to, we've built a wall between us and our girls. We're doing things differently with Takuya, though," Marcia said, smiling at her son who, not understanding what we were saying in Portuguese, wiled away the time playing video games on his cellular phone. "The thing is, our children might as well be Japanese," added Elio, who at the time was employed as a manager of Brazilian workers at a nearby factory. "They grew up here, and they don't want to go to Brazil. We're thinking of naturalizing to make things easier for the kids, but. . . . We're Brazilian, in the end. We miss our parents, too, and we're worried about what to do in case we need to return to São Paulo to take care of them."

In April 2010, just a few months before we met, the Matsudas had in fact filed an application for naturalization. To do so, they spent over a year collecting the supporting documents requested by their local Office of Legal Affairs. According to Article 5 of Japan's Ministry of Justice Nationality Law, a foreign resident may naturalize to Japanese citizenship provided:

(1) that he or she has domiciled in Japan for five years or more consecutively;
(2) that he or she is twenty years of age or more and of full capacity to act according to the law of his or her home country;
(3) that he or she is of upright conduct;
(4) that he or she is able to secure a livelihood by one's own property or ability, or those of one's spouse or other relatives with whom one lives on common living expenses;
(5) that he or she has no nationality, or the acquisition of Japanese nationality will result in the loss of foreign nationality; and
(6) that he or she has never plotted or advocated, or formed or belonged to a political party or other organization which has plotted or advocated the overthrow of the Constitution of Japan or the Government existing thereunder, since the enforcement of the Constitution of Japan.[2]

Once a complete application for naturalization is successfully filed, it normally takes the Japanese Ministry of Justice six months to a year to reach a decision on the case. When Sayuri traveled to Brazil with Rafael the same year they applied, however, the file was put on hold to see if "her feelings about becoming Japanese had changed" while she was away. She was also interviewed three or four times by telephone while she was in Brazil so that officials could confirm her whereabouts and what she was doing during those six months: "They asked me why I went to Brazil, whether I wanted to become Japanese or not, when I was coming back, what my boyfriend does." she explained to me in Japanese. Actually, since Sayuri could only call from Skype while she was in Brazil, Marcia had to bring her smart phone to City Hall so that she could call her daughter and pass the phone directly to the officials in charge of the family's case. When she returned from her trip, the purpose of which was to meet Rafael's family and visit her aging grandmother, Sayuri was asked to report to City Hall and reassure officials that yes, she "still wanted to become Japanese."

When I asked her what had led the family to naturalize, Marcia first explained:

It's because Takuya was born here in Japan and in his head he doesn't understand why he's Brazilian. When they were younger, the girls didn't understand why they were Brazilian either. Speaking only Japanese with a Japanese face, with eyes like this—"Why are we Brazilian?" they asked. But you see, in Takuya's case, since he's a boy [and, presumably, the potential head of a family], in the future—at school, at work—it might help him if he's Japanese.

The real catalyst, however, took place when Sayuri turned twenty (the legal age of adulthood in Japan) and her father went to inquire about the possibility of her naturalizing. The official on duty that day asked Elio why he himself did not naturalize,[3] to which he responded that he did not know enough Japanese. Once he saw a sample of the language test required for naturalization, however, Elio realized he understood most of it. That was when the family's interest truly bloomed, but because it required so much documentation to apply, it took time for the Matsudas to set their file in order. I asked Sayuri what had given her the idea to naturalize upon reaching the official age of adulthood:

I had done so many things and been in Japan for so long already. I had bought a car, rented an apartment. And it's a lot easier to do those kinds of things as a Japanese than a Brazilian. I also only speak Japanese, and at the time I thought of myself as staying in Japan forever. So I thought, I want to become Japanese. Even though people at work would tell me, once they found out I was Brazilian, that it didn't make any difference, it was still . . . *mendokusai* [a nuisance] to be Brazilian. You have to carry your *gaijin tōroku* [foreign resident ID] on you all the time, that kind of thing.

While Sayuri understood naturalization as a practical necessity, and the natural extension of having spent nearly her entire life in Japan, her parents rationalized the decision on more explicitly ethnic grounds: "We have only Japanese blood, and the girls were teased in Brazil for their Japanese faces, and then teased in Japan for being Brazilian," Marcia explained in Portuguese. "I always told my children they were Brazilian, but they still didn't understand why they were different from the others. Our blood isn't mixed at all, we only have Japanese ancestors. Maybe if our blood had mixed with Brazilian blood it would be different, but as it is, it was hard for the kids to comprehend."[4] In other words, for Marcia and her husband, naturalization was a means of showing their children both that they belonged where they lived and that they were truly Japanese in every sense—something that, having grown up in Brazil and moved to Japan as adults, they never quite felt themselves. As Elio explained in Portuguese: "In Brazil we're kind of *sem pátria* [without a homeland]. The Japanese left Japan, and went to Brazil, but there's no denying this appearance. We'll always be Japanese. But for the Japanese [of Japan], we're Brazilian, we're *gaijin* [foreigners]. We will always be foreigners." To which his oldest daughter Sayuri added, cheerfully, having understood her father's Portuguese but speaking only in Japanese: "Now it's different though. Because in Japan [having naturalized], people will call us Japanese."

The first official interview for naturalization took place in Japanese, and was only intended for the parents, although the Matsudas submitted an application for the entire family. "We figured, well, since we're not going to go back to Brazil, we might as well all naturalize, for the kids' sake. It's easier to rent an apartment and that kind of thing if you're Japanese, so we did it with their future in mind," Elio further explained. Each member of the family submitted official documents, and all documents in Portuguese had to be translated to Japanese. Since many Nikkei-Brazilians registered in the *koseki* (Japan's national family registry) die in Brazil, the information never reaches Japan and, as a result, the *koseki* is often out of date. This was especially complicated for Elio who, as the youngest of his family, had to provide documents proving the existence of all his older siblings. Marcia, as the oldest of her siblings, only had to show documents for her parents. In order to naturalize, she was also asked to provide consent from her father and her father's mother because they were still alive. "This is because I was giving up the nationality that my parents gave me," she explained, "and I needed proof of their approval." Since the Matsudas translated all supporting documents on their own (saving money in the process), however, and wrote in Japanese in front of the officials in charge of the case, they were exempted from the Japanese language test, and there was no police visit to their home.

In addition to the interviews, first with Marcia and Elio, and then with the family as a whole, the Matsudas were asked to draw a family tree with everyone's names written in *katakana* (the Japanese phonetic alphabet used for foreign words), demonstrating their exact generation of Nikkei-ness. This requirement was, of course, asked only of Nikkei residents filing for naturalization (not other foreigners), and had parallels with the application for a working visa in Japan based on Japanese descent. Thus, we see that, just as in Japanese immigration policy, so too in the process of naturalization was common ethnic ancestry emphasized through the idiom of family. Whether or not a sense of shared ethnicity also justified preferential treatment during the process of naturalization, however, is beyond the scope of this research.

After drawing the family tree, and thereby performing their shared Japanese-ness for officials, each member of the Matsuda family was asked to write an individual essay in Japanese about why she or he wanted to naturalize. Sayuri remembered writing about how she was bullied when she first arrived in Japan and, because she did not want to be singled out, learned Japanese to the point that she could no longer speak anything else. She also wrote about how her face was Japanese, and there was not much meaning to her being Brazilian anymore. Elio, for his part, wrote about the children, and how everyone in the family was together in Japan, so that for their future it would be better to become Japanese citizens. Marcia wrote that they had already been in Japan a long time, that the children all went to Japanese school, and that she wanted to avoid *ijime* (bullying) against her youngest child, Takuya. She also mentioned that they planned to stay in Japan forever, in order to make their request more convincing. As a minor, Takuya was not asked to write an essay.

On November 4, 2011, one month after Sayuri returned with Rafael from her trip to Brazil, the family's application for naturalization was approved. The entire process took a total of one year and eight months to complete. An official from the *homukyoku* (Office of Legal Affairs) called, and the Matsudas went together to pick up the certificate, which was read aloud to them before being handed over. After being congratulated on their new citizenship, the Matsudas went to a nearby McDonald's for a casual dinner. Over fries and soda, Takuya asked what would change in their lives, but beyond that the Matsudas did not remember the evening as anything out of the ordinary. "Because in terms of our day-to-day life nothing much will change," Marcia pointed out, though she—like Elio and their daughters—officially discarded her Portuguese given name, and registered the *kanji* (ideograms) for both her first and last names.[5] Besides this, the family was also asked to bring their foreign resident IDs into City Hall and to change their names on all official documents such as bank accounts, car insurance, etc.

In 2013, when I asked Marcia if anything had changed in the year and a half since the family naturalized, she said that she felt it was now a lot easier to obtain loans. She and Elio had also voted in local elections for the first time. But mostly, what had changed was how inclined they felt *a se integrar* (to integrate themselves) in Japanese society. In other words, since they were Japanese now, Marcia felt they could not rely on the excuse of being Brazilian anymore when, for example, they did not understand something in Japanese. "It's embarrassing not to be able to read or write something; we need to learn Japanese like all other Japanese people," she explained.

For Sayuri, she said that not much had changed because no one ever questioned her Japanese-ness to begin with. She just found it irritating to have to change her name on all her documents. Marcia believed that for Takuya, however, things would change when he went to high school. They would no longer have to inform authorities at the new school that he was Brazilian, as they had to for elementary and middle school. In fact, soon after they naturalized, Takuya asked his parents, "So now I can tell everyone I'm Japanese?" "You can," his mother replied, "but your friends will ask you why you're suddenly saying that, and then will you be able to explain?" Takuya decided it would be better not to tell them about naturalizing. After all, it was too *mendokusai* (troublesome) to explain.

NATURALIZATION IN CONTEXT

As Atsushi Kondo (2002) points out, most of the foreigners who opt for naturalization in Japan are ethnic Koreans and Chinese, and the naturalization rate remains relatively low compared with other Organization for Economic Cooperation and Development countries around the world. Although there is no official data available on the number of Brazilians who have naturalized to Japanese citizenship, the Japanese Ministry of Justice reported that between 2003 and 2012, a period that overlapped with the highest numbers of Brazilians in Japan (with the population reaching its peak of over 300,000 between 2005 and 2008), less than 2000 foreign residents of "other" nationalities besides Korean and Chinese successfully naturalized each year.

As mentioned earlier, far more common among Brazilians during this period was the decision to become permanent residents in Japan. Until the year 2000, less than 5 percent had become permanent residents; in 2003, the number had reached 15 percent (41,788), and by 2008, 35 percent (110,293)—or over one-third—of Brazilians in Japan were registered as permanent residents. Even in 2009, just one year later, when the number of Brazilians dropped for the first time since they began moving to Japan in the 1980s due to the global financial crisis, the number of permanent residents actually increased—to 43 percent (116,250) (Ministry of Justice, Japan).

For foreigners of Japanese descent, the process of acquiring permanent residency in Japan is simpler than it is for most other foreigners, who are generally required to reside in Japan for ten years before they can apply. For *nisei* (second-generation Nikkei), for example, they must have resided in Japan for at least a year, while for *sansei* (third-generation Nikkei) they must have been there for at least five years and already possess a *teijūsha* (long-term resident visa). In the same way, then, that visas to Japan are granted more easily and for longer periods of time to *nisei* than to *sansei* (and only to *yonsei*, or fourth generation, if they are already residents or dependents of residents in Japan), when it comes to permanent residency requirements, besides offering preferential treatment to people of Japanese descent, Japanese immigration policy also implies that the Japanese-ness of these descendants diminishes with each generation (Roth 2002).

According to the numbers, then, the Matsudas's trajectory was uncommon in that naturalization to Japanese citizenship remained relatively rare for Brazilians in Japan. Indeed, of the Brazilians I interviewed, even those who did not speak Portuguese or could not imagine returning to Brazil, most had never seriously considered the possibility of naturalization. For one, people considered it a lengthy and difficult bureaucratic process, and felt secure enough in Japan in their status as permanent residents. Many of them were also under the impression, as Elio had been, that the Japanese language test would be beyond their ability or—as will be explored in greater detail in the next section—that they would have to renounce their Brazilian citizenship upon naturalization. Still others explained their hesitancy to naturalize based on national affiliation and loyalty—"I am Brazilian and will always be Brazilian"—though they did not share the same experience of colonialism and discrimination in naturalization in Japan as, for example, Zainichi Koreans (Fukuoka 2000; Kim 1990; Kim 2006).

The Matsudas's decision to naturalize may be viewed as the extreme point on a continuum from temporary resident to fully incorporated citizen, whereby Brazilians in Japan have increasingly been drawn to the option of permanent residency. Like the Matsudas, many Brazilians raised children in Japan who, whether they were educated in Japanese or Brazilian schools, often considered Japan to be their primary home. For Brazilians who considered Japan their primary home, then, naturalization represented the furthest extension possible of permanent residency. While most of them did not go as far as to naturalize, an increasing number of Brazilians saw themselves as long-term or permanent residents in Japan (see also Chiavacci 2016; Kajita et al. 2005).

It is also important to note that because the Matsudas were "pure" Nikkei (in other words, they had not intermarried with non-Nikkei Brazilians) and, after many years in Japan, could communicate in spoken and written Japanese, this surely helped them both in their confidence during the application process and in the impression they made on the officials in charge of their case. Would their experience during the naturalization process have been different if, like Sayuri's husband Rafael, they were deemed *mestiço* (of mixed descent) or carried themselves in a more "Brazilian" way in terms of dress, body language, and/or speech? Since the Japanese Ministry of Justice is not required to justify its reasons for refusing a person citizenship (Kim 2006), the answer to this question can only be conjectured.

NATURALIZATION ≠ ASSIMILATION

At the end of his monograph (2003), Takeyuki Tsuda predicted that most second-generation Nikkei-Brazilians in Japan would eventually assimilate on a cultural level and escape low-class immigrant occupations.[6] More recently, David Chiavacci (2016) has argued that, based on net income, Nikkei migrants have integrated rather well into Japanese society as part of its lower middle classes, though "the low school achievements of their children carry the risk of becoming a future ethnic underclass" (234).

At first glance, it appears that Marcia wished for her children—particularly her son Takuya—to be able to pass as Japanese in every respect, and that naturalizing might provide the ticket to erasing the Matsudas's Brazilian heritage altogether. She even recounted how, when Takuya entered preschool, Marcia did not tell the other parents they were Brazilian, only the teachers, because of what her daughters had already been through. By the time we last met in 2013, many people in her large apartment building were still unaware of the family's Brazilian origins.

At Takuya's middle school, however, Marcia had begun making Brazilian food for the school fairs—albeit "adapted to Japanese taste, with less salt and less sugar"—and all of Takuya's middle school classmates were now aware of his Brazilian background. With more time on her hands and better Japanese language abilities than she had when her daughters were in school, Marcia participated regularly in PTA meetings and, the same year she and the rest of the family naturalized, took on the role of "foreign representative" at the school's five-year-old *gaikokusei* (international committee). "Only when I did this did people find out that I—and therefore Takuya—are actually foreigners," she explained.

Takuya, for his part, told me that he now had Brazilian and Chinese classmates at school, and that one of his good friends who also lived in the same building as him was half-Korean, or *hāfu* (lit. "half," referring to having one Japanese parent from Japan). Like his sisters, though, most of Takuya's friends were Japanese. Marcia felt it was important for Takuya to learn some Portuguese, not because he would need it in his day-to-day life or because he might return to Brazil one day but because she wanted him to meet other Brazilian children like himself:

> I think it's important, not to hide that you're Brazilian. I know a lot of parents here who hide it. I never hid it from my kids. When they were young, they rebelled against it, though, and our oldest daughter suffered a lot because she didn't speak any Japanese at first. But with Takuya, he entered right from nursery school and was so well accepted—he left the school as though he were Japanese already. I think that's why he's not embarrassed about speaking a little Portuguese, like the girls are—for him it was never a source of shame.

Even after naturalizing, then, Marcia and Elio continued to perform small, everyday acts of Brazilian-ness. They continued to tell some people that they were Brazilian, spoke primarily in Portuguese with one another, and often referred to themselves as *nós brasileiros*, or "we Brazilians." At work people still called them by their Portuguese given names. Marcia liked to joke that she and Elio were *japoneses falsificados* (fake Japanese), while their children were really the Japanese ones of the family. Having secured a relatively comfortable lifestyle for themselves in Japan, and with the added advantage of hindsight over how they had raised their two older daughters, Marcia and Elio increasingly encouraged their teenage son Takuya to express his Brazilian-ness, whether through a peck on the cheek or Saturday morning Portuguese class. Their goal was not to prepare Takuya for an eventual return to Brazil, however. Rather, it was to provide him with positive enforcement of his Brazilian heritage,[7] should he one day choose to embrace or, possibly, use it to his advantage as a marker of international or global status.

From the Matsudas's experience, it is clear that naturalization did not necessarily signal assimilation, and that, at least for first-generation migrants, symbolic ethnicity[8] continued to be relevant even after decades living in Japan.[9] While Marcia and Elio's daughters still felt shame at speaking Portuguese, this had more to do with their experience as children of the 1.5 generation, who came to Japan at a young age and experienced bullying and negative identity reinforcement at school, than it did with their parents' example. Takuya, who was born in Aichi and therefore fully part of the second generation of Brazilians in Japan, did not experience the same pressures his sisters did. In his case, were he interested, Brazilian-ness and the Portuguese language could be a source of pride and/or curiosity—albeit at a safe distance.

PASSING AS JAPANESE

Whether or not they were legal citizens of Japan, a number of Brazilians—
particularly those who, like the Matsudas, had been in Japan for many years
and could not easily imagine living in Brazil in the future—"passed" as
Japanese in their appearance, dress, language, demeanor, and so on (in other
words, their habitus). This was, of course, easier for non-*mestiço* Nikkei-Brazilians, or those who otherwise appeared fully Japanese. However, passing as
Japanese was not, as Takeyuki Tsuda (2003) suggests, necessarily equivalent
to assimilating. Rather, it served as a strategy in adapting to Japanese cultural
majority surroundings, all the while maintaining a certain orientation toward
Brazil in case life became too precarious to stay.

As a point of comparison to the Matsudas, consider Yuko, *sansei* and in her
early forties, who, though she had not yet naturalized to Japanese citizenship,
was in many ways more "invisibly" Brazilian than the Matsudas even after
they legally became Japanese. Yuko was the mother of two teenage children
who were born in Japan and raised speaking only Japanese. She and her husband, also *sansei*, met in a factory in Japan. She was raised in an agricultural
community in the interior of São Paulo, and grew up speaking Japanese with
her grandparents and other members of the Nikkei community until she went
to school. Yuko learned more about Brazilian food in Japan, she said, than
in Brazil, because growing up her family made mostly only Japanese food.
Her siblings and parents all tried out life working in Japan, and she and two
siblings ended up staying since the early 1990s, while her parents retired back
in the São Paulo countryside.

Yuko originally came to spend a maximum of one year working in a factory and learning about Japan before returning to Brazil to finish university.
After falling in love with another Nikkei-Brazilian factory worker in Hamamatsu, however, she married, and stayed for over twenty years. Once her
children were old enough, she returned to work, this time as an interpreter at
an employment brokerage firm. As a result of the financial crisis, however,
she lost her job in 2008. After that, Yuko accepted short term contracts at
various local city halls before again losing her job in 2010. At the time of
our last interview, she had taken on *naishoku* (contract work done at home),
wrapping packages of screws for three or four hours every day while her
children were at school.

When her children were young, Yuko spoke to them in both Japanese and
Portuguese, but when she discovered that teachers at school had difficulty
understanding their mixed speech, she began using only Japanese at home.
The children were registered with a Portuguese first name and a Japanese
middle name, something Yuko wanted because in Brazil she had never had
a Portuguese sounding name and wanted her children to have more of a

choice. In Japan, though, similarly to the Matsudas's daughters, her children felt embarrassed when their full names were called at school and preferred to go just by their Japanese names. Yuko recalled how her children would often say to her: "I don't know why I am Brazilian. I don't speak the language, I have never been there."

As a child in Brazil, looking Japanese and speaking with a Japanese accent because it was the first language at home, Yuko had often felt bullied at school. "I was really shy as a child, I couldn't express what I felt. I was always holding back, I never felt at home. I thought that was normal. But then I came here, and . . . I found myself," she told me, preferring to speak only in Japanese. For this reason, and because her children had grown up entirely in Japan, Yuko could not easily imagine returning to Brazil. She was considering naturalizing the entire family, too, because she felt it would allow her children better opportunities in the future, especially if they were to attend Japanese university and attempt white-collar jobs instead of factory work.

Still, Yuko felt that even if they stayed permanently in Japan, they would always be Brazilian, and that it was important to keep their options open:

> As foreigners, we never know what will happen tomorrow. We might have to leave Japan, and we always have to be prepared for the worst. I think people should always keep one foot behind them, whether they're foreigners or not. But as foreigners, we have to even more. Today I say I don't intend to return to Brazil, but I also don't completely throw away that possibility, because you never know what might happen.

No matter how much she was able to and preferred to pass as Japanese in Japan, then, Yuko, like Marcia and Elio Matsuda, nevertheless kept Brazilian-ness "on the back burner," both in the sense of her own ethnic expression and life options, and her awareness that, especially in times of crisis, she and her family were unequal to majority Japanese and might have to return to Brazil should life in Japan become unviable. Yuko also gave her children both Japanese and Portuguese names so that they could enjoy greater flexibility than she had had as a child in Brazil, even though they—like the Matsudas's children—preferred to use only Japanese names in Japan.

ZAINICHI BRAZILIANS OR BRAZILIAN-JAPANESE —OR NEW BRAZILIANS?

In *Lives of Young Koreans in Japan* (2000), Yasunori Fukuoka lays out a useful typological framework according to which people are commonly judged to be Japanese or not. In this, the three variables he delineates are lineage (or what is perceived to be a common Japanese blood line), culture (or that which is perceived to be a common Japanese language, customs, values, and lifestyle), and nationality (Japanese citizenship). Thus, he comes up with eight "types" of Japanese: (1) "pure" Japanese; (2) first-generation Japanese migrants (i.e., *issei*); (3) Japanese raised abroad; (4) naturalized Japanese; (5) second- and third-generation Japanese emigrants (i.e., *nisei* and *sansei*) and war orphans abroad; (6) Zainichi Koreans (ethnic Koreans and their descendants residing in Japan) with Japanese upbringing; (7) the Ainu; and (8) pure non-Japanese.

According to this framework, Marcia and Elio grew up in Brazil as Type 5, that is, as Brazilian citizens with Japanese lineage but mostly Brazilian customs (though one could argue that they were actually closer to Type 2 because of the strong Japanese cultural influence of the tight-knit Nikkei communities in which they happened to be raised). Once they moved to Japan, however, and the years passed, Marcia and Elio grew closer to Type 2, absorbing more and more Japanese culture until finally, upon naturalizing, they could be seen to have transitioned to Type 1, or "pure" Japanese. Marcia and Elio's children, for their part, could be said to have begun their young lives in Japan already as Type 2: Brazilian citizens of Japanese lineage growing up culturally Japanese until they, too, naturalized, and shifted to Type 1.

What this typology does not account for, of course, and what is missing from such a story—and, one might argue, commonsense notions of what makes a person Japanese, Brazilian, or any other ethnicity/nationality for that matter—is the idea of *double* or *multiple* lineages, cultures, and nationalities. As we saw at the dinner table at the beginning of this chapter, the Matsudas ate a mix of Japanese and Brazilian food and spoke a mix of Japanese and Portuguese together. Marcia and Elio, even after they naturalized and took only Japanese names, continued to refer to themselves—among many Japanese and non-Japanese alike—by their Portuguese names. And, as we will soon see, everyone in the family kept their Brazilian passports along with their newly acquired Japanese ones.

Since the early days of labor migration from Brazil to Japan, the ways in which migrants and their children express ethnicity and belonging have grown infinitely more complex. What new label, then, might apply to people in Japan like the Matsudas, or Yuko and her family? Even if they generally passed as Japanese or went so far as to naturalize, they still maintained a heritage and history different from the majority Japanese, and in many cases continued to perform acts of symbolic ethnicity, whether through dress, food, language, naming, etc. Has Japan embraced its inner diversity enough to consider the Matsudas "pure" Japanese nonetheless? Or is the idea of pure Japanese in itself a negation of that very diversity?

In the United States, it is common today to refer to people by a two-part, hyphenated label, as in "African-American," where the first part signals ethnicity or lineage and the second part nationality and/or culture. In Japan, however, it is common to refer to people deemed not Japanese by either their nationality or ethnicity, or simply as *gaikokujin/gaijin* (foreigner). Finally, in Brazil, people perceived as other than the commonly imagined mix of European, African, and Indigenous heritage are usually referred to by their perceived ethnicity (e.g., *japonês* or *árabe*—Japanese or Arab) or, if they appear to be white tourists from the Global North, simply as *gringos*.

Although *Nikkei Burajirujin* (Nikkei-Brazilian) might make sense (and is often used by both Nikkei-Brazilians and Japanese) in reference to Brazilians of Japanese descent living outside Japan, it does not capture the long-term orientation of many Brazilians who have since come to settle more or less indefinitely in Japan. The term *Burajirukei Nihonjin*, or Brazilian-Japanese, also does not quite fit since, following a more North American framework of ethnicity, it implies that the person is of both Brazilian ethnicity and Japanese nationality. Finally, Daniel Linger's suggestion that the children of Nikkei-Brazilian labor migrants be referred to as "New Brazilians, or something else perhaps" (2001: 313) is also problematic in that it takes the Brazilian nation as its focal point, when many youth in fact align their experiences and aspirations more closely with Japan, or even the Global North.

The term *Zainichi Burajirujin*, or Zainichi Brazilians, on the other hand, might be the most apt when applied to Brazilians living long term in Japan, even those who, like the Matsudas, end up naturalizing to Japanese citizenship. The term Zainichi is made up of two characters, 在 (*zai*—"stay") and 日 (*nichi*—"sun," or that which is related to the "sun origin," or Japan) and so refers to long-term residents of Japan. While Zainichi is usually used in reference to people without any Japanese heritage (Nikkei being the term reserved for people of Japanese heritage), and most commonly the descendants of former colonial subjects from Korea, the term Zainichi Brazilian signals long-term orientation in Japan, and is also inclusive of all Brazilians—be they "pure" Nikkei, *mestiço*, or non-Nikkei partners and dependents. Still, because it only applies to the Japanese—and not the Brazilian—context, even this label implies an end point along the binary spectrum of migration versus settlement, and fails to capture the contextual, ever-shifting nature of national and ethnic expression and belonging. What is more, it is likely to be used, if at all, primarily only in academic circles, rather than by Brazilians or most majority Japanese.

CONCLUSION

Not the End of the Story

Although Japanese law still requires that dual citizens renounce their second citizenship by the age of twenty-two[10] or within two years of naturalizing, other countries (including Brazil)[11] permit the possession of multiple nationalities without restriction. In reality, dual citizens of Japan and other countries such as Brazil often keep both passports, even after naturalizing. In this case, they simply do not show evidence of their second citizenship to authorities in Japan, employing a strategy described by Aihwa Ong (1999) as "flexible citizenship"—albeit leaving themselves in violation of Japanese law. As Nina Glick Schiller et al. note, "no one place is truly secure, although people do have access to many places" (1992: 12). Keeping multiple passports is a way to keep one's options open, and it is not only limited to the transnational elites Aihwa Ong describes. Rather than necessarily signaling loyalty to a nation-state (or in this case multiple nation-states), passports can signal "claims to participate in labor markets" (Dikötter 1992) and, I would add, in possible futures.

The Matsudas, for their part, decided to keep their Brazilian passports even after naturalizing. After all, Marcia and Elio still had their parents to think about in Brazil, and wanted to be free to go back and forth if and as they pleased. Elio, who had experienced unstable employment since the economic crisis hit and he lost his factory job, considered his Brazilian nationality a safety net in case of further job insecurity in the future. Fortunately, thanks to a bilateral agreement between Japan and Brazil that went into effect in 2010, Elio was reassured by the fact that, should he wish to, he could eventually move back to Brazil and still receive the retirement pension he had earned in Japan.

Sayuri, since she had married a Brazilian citizen, also wanted to keep her options open in terms of being able to live and work in both countries. For her younger siblings, though, Brazil was imagined primarily as a vacation destination but not a place to live:

Sarah: Would you like to go to Brazil one day, Tomoko?

Tomoko: Yes, I want to go. *Asobini* [to play]. I don't want to live there. Since I haven't lived there all I have is a scary image of it. There aren't things like karaoke, or *konbini* [convenience stores].

Sayuri's husband Rafael: No, there are convenience stores, but they're different.

Tomoko: So that's why I don't want to go!

Marcia, turning from her daughter to me: It's that we've already gotten used to life here, and here there is everything, and everything is easy to get. You want to eat something, all you have to do is go out and there's a *konbini* [convenience store]. Now in Brazil, that's not the case.

Marcia told me that, like her children, she could not easily see herself living in Brazil. Without a house in Brazil, if they were to return there one day, they would have to start all over again. "That's what makes me a little uneasy," she said, using the Japanese word *fuan* (unease) in an otherwise Portuguese sentence. She went on to say, speaking with me primarily in Portuguese:

> Maybe if we had a house or something to go back to things would be different but we have nothing. Imagine, we would have to start from zero. My experience here wouldn't mean much in Brazil either. And since I saw how difficult it was for the girls to adapt here, I'm afraid what it would be like for Takuya to go through the same thing in Brazil. My hope is that he will continue with his studies and be able to be a proper breadwinner one day, since he is a man, and will have to support a family eventually.

Thus, although the Matsudas kept their Brazilian citizenship as a kind of insurance against possibly needing to leave Japan one day, they by and large did not imagine themselves returning permanently to Brazil. As Marcia said, she and Elio had invested in an apartment in Japan and did not own property in Brazil, nor did they possess significant economic capital. Furthermore, they were concerned about their and their daughters' limited educational credentials and occupational skills, should they try to find work in Brazil, as well as whether or not their children, lacking proper linguistic capital and cultural know-how, would be able to adapt to life there. Even though Marcia and Elio worried about their parents, and considered the possibility of returning to São Paulo to take care of them one day, their children's lives were primarily oriented to Japan, the country where they were raised and educated, and where they had grown accustomed to the comforts of a middle-class, albeit largely blue-collar, lifestyle.

Return to Brazil, then, whether a myth, a reality, or a distant possibility, meant different things to different generations of transnational migrants and their children, and even for a single individual these meanings often changed according to shifts in life circumstances and objectives. Marcia and Elio, for example, though they originally intended to return to Brazil after a few years, ended up changing plans when their son Takuya, born in Japan, was diagnosed with leukemia at the age of two. The intensive yet accessible medical treatments and fragility of Takuya's health eventually led Marcia and Elio to reconsider. Years later, having bought an apartment in Japan and raised their three children speaking primarily Japanese, the family decided to naturalize to Japanese citizenship.

Meanwhile, the Matsudas's oldest daughter Sayuri, who had grown up hiding her Brazilian background from most people around her and was the first of the family to seriously consider naturalizing, met and married a recently arrived Brazilian labor migrant and, for the first time in her life, began imagining a future for herself in Brazil. As Marcia well knew, the future was never guaranteed, and the vicissitudes that had altered her parents' lives before her might well affect her or her children's own expected trajectories:

> What we'll do in the end, we still don't know. We're experiencing here what our parents experienced in Brazil. And now we came here and left them there, so who knows, maybe we'll stay here and our kids will go to Brazil. When Sayuri was twenty she wanted to be Japanese. Now she's twenty-four and she wants to go to Brazil! The pain we'll feel if she goes away is the same pain our parents felt when we left them behind.

Thus, while naturalization might carry with it connotations of assimilation, or signal the end point along a path from migrant to immigrant, labels and categories, as well as affinities and aspirations, continued to shift over time. No matter how long they stayed in Japan, or which new ethnic labels were applied to them, Brazilian labor migrants adopted multiple identities and orientations that challenged the singular meanings of what it was to be Japanese and/or Brazilian, as well as migrants and/or immigrants. At the same time as they may—in certain situations and at various points in their life—have passed as Japanese in Japan as a strategy toward gaining greater acceptance from mainstream Japanese, they also had the option of using their transnational flexibility as both Japanese and Brazilian in order to negotiate the shifting opportunities of a precarious global economy.

As the cases of both the Matsudas and Yuko further demonstrate, people's positionings vis-à-vis Japanese and Brazilian ethnic and/or national belonging shifted not only over time but also according to context. People often presented themselves as more Brazilian or Japanese depending on the situations they found themselves in. Tomoko Matsuda, for example, despite her limited Portuguese and identification with things Brazilian, capitalized on external perceptions of her Brazilian-ness in order to get a job translating Portuguese at the local City Hall. Her parents, in turn, emphasized the family's Japanese-ness when filling out an application for naturalization, since multiple identities were surely not the ticket to obtaining Japanese passports. These small acts point to what Michael Jackson (2013) so eloquently described when he wrote: "[r]ather than implying that people necessarily find fulfillment in being settled in one place or possessing a single core identity, I consider it imperative that we complement this view of a stable self with descriptions of human improvisation, experimentation, opportunism, and existential mobility" (202).

Finally, for the children of Brazilian labor migrants who grew up primarily or entirely in Japan, even if they did not speak Portuguese, identified only as Japanese, and/or eventually became Japanese citizens, still their lives were shaped by the transnational constraints and opportunities of the families into which they were born, or into which they married. Though the Matsudas might stay in Japan for the rest of their lives, their ties to Brazil remained real—ties reinforced through family history, relatives scattered throughout São Paulo, and the Brazilian passports they kept quietly tucked away in a drawer at home, even as they used Japanese names and identification in many of their day-to-day exchanges.

At the same time, however, as Dennis Conway et al. (2008) have cautioned, it is important not to conflate transnational migration with identities, belonging, and multiple citizenships. Just because the Matsudas kept their Brazilian passports did not mean they were acting out ethnic resistance in Japan—though by refusing to give up their original citizenship, they were arguably engaged in a quiet kind of resistance against Japanese state control. Similarly, Yuko's desire to keep return to Brazil as a potential option for the future had little to do with a sense of belonging in Brazil. And, as we saw in the case of the Silvas in chapter 1, Carlos kept his permanent residency in Japan in case he should need to return there one day, not because he necessarily identified strongly with Japan. In all of these cases, then, migrants and their children engaged in a kind of flexible, transnational living, resourcefully "negotiating the limits that had been set upon [their] freedom" (Jackson 2013: 77) through "improvisation and opportunism" (ibid: 202). For them, citizenship may have signaled not ethnic or national belonging per se but rather a sense of inclusion in the global economy of desire, "in which the hope that our lives may be made more abundant, for ourselves and those we love, constantly comes up against the limits of what we may achieve and the despair into which we may be plunged when we find ourselves unable to achieve [a] state of well-being and flourishing" (ibid: 6).

In sum, in this chapter, we saw a Brazilian family whose decision to stay in Japan long term, and ultimately to naturalize to Japanese citizenship, was influenced by a constellation of factors, including lifestyle comforts and aspirations, family concerns, and imagined future opportunities. At the same time, these decisions did not signal the fixed, end point of ethnic expression, as an imagined differentiation/assimilation scale might presume. In this way, the example of the Matsudas points to the importance of life histories as a medium of research in contemporary studies of migration (Olwig 2007), since "the ramifications of citizenship . . . emerge through the unstable intersections between idiosyncratic and unfolding life histories on the one hand, and changing institutions and regulatory regimes on the other, [suggesting that], over the life course, the various entailments of citizenship status will likely shift repeatedly" (Amit 2014: 407). In the next chapter, I explore how the educational system in particular shaped children's sense of limitations and possibilities, both in Japan and Brazil, as well as their experience of ethnicity and transnational (im)mobility over time.

NOTES

1. Citizenship is a form of membership in a political and geographic community and can be disaggregated into four dimensions: legal status, rights, political and other forms of participation in society, and a sense of belonging (Bloemraad et al. 2008: 154).

2. A full English translation of Japan's Nationality Law is available online at: http://www.moj.go.jp/ENGLISH/information/tnl-01.html.

3. Administrative guidance of the Justice Ministry encourages naturalizing household members as a group rather than a specific individual within a family, to avoid members of the same household holding different nationalities (Kashiwazaki 2000: 443).

4. As seen in the case of Angela Silva in chapter 1, this differentiation between "pure" and "mixed" came up time and time again in interviews as a means of arguing just how unfair it was that, despite their ethnicity, most Nikkei-Brazilians did not gain full social acceptance among majority Japanese. At the same time, it also served to reproduce race-based notions of "rightful" membership and belonging and, in some cases, justified a sense of superiority over other, non-Nikkei or mixed-heritage Brazilians.

5. The amendment of the Citizenship Act in 1985 has eliminated the phrase "Japanese name only" in the administrative guidelines on naturalization. However, it is still necessary to write the name with Japanese characters—*kanji, hiragana*, or *katakana* (Kondo 2002). See also Kim (2006) on the legal treatment of foreigners in contemporary Japan.

6. Takeyuki Tsuda's conclusion tends toward an assimilationist paradigm (Cordero-Guzmán et al. 2001), and does not fully account for the racialization process that occurs especially among Nikkei-Brazilians of mixed descent in Japan.

7. This might be a useful strategy in countering what Takeyuki Tsuda (2003) considers the consequences of passing: "ethnic alienation and self-hate" (344). Though at the time I knew him, Takuya did not appear to struggle with these negative consequences, nor did he appear much interested in his parents' project of instilling ethnic "self-love" in their youngest child.

8. Takeyuki Tsuda (2003) writes that "ethnicity becomes 'symbolic' precisely when a well-integrated and culturally assimilated positive minority finds it beneficial to continue asserting their ethnic differences instead of becoming subsumed in the majority" (80). Although Brazilians were not, for the most part, seen as a "positive minority" in Japan, in the case of the Matsudas, one could argue that they had become relatively well integrated into Japanese society.

9. Similarly, Hélène Le Bail (2012) found that Chinese entrepreneurs who acquired Japanese nationality did so primarily for business reasons (e.g., ease of international travel), not because they were more or less assimilated than other newcomer immigrants in Japan.

10. Article 14 of the Nationality Law, last amended in 2008, states:

> A Japanese national having a foreign nationality shall choose either of the nationalities before he or she reaches twenty two years of age if he or she has acquired both nationalities on and before the day when he or she reaches twenty years of age or, within two years after the day when he or she acquired the second nationality if he or she acquired such nationality after the day when he or she reached twenty years of age. (see http://www.moj.go.jp/ENGLISH/information/tnl-01.html)

11. See, for example, information on Brazil's Ministry of Foreign Affairs website at http://www.portalconsular.itamaraty.gov.br/outros-servicos/nacionalidade-brasileira. According to Thomas Faist (2007), more than half of all countries in the world now tolerate some form or element of dual citizenship.

Chapter 4

Learning to Labor or Leave

As one drives through Gifu and Aichi, in central Japan, the signs of Brazilian life can be easy to miss. In the years since the global financial crisis of 2008–2009, many Brazilian-run enterprises, including restaurants and supermarkets, churches and schools, have shut down suddenly, leaving traces of Portuguese language—faded cedillas, silenced tildes—barely legible against the broader urban landscape of *kanji* (ideograms) and Romanized script. In many ways, the fate of ethnic Brazilian businesses in Japan reflects that of smaller industrial cities found throughout the country: economically unstable, if not stagnant, and intimately tied to the vicissitudes of global supply and demand.

Despite a significant decrease in number since their peak in 2007, however, Brazilians have continued to work and live alongside Japanese and other foreign residents, including Chinese, Filipino, and Peruvian nationals. As illustrated in previous chapters, over the last nearly three decades, some brought children with them; others gave birth to daughters and sons in Japan. These 1.5 and second-generation Brazilian-Japanese, or *Zainichi Burajirujin*, as I suggested they might be called, grew up partly or primarily in Japan. While their parents worked—mostly in unskilled labor—the children of Brazilian labor migrants living in Japan had the option of attending Japanese, Brazilian, or international school. By 2008, an estimated 33,000 Brazilian children of school age were living in Japan, about one-third of whom attended Japanese school, while the rest enrolled in Portuguese-language school or did not attend school at all (Sasaki 2009).

For Brazilian youth in Japan, private international school, often operating in English, remained the most expensive and least available option, especially in the smaller cities where most *dekasegi* lived. As a result, the choice usually came down to either Japanese or Brazilian school, or else some combination of the two (e.g., Japanese elementary school followed by Brazilian middle school, since accredited bilingual Portuguese-Japanese schools still did not exist at the time of my research). In this chapter, I focus on the experience of education among Brazilian labor migrants' children, especially in the context of national (Japanese or Brazilian) schooling options in Japan. As I aim to demonstrate, whether they stayed in Japan, returned to Brazil, or engaged in repeat migration between the two countries, the educational options available to them tended to push students either to labor in factories, thereby reproducing the social/class relations of their parents, or to return definitively to Brazil. In other words, educational institutions were important vehicles in reinforcing the ideological binary of temporary migrant versus immigrant, as well as the idea that the children of Brazilian labor migrants were necessarily bound to be Brazilian (ethnically segregated/differentiated) *or* Japanese (assimilationist), instead of a constantly shifting combination of the two. In fact, many 1.5 and second-generation Brazilian youth in Japan fell somewhere in between—or beyond—these poles. Rather than view them as necessarily "caught" or "lost," however, I show the ways in which they creatively navigated life constraints and opportunities even in the face of limiting, single-state oriented structures.

THE ROLE OF SCHOOLS

Social scientists have long been aware of the role of educational systems in promoting national solidarity and cohesion. Drawing on Émile Durkheim and others, Louis Althusser, and, later, his student Pierre Bourdieu, both recognized the central importance of school in teaching children the rules of the social game (Althusser 1971: 89), and in reinforcing and reproducing ideological positions. Contrary to the liberal ideal of emancipatory education, then, Althusser and Bourdieu believed that schools function to propagate knowledge construction and cultural transmission, and are essentially conservative, traditional institutions aimed at self-preservation and replication (Reed-Danahay 2005: 49). Their work is illuminating in its ability to unmask the legitimations, misrecognitions of power, and symbolic violence inherent in the functioning of any social system (DiMaggio 1979: 1460). Bourdieu's notion of habitus, or the "durably installed generative principle of regulated improvisations" (1977: 78), in particular, helps explain how children embody ideologies from an early age, from their relatives and at school, such that "the habitus acquired within the family forms the basis of the reception and assimilation of the classroom message, and the habitus acquired at school conditions the level of reception and degree of assimilation of the messages produced and diffused by the culture industry" (1990: 43). In insisting on a unified habitus, however, Bourdieu did not account for different, competing sets of regulative principles, as people from mixed cultural or class backgrounds often experience.[1]

Althusser's Marxist work also demonstrates the ways in which educational systems serve to reproduce the diversified skills of labor power necessary to a capitalist regime (1971: 88). All ideological state apparatuses, from family to schools, "contribute to the same result: the reproduction of the relations of production, i.e., of capitalist relations of exploitation" (ibid: 104). Paul Willis's 1977 classic *Learning to Labor: How Working Class Kids Get Working Class Jobs*, to which I allude in the title of this chapter, is a clear extension of this idea, demonstrating how schools in industrial Britain aided in the reproduction of a manual workforce.

In the context of Japan, as Ishida & Slater (2010) argue, "the educational system . . . is usually considered to be the primary mechanism for the reallocation of individuals through the class structure" (21). Among the important early works linking social class, educational structures, and socialization in Japan are Thomas Rohlen's *Japan's High Schools* (1983), which shows how, through the educational system at the secondary level, "the Japanese are producing an average adult citizen who is remarkably well suited to [the] requirements of modern industrial society" (305), and Roger Goodman's *Japan's "International Youth": The Emergence of a New Class of Schoolchildren* (1990), which looks at returnee students as new international elites. Kaori Okano's *School to Work Transition in Japan* (1993), for its part, highlights the reproduction of social class by focusing specifically on vocationally oriented day high schools and how working-class students, as a result of their particular habitus, adjust their aspirations and hopes about their employment as a result of past experiences and material conditions. More recently, David Slater's (2010) work looks at the ways in which Japanese secondary students are tracked into high schools that prepare them for, and predispose them to accept as legitimate, very different social destinations, and Amy Borovoy (2010) examines how different tertiary educational institutions prepare students for different positions in Japan's occupational structure.

But what of foreign—or migrant/immigrant—youth in Japan? Many studies, especially those conducted by education experts, are primarily concerned with second-language acquisition and children's overall integration into Japanese society. Others focus on how ideologies of ethnicity, national belonging, and language serve unwittingly to exclude non-Japanese citizens attending public Japanese schools. Yuko Okubo's (2009) work on "newcomer" children who attend Japanese schools, for example, looks at the ways in which the native speaker concept marginalizes them as others because it is associated with both citizenship (being Japanese nationals) and ethnicity (having Japanese parents). In a similar vein, Michiyo Takato's (2009) study on Latin American children in Japan focuses on the ways in which the commonsense notion of native speaker competence in speech makes teachers overlook the problems foreign-born Nikkei students have writing Japanese.

Although these are important contributions, the topic of education for foreign youth in Japan has been analyzed primarily from the perspective of those attending Japanese public schools. In terms of ethnic education (or minority schooling), Sonia Ryang's (1997 & 2000) work on North Korean schools in Japan is a valuable exception in showing how social reproduction occurs through codified, rule-bound language, and how students use language to resist the cultural domination of both majority Japanese and Mindan (South Korean) populations. As far as newcomer foreigners such as Brazilians are concerned, however, studies continue to focus on children attending Japanese schools (e.g., Morita 2007; Sekiguchi 2003) and, in this way, approach their subjects as immigrants to Japan, rather than as people who might (and often do) move between Japan and Brazil.

As Tiago Minami points out in his chapter "The Social Costs of Labor Migration and Global Recession on Brazilian Schools in Japan" (2012), in the academic literature thus far, only a handful of works have addressed Brazilian schools in Japan, usually with an ethnographic approach focused on students' identity (e.g., Fujiwara 2008; Sugino 2008). In this chapter, based on fieldwork at a Brazilian school in Aichi and interviews with interlocutors who grew up attending Japanese or Brazilian schools (or both) in Japan, I aim to sketch the role that educational institutions played in shaping and (re)producing younger Brazilians' national orientation, sense of future opportunities and mobility in Japan and Brazil, and social/class positionings across national borders. At the same time, however, I avoid the approach that views these 1.5 and second-generation Brazilians as either lost/in crisis or completely assimilated, and instead demonstrate how, while they may have experienced difficult odds in terms of upward mobility, they also crafted multiple, flexible means of belonging, as well as resourceful strategies in living transnationally between Japan and Brazil.

BRAZILIAN SCHOOLS IN JAPAN

Between 2010 and 2013, during the main years I carried out fieldwork in Japan, I made regular visits to a private Brazilian school in Aichi, where, as a result of working as a volunteer teacher in 2011–2012, I came to know and interview staff and students alike. For comparison, I also interviewed staff and students at Brazilian schools in Gifu, Shizuoka, and Ibaraki, though I maintained the Aichi school as my base. I have chosen to call this school by the pseudonym *Mundo do Conhecimento* (World of Knowledge), or MdC, in order to protect the identities of the people who worked and studied there.

When I first sat in on a Grade 10 Portuguese class at MdC, I understood viscerally what Daniel Linger meant when he wrote of school as "a fascinating opportunity to explore what, unaccountably, anthropologists often neglect: the worlds of young people" (2001: 65). There is good reason anthropologists often neglect this world, I realized, glancing timidly at the fifteen- and sixteen-year-olds around me. While the teacher lectured about *Vidas Secas* (Barren Lives), a story written in 1938 about poverty and desolation in northeastern Brazil, students texted furtively with each other on their cell phones or else toyed absentmindedly with the hair—some of it dyed blue, some purple—falling into their eyes.[2] Approaching thirty, I was no more likely to blend in as a Brazilian teenager in Japan than I was a teenager anywhere else in the world. As Merry White concluded during her own fieldwork in Japan, "I could not take on the activities let alone the age-stage definitions and identities of the young" (2003: 28). How, then, could I access 1.5 and second-generation Brazilians in Japan? The answer, I found, was through regular and sustained contact with them, not necessarily as a peer—I could not, in practice, study alongside them—but as a voluntary English teacher at MdC. In this way, I came to learn not only about students' experiences and aspirations but also about the structure, organization, and overall social world of the school.

In 2013, on my last visit to it, MdC was one of forty-five Brazilian schools in Japan officially recognized by the Brazilian Ministry of Education and Culture (MEC), with twelve more listed as in the process of recognition.[3] A number of schools were neither recognized by the Brazilian government nor in the process of recognition and, consequently, were excluded from official data. Still, according to data from *the Associação das Escolas Brasileiras no Japão* (AEBJ, or Association of Brazilian Schools in Japan), in 2006, at the peak of Brazilian migration to Japan, there were a total of ninety-seven Brazilian schools in Japan, fifty of which were officially recognized by MEC. This was a huge leap from 1998, at which time there were only twelve Brazilian schools in Japan, none of them officially recognized by MEC. By 2009, many Brazilian schools, especially those not officially recognized by the government, had shut down as a result of the global economic crisis.[4] Table 4.1 shows the geographic breakdown of the forty-five *escolas homologadas*, or recognized schools, still remaining in 2013.

Table 4.1   Brazilian Schools in Japan Officially Recognized by MEC (2013)

Prefecture	Recognized
Aichi	10
Gifu	4
Gunma	4
Ibaraki	3
Mie	3
Nagano	3
Saitama	2
Shiga	3
Shizuoka	12
Yamanashi	1
Total:	45

It is important to note that until 1999, Portuguese-language schools in Japan were not officially recognized by either the Japanese or Brazilian governments, making it difficult for students wishing to apply to university after finishing high school there. The Brazilian MEC ultimately changed its policy in response to demands voiced during symposiums in 1997 and 1998 on Brazilian children's education in Japan. Also, in 2004, the Japanese Ministry of Education decided to accept university applications from candidates who had finished high school in MEC-certified Brazilian schools in Japan. As Thiago Minami (2012) points out, however, this measure proved largely ineffective, since the lack of knowledge of Japanese language and school curriculum made admittance to highly competitive public universities impossible, while private universities, usually expensive, proved an unviable option for many Brazilian families in Japan.

THE MUNDO DO CONHECIMENTO (MDC) SCHOOL

MdC was founded by a Nikkei-Brazilian family, who opened the school's first unit in Toyota City in 1995. At the time, the demand for private Brazilian schools in Japan was already evident, as many 1.5 and second-generation children of Brazilian labor migrants struggled to fit in or keep up with Japanese school, or else preferred instruction in Portuguese in case they should return to Brazil. According to interviews with staff at MdC, in the beginning, the director in Toyota acted as a teacher as well, instructing students in Portuguese through the sixth grade. She was the only teacher at the time, and her husband worked as a bus driver for the students, while her mother served as school secretary. The three of them stayed after school to clean the building and prepare it for the next day. As the number of enrolled students continued to increase, the school's director hired two of her brothers and sisters-in-law—all of them former *dekasegi*—to help with the growing demand.

By the time I conducted fieldwork, MdC had expanded to include five different units and approximately 2,000 students spread throughout Aichi, Shizuoka, and Mie, and was in the process of purchasing a sixth unit in Gunma. It continued to be a family-run affair until 2007, when the director sold the school's five units to a young Japanese entrepreneur, whose father owned a successful *juku* (cram school) chain. The following year, in 2008–2009, the economic crisis hit hard in Japan and roughly 55 percent of the students at MdC withdrew their enrollment, either because their parents could no longer pay tuition or because they had lost their jobs and decided to return with their families to Brazil. As a result, salaries at the school decreased significantly, and a number of the staff had to be let go. As one science teacher at MdC put it: "Here it's all improvised, even the teachers are improvised—many of them aren't trained to teach, or they haven't gotten their university degrees yet, but there's no one else here in Japan who's eligible. After the crisis, things only got worse, because a lot of teachers were laid off or decided to go back to Brazil anyway." At the particular unit where I taught in 2011–2012, what was once a two-building unit turned into one, serving 201 students, preschool through high school, a significant decrease from just three years before, when there were over 500 students.

The school itself was divided into two stories, the first one serving as a preschool, and the site of administration and reception, and a cafeteria, while the second story housed the elementary, middle, and high school classrooms. There was a small teacher's room on the second floor, and all employees were required to use a machine on the wall to punch in their name card when they began and ended work. The main entrance of the school led to the secretary's desk, set off from the rest of the room by a long reception counter. Here one could thumb through free magazines or newspapers such as *Alternativa*, *Empregos*, *Akitem Bom Negócio*, and *Boa Dica*—all of them aimed at Brazilians living in Japan, and filled with advertisements placed by employment brokerage agencies—or pick up a pamphlet with information pertaining to the next student soccer tournament or museum visit. The director's office, the principal's office, and the financial registrar were marked on the outside by a simple paper sign printed in Portuguese, *kanji* (ideograms), and *hiragana* (basic phonetics). Students who were sick often lounged around on one of the two weathered leather sofas in the reception area, next to a case of dusty soccer trophies and the first-floor bathroom. At lunchtime and recess, students either conglomerated there or in the cafeteria and sports field, the latter of which consisted of a narrow cement soccer and basketball court. Outside the cafeteria was an automatic vending machine selling Japanese soft drinks and Guaraná soda from Brazil,[5] and the student-run canteen served the role of a small *konbini* (convenience store).

The sports area, demarcated by high netting, was large enough for students to kick a ball around, or shoot a basketball but was hardly a field per se. Also, while the school technically had a library, there was no librarian and the books MdC owned—most of them donations from individuals, NGOs, or other schools—were shelved in the same room as the director's office. Although students could technically borrow or refer to books, it was hardly a space they could study in, and materials were, for the most part, haphazardly collected and out-of-date. The computer lab, for its part, located in a locked room within the cafeteria, was only available to students during allotted class time.

MdC followed a calendar that ran from February to December, with breaks occurring three times throughout the year, in accordance with Toyota's work schedule: one week in May (Golden Week), one week in August (coinciding with the Japanese Obon holiday), and one week at the end of the year. Brazilian national holidays were acknowledged and at times celebrated but not observed in terms of time off from school. At the same time, the regular class schedule alternated between even and odd weeks, with students studying either in the morning (*matutino*) or the afternoon (*vespertino*), a system found throughout public schools in Brazil, and otherwise unknown in Japan. Monthly tuition fees for half-day schooling totaled 290,000 yen/month (~US$300) for elementary and middle school, and 40,000 yen/month (~US$400) for high school, with additional fees for school transportation, full-day (*período integral*) schooling, school materials, insurance, and the compulsory school uniform.

MdC, like most Portuguese-language schools in Japan, followed an educational model based on what one might commonly find in Brazil. Students used textbooks and other materials from Brazil, took classes in Portuguese, learned Brazilian (but not Japanese) history, sang the Brazilian (but not Japanese) national anthem, wore typically Brazilian-style school uniforms, and went to school either for morning or afternoon sessions but rarely for the full day. Japanese, for its part, was taught only as a second language, in the same way that English and Spanish were. Furthermore, school lunch usually consisted of typically Brazilian food (rice, beans, and meat), and, as noted earlier, even the vending machine on campus sold Brazilian soft drinks.

At the same time as it was oriented to Brazil and Brazilian educational models, however, MdC was also clearly shaped by a culture of labor migration. Many of the teachers and staff there had previously worked in factories in Japan, and the numbers of students and staff—as well as the physical size of the school—depended on ebbs and flows in factory production and, therefore, the availability of jobs. What is more, the documentation shop at the entrance of the school, the Portuguese-language magazines in the reception area aimed at Brazilians looking for jobs in unskilled labor in Japan, and even MdC's academic calendar—which, in terms of holidays, followed the schedule of Toyota factories in Japan, and not the regular Brazilian school year—all pointed to an educational apparatus set up specifically as a kind of holding place for the children of temporary migrants until they returned to Brazil. Even school transportation, as I will demonstrate next, followed a model based on the segmented labor system through which most Brazilians commuted to/from work in Japan.

SEGMENTED TRANSPORTATION: THE BUS RIDE TO SCHOOL

Every Thursday at 6:50 in the morning I waited groggily for an MdC school bus to pick me up from the convenience store near my apartment in Aichi. I was the only teacher who rode the bus, together with fifteen students ranging from preschool to high school age, all of them dressed in the standard, obligatory school uniform: a white shirt and green gym pants, with the yellow, green, and white school emblem—almost exactly the same color scheme as the Brazilian national flag—clearly in view. The bus driver was an elderly Nikkei-Brazilian man who picked up children from throughout the region to bring them to MdC. In all, it took us nearly an hour and a half to get to school in the morning and two hours to get back in the evening, because of all the different places the driver had to stop. For some of the children on the bus, the journey took longer, as they lived even further from the school than I did. Most of the students at MdC took one of the five available private buses to school (each one serving a different region in Aichi or Shizuoka Prefecture), with a few of the older students opting to arrive by motorbike. In my time there, however, I did not encounter a single MdC student who took public transportation or their own bicycle to school, although these forms of transportation are extremely common among Japanese school students throughout the country.

For part of the bus ride through western Aichi, we rode parallel to a Meitetsu commuter train, the red ribbon of it winding through the green hills and rice paddies until it was out of sight. In many ways, the fifteen feet or so of space within the bus was itself a parallel to the world outside. Here, children chatted in a mixture of Japanese and Portuguese, played video games, and showed each other photos on their cell phones. Some of them were born in Japan, and had never been to Brazil. Others remembered Brazil, or expected to go there soon. One particular day, a student with a long earring spiked through his left ear complained about the rain and wondered how he would get to his *arubaito* (part-time job) shift later that afternoon.[6] Another student turned around to complain about the song her friend was playing loudly from his iPod: "*Que chato! Dame!*" she exclaimed, expressing her irritation first in Portuguese, then in Japanese.

The MdC bus was an extension of the school, and in many ways, it acted as the child's version of the employment brokerage firm buses that carried adult Brazilians to and from factories. In other words, the school buses served to pick students up directly from home and drop them off at Brazilian school, without them having to interact with the majority Japanese environment that surrounded them. Many of the students' parents experienced the same thing at work, picked up by company-provided *sōgei* (transfer) buses and dropped off at factories where they worked side by side with other Brazilians—as is often the case in a brokered, segmented labor system—without much time or opportunity to interact in Japanese. In *Bicycle Citizens* (1999), Robin LeBlanc argues that what we see and who we are in terms of our identity depends in part on the social transportation that we use. Like the housewives she studied peddling their way through Japanese politics by bicycle, the private MdC school buses reflected a particular *dekasegi* experience and perspective.

The students who rode private MdC buses had little contact with students from Japanese schools, just as their parents often had limited contact with Japanese coworkers. The buses were not, however, an airtight space operating independently from a broader Japanese setting. Rather, the bus, just like the school, represented a space for students to perform and explore *both* their Japanese and Brazilian identities, as well their position as the children of foreign labor migrants in Japan. Together with other students from a similar background, children at MdC could relate to one another about being a visible minority in Japan, about speaking Portuguese at home, about watching TV shows in Japanese, and about what they might do after graduation, regardless of whether they imagined staying in Japan or eventually returning to Brazil. In other words, private Brazilian school offered students the chance to spend their day-to-day lives with other children just like themselves, from the time they stepped on to the bus to the moment they arrived home from school. For many of them, this offered a sense of reassurance and comfort, as well as deep ambiguity about the future.[7]

A DAY AT THE SCHOOL

Other than Monday mornings, when everyone was asked to sing the Brazilian national anthem outside on the school court, students played ball and hung around in the cafeteria and reception area until classes started. Staff meetings began at 8:45 every morning and included twelve to fourteen people: the principal, the financial secretary, a Japanese instructor and her translator, and the school's full-time teachers. Other staff—the school secretary, the bus drivers, and the janitor—did not participate, though the part-time teachers (e.g., English, Art, and Spanish) did on the days they were present. Female staff, with the exception of the gym teacher, wore a uniform of black pants and grey vests over colored, short-sleeved shirts, while men had greater freedom in their dress. Most employees were Nikkei-Brazilian, or the spouse of a Nikkei-Brazilian, and had worked in factories in Japan before finding a job at the school. Most of the teachers had university degrees, or were in the process of obtaining one online at the time I met them.

Renato, the school principal, would usually lead the staff meetings in Portuguese, with a translator whispering in the ear of the Japanese instructor in order for her to follow along. Once in a while, however, the Japanese owner of the school—or a Nigerian teacher, fluent in Japanese, who worked for the school's various units—showed up with an important announcement, which would then be communicated to the staff in Portuguese by the school's translator and only fully bilingual employee. Regular meetings touched on a range of topics, from teacher-parent interviews and exam periods to students who had to return to Brazil or had a difficult time adjusting to Portuguese after transferring from Japanese school. Renato ended every meeting with an upbeat *"Vamos para o dia, bom dia para todos"* ("Let's get on with the day, and a good day to you all") as the school music sounded at 9 a.m. and students shuffled to class.

Around 11 a.m. every morning a former *dekasegi* worker dropped off Brazilian *bentō* (boxed lunches)—usually a mix of rice, beans, and a cut of meat—for those who preordered them. Students and staff would eat their lunch together in the cafeteria, beginning around 1 p.m., and students who studied in the morning (*matutino* session) got on the bus to go home while those who studied in the afternoon (*vespertino* session) began arriving for class. Although it was more expensive, some parents also opted to leave their children at school for the entire day (*período integral*), allowing them greater flexibility with their own works schedules. Afternoon classes ended at 5 p.m., and by 6 p.m., buses began shuttling students home. The same music chimed every day, in Portuguese, signaling the end of the school day on the following, almost cautionary note: "You need to discover your path, find your own way of being, arrive on time. The future doesn't wait . . . for tomorrow."

THROUGH THE EYES OF SCHOOL
ADMINISTRATORS, STUDENTS, AND ALUMNI

The principal of MdC, Renato, had studied to be a gym teacher in Minas Gerais and worked in Brazilian schools in Japan for five years before becoming principal. When I met him in 2011, he had just recently been promoted from teacher, and was eager to improve the overall quality of the school. Tall and gregarious, he gave the impression of a friendly basketball coach, delivering high fives to students in the hallways, picking up the younger ones and throwing them into the air, and jokingly (though not unproblematically) calling out *gata* (sexy/pretty) to some of the older girls. During lunch he brought Brazilian red peppers he grew from his apartment in Hamamatsu to share with the other teachers, and spent most of his breaks chatting casually in the hallways with students and staff.

Six months into his new position as principal, Renato was less upbeat than he had at first appeared. As much as he joked around with students in his free time, when we chatted alone in his small office, Renato took on a more serious, concerned tone:

> Now that I've been here for a while, I have a good idea of what the school's real problems are. The essence of my thinking hasn't changed. This is a piece of Brazil that's been transferred here and we're living in a bubble. The whole Brazilian community here is. Interaction with Japanese culture is limited. At the same time, students are also losing Brazilian culture, their home culture, because their parents work so much, that's their whole life, they don't encourage their kids to read, they don't teach them about their history. These kids don't even know where they're from in Brazil, what their grandparents did. So the school has to play this role that goes beyond just education. It has to contribute extra-curricular activities as well, because the parents don't have time for that. The school has to be more than just an educational institution. I already felt this as a teacher, and now as principal, I have more contact with families. I know their problems, and so when I look at the kids, I don't just see them, I see the families and the contexts they're coming from.

Renato was especially concerned about the older students, pointing out that of the twelve students in their final year of high school at MdC, only two were planning to return to Brazil immediately following graduation to continue their studies. As for the rest, he said, they would start working at a factory just like their parents, make money, become independent, and forget about furthering their studies:

> I say to them, you're going to get swallowed up by the system, I know it. I offer examples, I tell them, don't do what your friend did, who went back to Brazil.

No, no, they say, it's only for a year. But it's not just a year, it's never just that. As soon as they see how much they can buy with their own money, it's already started. Students who have already graduated come here and each one of them has their own car, name-brand clothes, name-brand sunglasses. They're happy for now. And time keeps marching on. If they go back to Brazil, what are they qualified to do? How are they going to be absorbed into the job market there? They didn't study here, they didn't specialize in anything. Potential employers are going to ask what they know how to do, and all they're going to be able to answer is this [*here Renato pounded the desk with his fist, imitating the repetitive movements of a factory worker assembling pieces together*]—this is all they've ever done all day long.

Of the various private Brazilian schools I visited, only a minority of the graduating students had concrete plans to return to Brazil or to continue on to university right away. As Renato had said, most of the students were eager to make a salary comparable to that of their parents. Few to none of them were properly prepared for the competitive *vestibular* university entrance exam system in Brazil and, consequently, stood a slim chance of entering free, public university there. In order to attend private university or to prepare for the entrance exams via a *cursinho* (an intensive preparatory course) in Brazil, they or their parents would have to pay high tuition rates, just as they would in order to attend private university in Japan. In the case of Japan, however, few students from the Brazilian schools had a high enough level of written or spoken Japanese to be admitted to a Japanese university, whether private or public. The choice for these students usually did boil down to the following: either return to Brazil immediately following graduation, using whatever funds the student or their family might have saved, or else stay in Japan to work. With only a high school education, most students would not be able to make more than the minimum wage in Brazil (755 reais in São Paulo in 2013, or approximately US$350 per month), whereas they could potentially make at least five times this amount working in a factory job in Japan. For most high school students studying at private Brazilian schools, then, working in Japan immediately following graduation appeared the easiest and most tempting of available options. The following profiles of students who attended or already graduated from MdC help demonstrate the broader horizon of possibilities and limitations for those who studied at private Brazilian schools in Japan.

VANESSA

From Student to Secretary

Vanessa, the twenty-seven-year-old secretary at MdC, came to Japan at age twelve with her parents, who, though they only planned to stay a few years, continued to work in factories fifteen years later. She attempted a few months of Japanese school but did not adapt well. As one of few foreign students, she felt lonely, and was worried that in middle school there would be no language aids to continue helping her with Japanese. Also, as a third-generation *sansei* of mixed descent, she felt she stuck out more than the only other Brazilian student, who was fully Nikkei, and found herself shunned and even bullied by her Japanese classmates. Thus, in 1996, Vanessa ended up commuting several hours a day to the very first MdC school, originally founded in Toyota, which at the time consisted of only a small room with a handful of students. Although she was supposed to enter sixth grade, the lack of students her age meant she had to enter fifth grade again, though later they adjusted for this and placed her with her own age group.

As early as eighth grade, Vanessa was hired part time as a secretary at the school, studying in the morning, and working four hours every afternoon for 600 yen/hour (~US$6). She continued the job through high school, at which point most of her classmates at MdC went on to work in factories. In fact, her class was the first to graduate from MdC—three or four students in all—although many left early, either back to Brazil, or to enter factories as soon as they turned sixteen. As she explained to me in Portuguese:

> I wanted to work in a factory too, I wanted to earn more money. So I got a job at Sony and worked there for one week, but then I quit. I was shocked, because when I was on the line, the woman who I was replacing, she told me she loved the work—putting together a camera in 30 seconds, using twenty screws and a wire that hurt your fingers—and so I asked her, why are you leaving then? And she told me that she was losing all feeling in one of her hands, due to the repetitive motions of work. And I was taken aback, I thought, God, is this what I want for myself?

Unlike most of the people around her, Vanessa was able to choose an option beyond unskilled labor in Japan because of her previous connection to and experience working for Brazilian schools (i.e., ethnic social capital). In this way, she was eligible to work for the "ethnic business" of a Portuguese-language school, though she did not otherwise envision many opportunities for herself in Japan. By the time I met her in 2011, she was completing an online degree in education from a private university in Brazil, and saw her future options as either continuing working in Brazilian schools in Japan, or returning to teach at an elementary school in Brazil (the former option paying a considerably higher salary than the latter).

Though she had been in Japan for over fifteen years, the fact that Vanessa was educated in Portuguese and still uncomfortable speaking Japanese meant that, as Renato said of other MdC students, she lived in a Brazilian bubble in Japan. In her case, though, rather than being "swallowed by the system," she found a way to acquire professionalization that she could use either within the Brazilian school system in Japan or in schools back in Brazil. Thus, in the same way that interlocutors sometimes used multiple passports or permanent visas as a means of "improvisation and opportunism" (Jackson 2013: 202) in the face of the class, work, and educational structures into which they were thrown in Japan and Brazil, so too did they use educational and professional training in both countries as a means of creatively navigating the national and transnational worlds of which they were a part.

ANA

Mixed Japanese and Brazilian Schooling

Ana was eighteen, *sansei* of mixed descent, and in her last year of high school at MdC when I taught her. She could understand a fair amount of Japanese but preferred to speak in Portuguese with me. In all, she had spent eleven years in Japan, and her younger siblings, twelve and nine, also attended MdC. Ana's parents had first come to work in Japan in the late 1990s, but when her mother got pregnant with her, they returned to Brazil. Then, when Ana was two, they came back to Japan to save more money, returning to Santa Catarina, in southern Brazil, when she was five. Her father was able to make a living working for a school bus company there, but when her younger brother was born and the company took a turn for the worse, they decided to return to Japan for a third time in order to save more money. Ana was nine at the time and, since then, she had only returned once to Brazil, in 2008, to visit family and celebrate her fifteenth birthday.

Ana remembered seeing very little of her parents while growing up. Both of them worked long hours at factories and, as the eldest child, she was responsible for taking care of her younger siblings. Ana had studied in both Japanese and Brazilian schools in Japan. When I asked about her experience studying in a Japanese middle school before entering Brazilian high school, she told me how, when she came back to Japan at age nine, she was placed in MdC for elementary school. Her younger brother and sister were sent to Japanese school, however, and Ana grew increasingly frustrated at not being able to understand what they were saying to each other in Japanese. She asked her parents to send her to Japanese school as well. At first, they resisted the idea, saying that they wanted her to go back to Brazil and enter university there, and that Brazilian school would better prepare her for such a move. Ana was determined, however, and entered a Japanese middle school for three years before returning to MdC for high school.

At first, Ana experienced *ijime* (bullying), but with time she grew accustomed to the language and the curriculum, and began to enjoy her time in Japanese school. Her decision to return to Brazilian high school was based on where she (and her parents) saw her in the future. Since the goal was to send Ana to university in Brazil, she and her parents believed it would be better for her to attend high school in Portuguese instead of Japanese. Overall, though, Ana expressed a preference for the Japanese school she attended, which she considered organized and clean, and with better facilities than MdC:

> They taught us to have responsibility there. To go to school on our own, things like that. In Japanese school I felt that they were preparing us better for life. They taught both boys and girls to cook, to sew, things like that. One thing that I really miss is how much they encouraged us to play sports. Here [at MdC] we don't have that. I used to go to dance club every day after school, on Saturdays, and sometimes even on Sundays. Swimming too. Here we only have basketball and it's only once a week.

Despite her reluctance to leave the Japanese school, Ana entered MdC again in 2009, and then in 2010 her siblings followed suit. Since both her brother and sister were relatively fluent in Japanese already, and the family intended to return to Brazil in the near future, her parents felt it was time to put all three children back in Portuguese-language school. Paying private tuition for three children put considerable financial strain on the family, however, and in 2012 they had still not saved enough money to return to Brazil. When I asked her about her feelings about returning to Brazil, Ana was ambivalent:

> It's something I really want, but I'm also a little afraid because I've lived here more than I have there. I always liked Brazil a lot though, more than Japan, even though I like here too. But I'm afraid because I'm not used to it, I'm afraid of going back and not being able to do things, like get around on my own, that type of thing. But I really want to go back to be able to study. I'm really attached to my family there, too, I like the people in Brazil, the *calor humano* [human warmth]. At the end of the day, I think I'm really Brazilian.

Thus, Ana, even though she identified primarily as ethnically Brazilian and struggled at first to fit into public Japanese school, found that it provided her with better resources than the private Brazilian schools could. Still, it was clear to her that since her parents intended to return to Brazil, and to send her to university there, she was better off improving her Portuguese and following a curriculum that would prepare her for Brazilian university entrance exams. In this way, Japanese school would prepare her to stay in Japan, while Brazilian school would prepare her to leave. The ambiguity and anxiety she felt about returning to Brazil were trumped by the longer-term goals of living near extended family, immersed in familiar cultural norms, and opening her future to better life opportunities and educational/professional mobility—all of which she could not imagine for herself were she to stay in Japan.

MASANA

From Brazilian School to Working in Japan

Masana was seventeen and in her final year of high school at MdC when I first met her in 2011. She was born in Aichi, was *yonsei* (fourth generation) on both her mother and father's side, and had lived back and forth between Japan and Brazil her entire life. In 2008, at age fourteen, she returned to Japan after ten years in Brazil, and entered MdC. Although she had never been to Japanese school, Masana was fluent in Japanese. In fact, at the McDonald's where she worked part time, customers usually assumed she was Japanese. She had learned Japanese as a child living with her grandmother in Paraná and also spoke it at home with her mother, who worked as a translator for an employment brokerage firm in Aichi. Masana was an extremely bright student, and besides being fluent in Japanese and Portuguese, she also read voraciously in English in her free time.

Meeting her for coffee shortly after she graduated from MdC, I chatted with Masana in a mix of Japanese and Portuguese about the possibility of furthering her studies in Japan before returning to Brazil. As she saw it, Japan would offer her the possibility of polishing both her Japanese and English, and this would be invaluable once she applied to university in Brazil. Still, she had never considered going to Japanese high school, even though she had mixed feelings about MdC. She felt relieved to be graduating but apprehensive about university entrance exams in Brazil: "School here wasn't good, it's weaker than it is in Brazil. The stuff we learned was OK but sometimes we didn't have enough teachers. We had to kind of make it on our own. Whereas in Brazil people are already set up to take the *vestibular* [university entrance exams]."

Masana's feelings about Brazilian school were shaped by the fact that in 2008, the same year she and her younger brother entered MdC, the global economic crisis hit and many people—faculty and students alike—left for Brazil. Nevertheless, she was justified in her more general critique of the limited resources available to students attending Brazilian schools in Japan. As discussed earlier, MdC—which was in fact one of the larger, wealthier, and long-accredited Brazilian schools in Japan—was by and large an improvised, under-equipped facility. Teachers often had little or no previous experience in education (also noted by Fujiwara 2008) and learning materials, focused mainly on university entrance exams in Brazil, were not designed "to raise discussions directly related to the lives of the students, on topics such as immigration, discrimination, and Japanese society" (Minami 2012: 235). Thus, even though the school attempted to prepare students for an eventual return to Brazil, it did not have the adequate material and human resources to do so. In the meantime, by focusing on a solely Brazil-oriented curriculum, it did not prepare students for life in Japan beyond factory work, and failed even to address issues pertaining more directly to students' lived realities.

Masana, because of her particular language abilities and experience (i.e., linguistic and social capital), was able to find non-factory work upon graduating from MdC. She was hired to work in administration for a private language school in Aichi, where she could use her Japanese, Portuguese, and English. One of her close friends from MdC, who also graduated with her, did not have the same luck, however. Because of his limited Japanese, he could not get a job he applied for at McDonald's. Like most of Masana's peers who stayed in Japan, he ended up in factory work immediately upon graduating from high school.

Though she felt comfortable in Japan and did not long to return to Brazil, Masana still hoped to attend university there one day. Because she did not have a strong background in academic Japanese, she believed that free, public universities in Japan were out of the question. Private university, on the other hand, though easier to gain admittance to, was prohibitively expensive, especially without significant help from her family. Thus, Masana aimed to save money to eventually return to Brazil, study for the entrance exams, and, if all went as planned, continue with her education there before moving to a third country outside of either Japan or Brazil. Ultimately, her resourcefulness was shaped and constrained by the employment and educational structures she faced as the child of foreign labor migrants living in Japan.

LARA

From Brazilian School Back to Brazil

Lara was sixteen turning seventeen and, like fellow classmates Ana and Masana, also in her last year of high school at MdC when I met her. Born in the interior of São Paulo, and *sansei* on the part of her father, she had lived in Japan for a total of nearly eleven years. Her family brought her to Japan for the first time when she was a year old; she stayed there until the age of five, returned to Brazil for two years, and then went back to Japan again in 2003. Lara never went to Japanese school, and she was the only one in her family to have gone to school in Japan. Her three older brothers, one who lived in Gunma and the other two who had since returned to Brazil, all arrived in Japan for the first time in their teens and immediately began working in factories, much like Carlos and Marcelo Silva of chapter 1. Though she could get by in basic Japanese, Lara was much more comfortable speaking her native Portuguese, and was also fluent in English, which she—like Masana—had largely studied on her own.

After graduating from MdC, Lara made plans to return to Brazil to live with her brother in Londrina and try out the *vestibular* entrance exams for the federal university there. First, though, she wanted to work at a factory in Japan in order to save up enough money for life in Brazil. After calling a number of employment brokerage firms in the area, she was finally placed in what she considered an easy but meticulous job, working alongside Brazilian and Peruvian women for 800 yen/hour:

> In the beginning, my first day to be exact, I was apprehensive I wouldn't make it, that nobody would like me and, since I was tense, everything and everyone seemed tense. I started with these two women, who taught me how to do the work that consists basically of sticking three sponges into a single piece. Actually, the older of the two women taught me for the most part. "Don't worry," she said, "for the time being just learn how to do it well. Then you'll master it and make 200 in a day, you'll see."

Lara soon did master her task at work but, after just a few weeks, she found it physically taxing, and began to look forward to leaving. After eight months working in the factory, she returned with her parents to Brazil.

In October of 2012, I visited Lara shortly after she had returned to her hometown in the interior of São Paulo. Her parents had quit their factory jobs in Japan and returned with her, partly because of Lara's grandmother's declining health, and partly because they themselves were getting older and tired from the physically demanding work. Lara was still recovering from jet lag when I met with her in Brazil, and her room was crowded with unpacked boxes from Japan. She showed me a magazine article on *síndrome de regresso* (return syndrome) as experienced by Brazilians returning from living abroad, and shared with me how difficult she felt it was to adjust to being back in Brazil. Like Masana, she too did not feel prepared to take the *vestibular* entrance examination for university. The books she used to study in Japan had still not arrived via ship from Japan. As far as she was concerned, she would try out for the *vestibular* in November, just to have a sense of what it was like.

In March 2013, I found out that Lara, then eighteen, had not passed the first *vestibular* exam she tried, and had instead joined a *cursinho* (preparatory program), to better prepare her for Brazil's competitive university entrance exams. "Well, little by little, I'm becoming more . . . Brazilian. However, I know I'll never be a true-true Brazilian, you know what I mean?" she wrote me in an email in Portuguese. Although she still struggled to adjust to life in Brazil, she was glad to have studied in Brazilian school in Japan. On their modest salaries in the interior of São Paulo, her parents could not have afforded to send Lara to private school in Brazil, but in Japan, working in factories, they could pay the fees for her to attend MdC. Lara believed that, given a choice between public Brazilian school in Brazil or private Brazilian school in Japan, the latter had provided her with better opportunities, at least in terms of her goals in applying to Brazilian universities.

Lara's mother, Carol, told me that working in Japan had been worth it because of the education she was able to provide her daughter with. Additionally, her two sons who had returned to Brazil in the late 1990s were able to put themselves through university there after the five years they spent working in factories in Japan. As Carol explained, speaking in Portuguese, "Those who go back to Brazil go to study. There's no way they'll work in Brazil if they can find work in Japan. And while Brazilian school in Japan motivates people to go back to Brazil, Japanese school is useful only for those who want to go on to university in Japan."

This sentiment was echoed, in fact, by many of my interlocutors, who believed that the purpose of Brazilian school in Japan was, essentially, to prepare the children of *dekasegi* for an eventual return to Brazil. Though it tended to provide students with fewer resources than public Japanese school, it was worth it, they believed, in terms of preparing children for further education in Brazil, as well as protecting them from bullying and the low self-esteem they might face as a minority in Japanese school. Still, others were of the opinion that even if families did not have concrete plans to return to Brazil, it was a waste (*mottainai*, many of them said, using the Japanese word for waste even if they spoke primarily only Portuguese) to send children to Brazilian school when they had the option of learning another language, and for free, in public Japanese school. As one fourteen-year-old interlocutor who attended Japanese middle school explained, in a mix of Japanese and Portuguese: "My Mom always says that as long as you're in Japan you have to learn Japanese." Still, Lara and her family were glad they had the option of sending her to Brazilian school in Japan, and hoped that it would help her eventually gain admittance to a first-tier university in Brazil—thereby expanding her future educational and professional opportunities.

DIOGO

From Brazilian School to Factory Work in Japan

Diogo, *sansei* on the part of his mother, graduated from MdC in 2006, having studied there from grades 8 through 12. When he arrived with his family in Japan at age thirteen, his mother asked him to choose between going to Japanese or Brazilian school. Because of his age, Diogo felt it would be easier to attend Brazilian school in case he wanted to return to Brazil to continue his studies there. He had already heard about MdC from friends who had studied there and then returned to his hometown in Brazil.

The choice to study at a Brazilian school, he believed, helped him adapt more quickly to life in Japan, because he was able to meet other people like himself. Although he learned basic Japanese at MdC, Diogo spoke with me mainly in Portuguese. Upon graduating from high school, he entered a factory in Aichi and, beginning in 2011, started an online degree from a private Brazilian university.

In 2006, Diogo had graduated with seventeen other students from MdC. Many of his classmates had since returned to Brazil, he said, studying in universities there or else working in factories in Japan. When I asked him how he felt about his time at MdC, Diogo replied:

> The school's goal is to prepare everyone to go back to Brazil. But whether they go back or not depends on their interests and goals, of course. I think the major difficulty most Brazilian teenagers face in Japan is just how easy they've got it here. Because if you go to work in a factory you make a good salary, right? Besides getting by, you can also just buy all kinds of things that in Brazil you'd kill to have. You'd never be able to get them there. So what happens in the meantime? People leave school, start working in a factory, and after experiencing the factory system, they start seeing a different system than the one offered by school. By that point, though, they're already trapped in the factory system, wasting their time, but they can't get out because they get used to the money they make.

In this way, Diogo's assessment of the role of Brazilian schools in Japan is similar to how MdC's principal felt about the issue. Once students graduated from Brazilian school in Japan, if they did not soon return to Brazil, it was tempting to continue for years in Japan earning the same wages their parents did. Diogo's experience was typical, then, in the sense that he stayed on after high school in Japan to work at a factory and save (as well as spend) money. Most of the students who graduated from MdC either began working in the same unskilled jobs their parents came to Japan for—with a few exceptions, as in the cases of Vanessa, the school secretary, or Masana, who worked for a private language school—or returned to Brazil, as Ana intended to do and Lara eventually did.

No matter which trajectory they took, though, most students at MdC felt they would have better overall opportunities in Brazil, especially in terms of education. Even if they had little to no memory of Brazil or did not feel particularly excited about the idea of returning there, they were often vocal about what they perceived as their limited options in Japan. Generally, they agreed that it was easier to imagine careers in Brazil than in Japan, partly because of language difficulties (negative linguistic capital), and partly because they felt disconnected (*desligado*), in terms of social and cultural ties, from other opportunities in Japan. As one tenth grade student at MdC put it, speaking only in Portuguese: "In Brazil when you go to [private] high school you're already prepared to go to university after. But here you only end up prepared if you go to Japanese school." She went on to say: "My parents say that if you don't study you have to work. They tell me to study because they weren't able to, they didn't have the money to do so. But they say that if it doesn't work out, well, I just have to work."

These experiences were hardly unique to students of MdC. In the various private Brazilian schools I visited in Japan, I heard similar stories and concerns about the future. At a Brazilian school in Gifu, for example, where I spoke at length with high school students age fifteen to seventeen, one student explained, speaking in Portuguese:

> In terms of material things and a comfortable life, I prefer living in Japan, but in terms of a better future, if you stay here and don't study, in other words, if you don't learn either English or Japanese, you're going to have to stay in factories. That will be your future. There isn't any choice. But if you go to Brazil, even if you don't have a university degree, you won't be forced into a life of going to and from the factory without seeing the sun.

Another student expanded, again in Portuguese, on this by now familiar paradox of growing attached to the material comforts available to Brazilian labor migrants while simultaneously feeling trapped by the lack of opportunities available to those who stayed in Japan:

> Since we grew up here, we have everything we want, when we want it, and our parents can give us everything. But if we go to Brazil knowing that we won't get into university right away, we're going to have to struggle a lot to get a degree. And in the meantime, we'd be in a country where we know we can't have what we want, where life is a lot tougher and we can't just get things easily, go out, buy clothes, that kind of thing. But if we do that and suffer now, later on we can reap the benefits. If we study, we can become whatever we want. And later on, we'll be able to buy things with our own money, say to ourselves, I made it, I graduated, I have a diploma. Here, on the other hand, we'll have to work, work as much as we want, but we won't have a diploma at the end of it. And money disappears. Knowledge stays. So that is what is bad about Japan and good about Brazil.

In other words, students were "torn" or "caught" less in terms of an ethnic identity crisis, and more in terms of what they perceived as, on the one hand, greater material wealth and comfort in Japan and, on the other, better, long-term occupational and educational opportunities in Brazil. Like the students at MdC, they felt there were few options for them in Japan besides unskilled labor, especially since, for the most part, they were not fluent in Japanese. Also, because many of them were *yonsei*, or fourth-generation Nikkei-Brazilians, they knew that if they were to go back to Brazil for too long they would lose their visa status as permanent residents and/or dependents of *sansei* (third-generation Nikkei) in Japan and be unable to return alone. As one student put it:

> At the end of the day, Brazil is our country, not Japan. We're Brazilian, not Japanese. We're also *mestiço*, but we're mixed in terms of our blood, not our documents. Brazil is our country. So if something happens Japan won't let us stay here. If tomorrow they say, hey, fourth generations can't stay anymore, we'll have to go back to Brazil.

Although this was an unlikely scenario, still students were aware of the relative precarity of their situation in Japan, and the fact that, as the children of *dekasegi*, limited in their Japanese language and educated primarily in Portuguese, they did not possess the same opportunities as Japanese-speaking youth their age, should they stay in Japan.

Even for those Brazilians who went to Japanese school, however, it did not necessarily mean they would escape a life of unskilled labor in Japan. As seen in the previous chapter, for example, neither of the Matsuda daughters had an easy time finding work outside of factories, even though they grew up in Japan, went to Japanese schools, and even naturalized to Japanese citizenship. The same was true of Claudia's two youngest daughters in chapter 2. In other words, even with positive linguistic capital, the social/cultural capital they possessed was still connected to the sphere of unskilled labor in Japan. Of the Brazilians I met who had graduated from Japanese school or were otherwise fluent in Japanese, the majority continued to work in unskilled factory jobs in Japan once they graduated or left school. Others worked in the service industry (beauty salons, bars, restaurants, etc.), or as go-betweens for ethnic enterprises (e.g., employment brokerage firms) or at local international centers (as Jessica Silva from chapter 1 did) and/or Japanese schools requiring Portuguese-language aids.

For many Brazilian youth growing up in Japan attending Japanese school, their parents often could not help them with their schoolwork, or be directly involved in their academic progress, either because of language and time limitations, or simply a lack of interest. What is more, as we saw in the case of Brazilians attending private Portuguese-language school in Japan, the option of working for the same wages their parents made upon graduating from high school was a tempting, accessible, and easily imaginable option. Thus, whether they were educated in Japanese or Portuguese, for those Brazilians staying on in Japan after school, they tended to reproduce the labor/

social positionings of their parents. This corresponds to the findings of scholars such as Eunice Akemi Ishikawa (2005) and Hirohisa Takenoshita et al. (2013), who observe very little upward mobility among Brazilian migrant children in Japan.

One of the few Brazilians I met in Japan to have gone on to Japanese university was Lucy. When I met her, Lucy was in her last year of Japanese university and preferred to speak with me in Japanese. From her appearance—both of her parents were "pure" Nikkei-Brazilian—and the fluent Japanese she spoke, she was almost never mistaken for a foreigner in Japan, though she did not have a Japanese first name. When she first came to Japan at the age of two, her parents put her in Japanese preschool and later elementary school. Then, when she reached the fifth grade, they placed her in Brazilian school, where she stayed for four years in order to improve her Portuguese. At the time, her family was considering returning to Brazil, and they were concerned Lucy could not speak the language. After a while, though, it became clear that they would continue living in Japan, and Lucy decided she wanted to return to Japanese school. In her third year of middle school, she entered Japanese school once again, where she passed the exams to enter Japanese high school.

Most of the people Lucy went to high school with started working once they graduated, and did not continue on to university. She worked hard on her own to study for entrance exams to Japanese university, and was ultimately admitted to a program in graphic design. Her mother helped assist Brazilian children at Japanese schools, and her father worked at a factory; neither imagined returning to Brazil anymore, especially now that Lucy had continued on to Japanese university. In her free time, Lucy also volunteered at an NGO helping Brazilian children who struggled to adapt to Japanese public schools.

Lucy did not have significant memories of discrimination in Japan, and she felt that her teachers at school encouraged her to continue with her education. However, she was quick to acknowledge that her advancement to university in Japan had to do with more than just hard work and intelligence:

> I think it really depends on how your parents think, that has a lot of influence. In my case I've always lived in Japan and my surrounding environment has been good, people haven't spoken negatively of Japan. But I think that for people who have had more experience being treated unequally, then their way of thinking might be different. My father is a *seishain* [regular employee], he was hired directly from the start, without going through a brokerage firm. Maybe for that reason he hasn't had such negative experiences, he's been treated relatively well, and doesn't say bad things about Japan. The things parents experience are

passed on to children, they really fix [*teichaku suru*] inside them, and so kids can feel bad about themselves if their parents do.

In other words, home environment (notably living with parents who did not find themselves marginalized via the usually segmented system of contracted foreign labor in Japan), as well as positive experiences and reinforcement in school, had as much to do with Lucy's success as her own hard work and skills. In her last year of university, Lucy already had a good idea of the design company she would work for upon graduating. She was surer than ever that she wanted to stay in Japan, in part because her family intended to stay there, and in part because she had secured a promising future for herself, outside of regular factory life.

Other Brazilian students who attended Japanese school, however, especially those of *mestiço* (mixed) descent, often cited discrimination or bullying based on their ethnic appearance as one of the primary reasons they struggled to feel accepted or supported in school. One sixteen-year-old *mestiça* interlocutor, Megumi, who was born in Japan and had always attended Japanese school, for example, remembered students in elementary school calling her "black bread" (*kuro pan*) because of her skin color. When she told her teacher, however, the latter responded by saying, "Well, you're dark [*kuroi*], so it can't really be helped." Deeply hurt, Megumi refused at first to continue going to school, but since her mother could not afford to send her to private Brazilian school, she eventually went back, and continued on through Japanese high school. Like Jessica in chapter 1, who also experienced bullying based on her mixed ethnic appearance in Japanese school, Megumi was aware that no matter how Japanese she might feel, she—unlike the Matsuda children of chapter 3 or Lucy earlier—could still never pass as a full insider in Japan.

CONCLUSION

In January 2012, I attended MdC's middle and high school graduation ceremony at a public facility near the school, followed by dinner and dancing at an upscale hotel in Hamamatsu (paid for by the students themselves). At the beginning of the ceremony, students were urged to bow to Japanese and Brazilian flags as they stepped up on stage, and to sing both the Japanese and Brazilian national anthems. During the Brazilian anthem, only some students sang, most of them half-heartedly, forgetting to keep their hands on their hearts, while during the Japanese anthem, they appeared confused and did not sing at all.

Next, a representative from the local City Hall offered a congratulatory speech, recited in Japanese and translated simultaneously by one of MdC's teachers. "For those of you who will return to Brazil, I hope you don't cause any problems to your society. For those who stay, I hope you contribute to our city," he said. Only once during the ceremony did Renato, the principal of MdC, mention the possibility of going on to university. The eleven grade 12 graduates, dressed in black formal attire, stood up to receive their diplomas to a background of popular Brazilian music. Then the nineteen grade 9 graduates, in blue formal attire, stood up, while Whitney Houston's "Greatest Love of All" rang out over the loudspeakers: *I believe the children are our future . . .*

I thought about the students on stage and their futures, whether in Japan or Brazil, and how they would lead the way for the next generation of Brazilian transnational migrants. In the epilogue of *Strangers in the Ethnic Homeland* (2003), Takeyuki Tsuda asks whether the children of Nikkei-Brazilians in Japan will "eventually overcome their socioeconomic marginalization as low-status, unskilled migrant workers through cultural assimilation and social incorporation and disappear into the mainstream Japanese populace" (380). In my fieldwork with 1.5 and second-generation Brazilians in Japan, I found that the question was rarely one of complete *differentiation* versus *assimilation*. What is more, even if the children of *dekasegi* did assimilate to Japanese language and customs (usually via the Japanese education system), it did not mean that they completely rejected their Brazilian background or that they necessarily moved outside of the unskilled labor sector. Furthermore, because many *sansei* and *yonsei* youth were in fact of mixed descent, and often perceived as such based on their physical appearance, they could rarely just "disappear" among majority Japanese.

What did stand out, however, was the fact that for the children of *dekasegi*, living transnationally meant in practice that they were generally either encouraged to *labor* (in the sense of contracted, unskilled labor) in Japan or *leave* for a better future in Brazil. As we saw from the case of MdC, most students attending Brazilian school in Japan did so because they (or their parents) imagined it would help them enter university—and later, the broader job market—in Brazil. Even so, many of them were "swallowed by the [labor migration] system" in the sense that, raised in an environment of labor migration and tempted by the possibility of earning relatively high factory wages straight out of high school, they often opted against returning to Brazil immediately and thereby entered the same class/social position that their parents occupied in Japan. For those who attended Japanese public school, on the other hand, though they faced assimilationist pressures, they were not necessarily more likely to enter the broader Japanese labor market than their parents. Often, knowledge of Japanese language and customs was not enough; exposed from a young age to the option and attractiveness of factory wages, and otherwise lacking social and cultural capital in Japan, Brazilian graduates of Japanese schools, unless they were particularly ambitious, well supported, and encouraged, at home as well as at school—as was the case of Lucy, for example—tended to gravitate toward unskilled labor.

Thus, educational institutions, by orienting students to return to Brazil or stay in Japan, reinforced their position either as temporary migrants (ethnically differentiated, via Brazilian schools) or immigrants (assimilationist, via Japanese schools), and tended to reproduce the labor/social relations of their parents.[8] At the same time, however, by focusing on whether interlocutors identified as Japanese or Brazilian (or were somehow lost between the two poles), rather than examining the larger social structures (e.g., local educational systems) in which they were embedded, earlier studies of Brazilian labor migrants might have obfuscated what appeared to be of greater everyday significance to youth than questions relating to ethnic or national identity (see Green 2012).

In fact, I found that 1.5 and second-generation Brazilians' attachment to Japan had as much to do with perceived life/lifestyle opportunities as it did with ethnic identification per se. What is more, even among those who returned or imagined returning to Brazil, they tended to be ambivalent about a country they had little memory of, and one they knew would not easily provide them with the kind of lifestyle they achieved by working in unskilled labor in Japan.[9] This did not mean, however, that the children of *dekasegi* were somehow lost between Japan and Brazil. Rather, whether they identified more as Japanese or Brazilian, or some combination of the two, they were very much aware of the particular set of limitations and opportunities they faced as the children of transnational migrants, educated in nationally oriented institutions, and subject to globally desired lifestyles of consumption and mobility. Like their parents, they creatively and resourcefully navigated the limitations imposed upon them by the various national structures of which they were a part. As Michael Jackson (2013) points out, migrant narratives serve as an allegory for human existence, since we all seek to ameliorate our lot within the confines of the world into which we are thrown. In the case of transnational migrants, however, they were often faced with the particular task of maneuvering within the structures and social worlds of not one but two or more national frameworks. This was the reality of what it meant for them to live transnationally. In the next chapter, I turn to the opportunities and limitations of actual "return" to Brazil, and show how this experience, too, was shaped by social contexts and concerns besides ethnic or national belonging.

NOTES

1. Shortly before his death, Pierre Bourdieu introduced the concept of *habitus clivé*, implying the possibility of a split or divided habitus. In a sketch for self-analysis, he said that "his was a divided habitus—a *habitus clivé*—as a consequence of the contradictions he experienced in coming from lowly social origins to achieve high scholarly distinction" (Bennett 2007: 201). Although Bourdieu did not have the chance to elaborate on this concept, still it points to the idea that people of mixed backgrounds are caught between worlds, as opposed to engaged in creating flexible forms of belonging.

2. The fact that students at MdC were allowed to dye their hair these colors was noteworthy to me given that Japanese public high schools tend to be very strict about hair color—so much so that, in one notorious news story from 2017, for example, a Japanese student in Ōsaka filed a case against her school for forcing her to dye her naturally dark brown hair to black (see https://mainichi.jp/english/articles/20171027/p2a/00m/0na/021000c).

3. Students who attended schools in Japan that were officially recognized by the Brazilian Ministry of Education and Culture could have their diplomas and transcripts validated at schools in Brazil, should they return to further their education there. Without official MEC recognition, however, their documents from Brazilian schools in Japan might not be acknowledged by schools in Brazil.

4. In fact, as Joshua Roth (2002) notes, writing well before the global financial crisis of 2008–2009, "the fragility of the [Brazilian] center [he came to know] evoked the ephemeral character of many Brazilian enterprises in Japan and of migrant life in general" (99).

5. Joshua Roth (2002) points out that: "like samba and coffee, this soft drink had been imported to Japan many years before the 'return' migration of Nikkeijin and was sold in cans and bottles by Japanese firms" (105). Still, the placement of a Brazilian soft drink at MdC was clearly intentional, and not a usual option in vending machines throughout Japan.

6. Similar to the example of hair color, noted earlier, the fact that students at MdC were allowed to wear large piercings and work part-time jobs outside of school was notably different from the rules that govern most Japanese high schools.

7. According to M. Kim (1995), attending ethnic classes—and, I would add, ethnic schools—can help youth regain the confidence to cope with identity threats in a positive manner on the labor market. However, as Kaori Okano (1997) demonstrates, in the case of third-generation Zainichi Korean students in Japan, most of whom attend Japanese schools, students downwardly adjust their aspirations to what they consider possible based on their collective understanding of the way in which the dominant society and employment market operate. Similarly, though Brazilian schools in Japan serve as a kind of safe space for students, like all schools, they also channel or in some ways limit students' understanding and aspirations of what is possible for the future.

8. Although there are parallels between what I observed and Yasunori Fukuoka's work (1996), which found that Zainichi Koreans tended to be more pluralist or nationalist, depending on whether they attended Japanese or Korean schools, both Japanese

and Korean schools by and large orient ethnic Koreans toward a future in Japan, while Brazilian schools in Japan aim in part to ease students' transition to working or furthering their studies in Brazil.

9. Ambivalence with regards to "returning home" has been well documented in migration studies. For example, Nicole Constable (1999) notes that for return migrants there is also the necessity of "reworking" and "creating another place [space]" upon their return: "Filipinas discover, like other return migrants, that it is not always easy to fit back into their old lives and relationships because they have changed and home has been altered by their absence" (223). In my own work, I find this ambivalence to be even more acute for those Brazilians who have spent little to no time in their so-called origin country.

Chapter 5

The Pereiras

Back to Brazil

Guy Standing (2012), in his studies of flexible, insecure labor relations and the global precariat of recent years, argues that the world is increasingly one of circulants, not settlers. Certainly, circular migration has always been a part of the *dekasegi* labor movement between Japan and Brazil, as migrants often moved multiple times between the two countries over the years, sometimes returning to places they had lived before, while at other times trying out new beginnings in places they either were not previously familiar with or did not remember at all. Whether they migrated once or many times, the issue of return to Brazil took on new meanings for *dekasegi* and their families in 2009, when the Japanese government decided, in response to the global financial crisis, to pay them to "go home." This event highlighted the precarity of their position in Japan, as well as the limits to their ongoing movement around the world.

As a result of the crisis, the Japanese government offered Brazilians and other *dekasegi* from Latin America who lost their jobs approximately US$3,000, on the condition that they go "home" and not return to work in Japan for at least the next three years. Consequently, between 2008 and 2009, the population of Brazilians in Japan decreased by at least 45,000. As seen in figure I.1 (introduction), following their peak of nearly 317,000 in 2007, by 2012 the number of Brazilians in Japan had dropped by a full third, down to only 193,571 (Ministry of Justice, Japan). For many, economic stagnation and drastically reduced job opportunities spelled a forced return to Brazil. Those Brazilians who intended to continue working and living in Japan for years to come had little choice but to leave the country after a prolonged absence from Brazil. The important point here is not, of course, who and how many people accepted the Japanese government's offer of money to go to Brazil,[1] but what return in fact meant and continued to mean to Brazilian labor migrants and their families after they left Japan.

Until now, scholars of Nikkei-Brazilian labor migration have tended to focus on the experiences of migrants and their families in Japan or Brazil but rarely the experience of circular migration and/or return to Brazil. Part of this omission stems, of course, from the financial and logistical difficulties of actually following people as they migrate back and forth between Japan and Brazil, or once they return to Brazil. An important exception to this is the 2011 documentary film, *Kodoku na Tsubametachi: Dekasegi no Kodomo ni Umarete* (Lonely Swallows: Living as the Children of Migrant Workers), which traces five *yonsei* (fourth-generation) Brazilians in Japan over a span of about 2.5 years (2007–2008), and picks up the thread with them again in 2010 after they have all returned to Brazil.

In the case of Brazilian labor migrants in Japan, most moved where the jobs were, or where employment brokerage firms placed them. Thus, they were concentrated in specific parts of Japan, especially in the industrial belt of central Honshū, spanning the area between Tōkyō and Ōsaka. Certain cities like Hamamatsu, Ōizumi, and Toyota had especially high numbers of Brazilians residing there. In Brazil, however, *dekasegi* and their families tended to return to where they had personal or family connections. Though many of them returned to the southeastern states of Paraná, São Paulo, and Mato Grosso do Sul, the distances between cities there are greater than in Japan, and returned labor migrants were rarely grouped together in terms of work or housing. Official resources for labor migrants were concentrated in capital cities, and in particular São Paulo City, even though most Brazilians never heard about or had access to them in the small towns and cities to which they returned.

Throughout the year of fieldwork I spent in Brazil in 2012, I followed a number of *dekasegi* during and after their return from Japan. Although I was based in São Paulo City at the time, I regularly traveled to small towns and cities in the interior of São Paulo and Mato Grosso do Sul to speak with interlocutors whom I had either previously met in Japan, or whose relatives I had gotten to know there. In São Paulo City, I also regularly attended seminars and workshops in Liberdade (the historically Japanese neighborhood of the city) put on by the Center of Information and Support for Workers Overseas (CIATE), and the related Kaeru and Tadaima projects, one aimed at reintegrating children who had grown up in Japan into Brazilian schools, and the other at helping returned adults ease into the Brazilian job market.

Thus, to locate returned labor migrants in Brazil, I largely relied on snowballing from the connections I had already made with Brazilians in Japan. In the cases I did not do this, approaching people instead for the first time at events or workshops, I generally found interlocutors to be less willing and open to share their experiences, especially if they had returned to Brazil without any savings, or else undergone a failed business attempt once they were back (not an uncommon experience). Having a previous connection to interlocutors or their relatives in Japan, however, usually paved the way toward greater trust and understanding of my purpose in interviewing them once I was in Brazil.

In this chapter, I examine return to Brazil after long-term residency in Japan as experienced by different generations of Brazilian migrants, and in particular the Pereira family: Wania (*nisei* and of mixed descent), her non-Nikkei husband Walter, and their five *sansei, mestiço* children, Stefanie, William, Cleber, Jefferson, and Raquel, whose ages ranged from the late teens to mid-twenties by the time we met (for a family tree, see figure 5.1). As I did with the Silva family tree in chapter 1, I have marked individuals without any Japanese lineage with grey symbols in order to illustrate the mixed heritage of various members of the family. Of the five Pereira children, Stefanie, who was married to Kenichi (also *sansei* and of mixed descent) and had two young daughters, was at the time the only one who lived and supported herself independently from her family (figure 5.1).

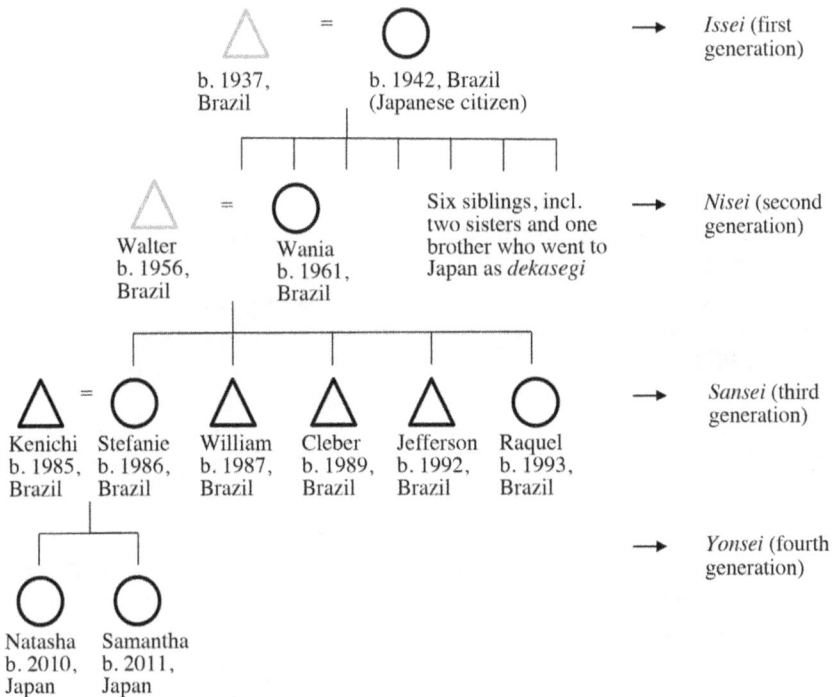

Figure 5.1   The Pereira family tree.

As will be explored in this chapter, the Pereiras possessed complex, shifting motivations for migrating to and staying in Japan, as well as returning to Brazil. Although religion figured predominantly in their lives, it was hardly the only force at play in their decisions and aspirations. As was the case for all Brazilian labor migrants and their children, locally embedded structures such as educational and employment systems, together with the kin and social communities they were a part of, helped shape their subjective experience of constraints and opportunities in both Japan and Brazil.

The Pereiras were practicing Evangelicals and held religion at the center of their lives. Although their experience of return was conditioned by religious motivation and belief, the trajectory they followed connected in more general ways to that of the thousands of labor migrants and their families who, in recent years, moved their lives back to Brazil, whether for the short or long term. Their story demonstrates the ways in which ethnic and national orientation—whether Japanese, Brazilian, and/or both—were inseparable from (if not subsumed by) contexts such as family and religion, and all these represented in terms of resources, pressures, and support. Furthermore, it explores the opportunities and limitations of return to Brazil—especially since it meant different things to migrant parents and their children—and the ways in which transnational identity and affiliation did not necessarily reflect the ability to move smoothly between countries (Appadurai 1996).

INTRODUCING THE PEREIRAS

Flying into Campo Grande, in the state of Mato Grosso do Sul in southwestern Brazil, I quickly discovered why the city is nicknamed *Cidade Morena*, or "Brown City." As rain beat down on the ruddy, sunbaked earth, the rivers winding through town quickly filled with the color of rust.

Cleber, Wania and Walter's middle child, was waiting for me inside the airport with his older sister Stefanie and her infant daughter Samantha, while Wania sat out in the old family Fiat with Stefanie's other young daughter, Natasha. This was my second time visiting Wania and her family in Campo Grande. Prior to that, I had last seen them in Gifu, as they prepared to leave Japan and pick up where they left off in Brazil over a decade earlier. The first thing we did that rainy August afternoon in 2012 was head to a nearby shopping mall to buy the ingredients for a large cake, which Wania's sister would make for the *churrasco* (Brazilian BBQ) goodbye party to be held in honor of her son and daughter who were soon to return to factory life in Japan.

Nearly all of Wania's immediate and extended family had experienced firsthand the impact of labor migration between Japan and Brazil, and had moved between Mato Grosso do Sul and Gifu multiple times over the years. When I first met Wania in her home in Gifu, in 2011, all five of her children still lived there, four at home and the eldest, Stefanie, nearby with her husband Kenichi and their two young children. Thinking back to Wania's cramped apartment in Ōgaki, where on several occasions I chatted with all ten members of the family standing around a wobbly kitchen table only big enough for two, I was surprised to note that less than a year later, all of them—save for Wania's second oldest child, William, who would eventually return too—had since moved back to Brazil.

FAMILY BACKGROUND

Staying with her in the home she and her husband Walter built over twenty years previously in Campo Grande, I learned that Wania had seven siblings, and was the only one among them to have completed university. Her mother, whose family had originally migrated to Brazil from Hokkaidō, in northern-most Japan, grew up on a farm in the interior of Mato Grosso do Sul, raised by her grandparents and uncles after her father died of typhoid fever and her mother remarried. When I met Wania's mother, a slight and quiet-spoken woman in her seventies with white hair pinned tightly in a bun and a long skirt and rimmed glasses, it was hard to imagine that at seventeen she had run away on horseback with Wania's father who, originally from Ceará, in north-eastern Brazil, described his ethnic background as "descended from Indians." The two then scratched out a living for themselves 300 kilometers away from the family farm from which she had escaped, certain that her relatives would punish her for choosing a man who was not Japanese.[2]

Although Wania's mother never went to school, she learned later how to read from the Bible. When I asked if her mother had always been a Christian, Wania explained to me in Portuguese that no, she used to be a Buddhist, like so many of the early Japanese settlers in Brazil:

She only stopped being a Buddhist when the doctors gave up on my sister. My sister was really ill and the doctors said there was no cure. She was small, and my Mom walked after the doctors all day carrying my sick sister with my brother and me trailing behind. We walked a lot in those days. My sister had a problem with her stomach and her blood was thin like water. We came to Campo Grande for a while, to live with my Godmother. My Godmother was a believer. She was Japanese too, a *descendente* [lit. a descendant]. And her husband was like my Dad, a northeasterner. She said to my Mom, let's go to the church, let's go. My Mom went to the Evangelical church and my sister was cured. So when my sister was cured my Mom saw that God does indeed exist and that we didn't need to do a novena—praying, praying, praying. We didn't need to sacrifice anything. There is a God, and a God who cures, regardless of whether you deserve it or not. He has power, and uses it on those who search for Him. And so my sister was cured.

As a result of this episode, Wania grew up in Campo Grande attending Evangelical church, though she claimed to have always had a keen spiritual intuition, something that she could just feel inside herself from a very young age.

Although only one of her parents was of Japanese descent, Wania looked so much like her mother that she was often mistaken for "pure" Nikkei. Like many *nisei* in Brazil, she was teased as a child for her ethnic appearance:

> I was bullied when I was a kid in Brazil because I had a Japanese face. The others would always call me *ceborinha* [a play on the name of Cebolinha, a popular cartoon character in Brazil known for saying the letter "l" instead of "r"]. So I didn't want to have anything to do with being Japanese. So much so that when my Mom officially got married to my Dad, I was 15 years old, they asked me if I wanted to keep her Japanese last name and I said no. I didn't want anything Japanese in my life. It was bad enough having to suffer because I had Japanese eyes.

From the age of twelve, Wania worked at a vegetable market in Campo Grande, and then switched to making soba noodles. The family was poor—her mother washed clothes to pay the rent and her father "would take from [them] and give to other women"—but she financed university by writing to Catholic priests to ask for a scholarship. When she met Walter, who later became her husband, she was almost finished with an undergraduate degree in social sciences. Her plan was to travel for six months throughout Brazil with a missionary group. She wanted to see if Walter would wait for her, and when she returned and he asked her to marry him, she agreed, and they set the date for five months later:

> People were suspicious, though, that I was pregnant because I got married so soon after getting engaged. So I prayed to God that I wouldn't have a child until a year after the marriage, and that was when our first child was born. Then I prayed that the baby would look like my mother-in-law, who has blue eyes, so that she would know for sure it was her grandchild. Sure enough, our daughter [Stefanie] was born with bluish eyes, the same color as Walter's mother's. God is good, you see.

Thus, for Wania, God made His presence known from the time she was a child and her younger sister recovered from a life-threatening illness to the moment her own daughter Stefanie was born, when and with the features she asked Him for.

Before moving to Japan for the first time in 1996, Wania described raising her five children in a comfortable, middle-class lifestyle very different from that of her own upbringing:

For years my husband had wanted to go to Japan. But I never wanted to. He wanted to build an addition on our shop [a construction business they started together in the mid-1980s]. He thought it was so easy to make money in Japan, that it nearly grew on trees there. That's how many Brazilians think. They think that people there are swimming in money, that it's easy to earn a living. No one thinks that people suffer from the work they do there, that kind of thing. And we earned good money here in Brazil, we had a shop. A fine life. Our three oldest kids were in private school, it cost the same as a person's monthly minimum wage for each kid we put in school, the best school in Campo Grande. On days I couldn't leave the shop I sent them home from school by taxi. With our shop we had bought a country house, a car, we had even built our house. So it was a small business but it did well.

Wania emphasized how well-off the family was in the 1990s, telling me only later—and indirectly—about the debts they ran into shortly before leaving for Japan. The trouble they experienced with the family business was only ever mentioned in passing, however, as though it were an insignificant memory to be brushed under the rug.[3] Indeed, in the same way that she explained most major life events to me, Wania narrated the decision to move to Japan for the first time as, above all, the will of God:

God used people to tell me that He wanted me to go to Japan, many times. And I didn't want to go. So I asked for proof from God. I said if it's really God's will then something will happen. And then things did happen, and that's why I went. I didn't go to make money to buy a house, to buy a car, to study, nothing like that. God started using people to speak to me. He wanted me to go to another country. And people began talking to me, people from church. I started to run into trouble with our shop. So many things happened at once, I said this really must be God's doing. So I said, OK, God needs to show me proof then. And in fact, right after I asked for the first sign, the next day at 9 a.m., a man came to ask if I would sell part of the [shop's] land to him, and I said to him, you are the first sign from God that I am going to Japan.

At first, in 1996, Wania and her husband Walter went to Japan without their children to work in Hokkaidō via an employment brokerage firm. Although her maternal grandparents had originally migrated from that very part of Japan, like most labor migrants to Japan today, she never attempted to track down or contact her Japanese relatives there (see Roth 2002; Tsuda 2003). At the time, Wania had five other siblings already working in factories in Kōbe and Ōsaka, but she and her husband chose to live far from all of them. They left their five children with one of Walter's brothers and sent money for him to take care of them, calling Brazil from a pay phone every week. Their youngest child Raquel was especially distressed over being separated from her parents: "I used to write letters to my father asking him to let me get plastic surgery so I could look more 'Japanese,'" she told me in Japanese. "I thought the reason I wasn't allowed to live with them in Japan was because I didn't look Japanese enough."

As it turned out, the employment brokerage firm had lied to Wania and Walter about—besides many other things—how close they would live to the factory and the fact that they would have to walk through the wintry weather at night, arriving home from work with feet and hands numb from the cold. After four months, Walter's mother fell ill and was put in intensive care, apparently sick with *saudade* (longing) for her son in Japan. Wania and Walter decided to return to Brazil to care for her, but it was not long before they decided to move again, this time to Hyōgo, in central Japan.

Wania and Walter then spent three years working in a *bentō-ya* (a boxed lunch factory) near Kōbe. There were no churches for them to frequent in Hyōgo Prefecture, where Kōbe is located, and Wania used to kneel down at home, crying, and asking God to send someone to speak about Jesus with her. In their fourth year, they moved to Saitama, north of Tōkyō. The first time Wania went to a church there—it was far from where she lived but people picked her up and brought her—she met a woman from Rio de Janeiro who had moved to Japan to proselytize. Wania did not know anyone in the church yet so she just stood outside looking in. After a while the woman approached her and inquired, "How long have you been in Japan?" Wania said, "I don't even know." The woman then went on to ask, "What did you come here to do?" and Wania replied, "Even worse, I don't know what I am doing here." So the woman told her to sit down, and she said, "God has a plan for your children, that's why you're here. You're the central reason, the spinal cord for them to come here. They could only be here through you. So don't think that you're here just because your husband wanted to be. God brought you here because he has a plan for your children in Japan. God has had this plan for many years. So tell your husband to bring your kids here." As Wania recounted the story, wonder filled her eyes, and she told me: "The woman didn't even know me. But God uses people, God is like that."

That very day Wania went home and told Walter, "God doesn't keep family apart. The God I know, the God that the Bible talks about, doesn't keep family apart. He doesn't leave kids behind." But Walter insisted, saying he would not bring their children to Japan. As Wania saw it:

> He was worried they would grow up in Japan, become independent, earn their own money, and lose themselves because of it. Which happens a lot. But he was also only thinking of money. He wanted to return to Brazil as soon as he could build the shop up. But then he saw it wasn't easy to save money, paying for five kids in Brazil too. So when I spoke with him I said, "Look, God used a

woman today to tell me that He has a plan for our children in Japan. And you won't bring them here? How long will they be cast aside? In one year I want to bring them here." And sure enough, a year later I brought my two oldest, in 2001, when they were thirteen and fourteen. The following year I went to get the other three. That's how it happened, it was the will of God.

Thus, despite her husband's reservations, and after several attempts at living in Japan without them, Wania—like Angela Silva and the Matsudas of chapters 1 and 3—was successful in bringing her children to Japan, where, beginning in the early 2000s, they stayed off and on for the next decade. God was the language she spoke and used to convince her husband that their family should not be kept apart. The youngest children, Jefferson and Raquel, were the only ones to go to Japanese school—both completed middle school in Japan before they began working in factories there—while the three older children, Stefanie, William, and Cleber, were placed in international Evangelical schools. None of the five attended private Brazilian school in Japan.

RETURN TO BRAZIL

When, in 2012, I first visited the home in Campo Grande that the Pereira family had built decades before and rented out while living in Japan, Wania and three of her children were just starting to make it theirs again while waiting for Walter to work his final few months in Japan. At that time in May, the house stood largely empty, an expanse of grey tile floors and plastic garden furniture lined up in the living room. One of the only boxes that had been unpacked contained a Japanese rice cooker, warm with the evening's *gohan* (rice). By the time I visited Campo Grande a second time, several months later, I found the home's mulberry tree in bloom, and the living room filled with a sturdy, middle-class sofa and chairs.

"How was the decision to come back to Brazil?" I asked Wania, as we leisurely picked ripe mulberries together from her increasingly flourishing back yard. "I didn't decide to come back," she said. "I decided to come when God spoke with me. I didn't ask any of my children to return either. Just to give you an idea, my husband wanted me to leave since last year. But I didn't leave Brazil because I wanted to, so I wasn't going to come back because I wanted to either. Or because he wanted me to. I was waiting for a word from God."

Although Wania believed firmly in the role God played in her decision to return to Brazil, it was clear, too, that she and her husband were tired of working in factories in Japan. As they grew older, manual labor grew more and more taxing on their health. Like many labor migrants in their fifties and sixties in Japan, Wania and Walter also found their work opportunities to be increasingly limited. Besides Japan's overall economic stagnation since the global financial crisis, factories were less interested in hiring older workers on temporary contracts than they were the young and physically fit. Without a home and extended family network to rely on in Japan, the reality of growing old and increasingly unable to perform manual labor (the only work available to them in Japan without more knowledge of Japanese) only added to the precarity of Wania and Walter's situation.

Since returning to Campo Grande, Wania had taken a job as bookkeeper for a supermarket in town, and could spend most of her time at work sitting down. Her youngest daughter, Raquel, eighteen years old at the time, was hired as a cashier at the same store. Raquel's education only went as far as the end of Japanese middle school. At fifteen she had taken a job at an electronics factory in Japan but suffered so much back pain from the repetitive work that she preferred to return to Brazil with her family. At first, she struggled with the names of the tropical produce she sold at her new job. Having left Brazil when she was just a child, she did not recognize *maxixe* (a kind of gherkin), for example, or *carambola* (starfruit). The names rolled off her tongue like unfamiliar flavors, and she missed speaking Japanese with her friends in Japan. Raquel's brother, Jefferson, only a year older than her, had also not continued past middle school in Japan. Capitalizing on his language skills, however, he was hired soon after his return to Campo Grande at a small travel agency to work with tourists at the city's new bus station. Both Raquel and Jefferson made far less money at their new jobs in Brazil than they did in Japan, as was the case for Wania, too.

Wania and her children explored Evangelical church options as soon as they returned to Brazil. Although they did not all attend the same church, or the same branch of Evangelical church they had attended in Japan, each member of the family found a way to continue practicing their faith on a regular basis. In *Transnational Religious Spaces: Faith and the Brazilian Migration Experience* (2013), Olivia Sheringham finds that Catholic and Evangelical churches not only helped Brazilian migrants create a sense of belonging in London, they also aided them in their re-adaptation to life "back home." Similarly, for the Pereiras, Evangelical churches served as an important locus of belonging and sociality upon their return to Brazil. On my second visit to Campo Grande, for example, I attended services at three different Evangelical churches, one with Wania and Raquel, another with Cleber, and a third with Jefferson. Although they were still "shopping around" for the right church, as Wania put it, Evangelical spaces were familiar and comforting, and had much in common with the churches they attended in Japan. Sharing a bedroom with Raquel, I listened every night as she fell asleep to light Christian rock music, and chatted online with a boy her age she had met at church who had also recently returned from Japan. Thus, for Cleber, Jefferson, and Raquel, although they missed Japan and in many ways struggled to adjust to life in Brazil, through religious spaces they were able to make new friends with similar values and beliefs, and thereby ease the process of "return."

When I asked her if she imagined her children would stay in Brazil or return to Japan one day, Wania replied:

> I can't really tell you. Since there is the option [i.e., a special visa for Japanese descendants and their dependents] for them to go there, one of them will always want to go, right? Who knows for how long. Even though it's all in the hands of God. And whether it's here or Japan, they'll get married and won't stay with us. It doesn't matter to me as long as they are firm in their faith in Jesus. Because one day we're going to leave this place. We're not going to take our house, we're not going to take our car. What we built will stay here. And we need to prepare ourselves to meet with God.[4]

Thus, although the entire family was now back or would soon return to Brazil, Wania was aware that they might not all stay there indefinitely. Return to Brazil was not a final destination, after all, but one of several different options available to her and her children until the work of life was complete. Even though Wania believed that God was ultimately responsible for their return to Brazil, family constraints and opportunities clearly played an important role in each person's individual decision and experience. What is more, in Campo Grande the Pereiras already owned a home, which could be used by everyone in the immediate family as a safe base to return to. Also, Wania's children could rely on her for help navigating Portuguese and the local job market, as well as pool resources with their parents even if they did not make enough money to support themselves independently from the family.

Despite the fact that everyone decided to return to Brazil at roughly the same time, return meant different things to the various members of the Pereira family. For Wania, for example, returning to Brazil appeared to be a smoother transition than it was for her children. She felt at home in both Japan and Brazil, she said, because of her faith in God: "When you move somewhere new and ask for God's direction, you adapt very quickly to your new home." In fact, Wania had moved back and forth multiple times between Japan and Brazil over the years, and although she did not imagine returning to work in Japan again because of her age, she could not be entirely sure. Still, she had a house and relatives to return to in Campo Grande, and with a university degree, Portuguese language capital, and varied work experience, had little difficulty being hired as a bookkeeper once she was back.

Wania's children, however, had mixed feelings about their return to Brazil. Like many of the Brazilians who grew up as part of the 1.5 and second generation in Japan, Wania's children were more ambivalent about their positioning in Brazil. Cleber, for example, Wania's middle son, was only seven when his parents first went to Japan in 1996, and twelve when he went to live there himself. Although he never attended Japanese school, at twenty-three Cleber identified more strongly with his Japanese heritage than his mother did:

> I feel Japanese. Because I'm helpful and polite. It doesn't matter how much people tell us we're only *yonsei* [fourth generation]—actually our blood is *sansei* [third generation] because my grandmother is pure-blooded, but since they brought her to Brazil and registered her here she ended up *nisei* [second generation]. I don't care how I look but if I could choose, I would like to have come out looking a little more Japanese. I like the way Japanese people look—their eyes, their appearance. When I was a baby I was a lot more *japonesinho* [like a little Japanese boy], but now that I'm older I don't look Japanese at all.

Perhaps because he did not appear as Japanese as his mother, Cleber suffered less teasing as a child in Brazil. While Wania rejected her Japanese appearance due to the more recent experience of discrimination in Brazil, Cleber embraced this aspect of his ethnic identity as something positive and valuable (i.e., positive minority status in Brazil). As a teenager in Japan, this was likely further reinforced by Cleber's status as a visible, negative minority there, such that he wished he could pass more easily as Japanese.

Cleber's identification with Japan had to do with more than ethnicity, however. Although he did not feel completely comfortable speaking Japanese, and for the most part spoke with me only in Portuguese, in Japan he discovered a certain amount of freedom and economic mobility that he would be hard-pressed to achieve in Brazil. With only a high school degree (that he ended up completing through a long-distance course), Cleber, like Marcelo Silva of chapter 1, felt at a distinct disadvantage on the job market in Brazil:

> I don't know what I'm going to do for work here. I started working in a factory in Japan when I was fifteen, and I got used to it. Since I really like to travel, I think Japan is the best place for me, it makes everything accessible. We can work for just one or two months, and already have enough money to go on a trip. We can go back and forth, work a little more, and then travel again. Here in Brazil it's hard even to survive on the money you make.

Cleber went on to explain that he was only really back in Brazil because of his grandparents, and his family, but that he would like to return to Japan one day. In reality, he appeared torn between the two places:

> I feel like both Japan and Brazil are my countries, I'm divided between them both. But in terms of quality of life, Japan is better. Here in Brazil we are more relaxed. If it weren't for the dreams we want to pursue, Brazil would actually

be the better place. Because here you can live fine without too many worries. But the thing is we have this desire to chase after our dreams, to work a lot, so I think Japan is better because we can work and earn more there.

Interestingly, Cleber's sense of inner division had less to do with a sense of dislocation in Japan and/or Brazil, and more to do with how attached he felt to both places. Also, when he spoke of his attachment to life in Japan, it was not necessarily in terms of ethnic belonging. Rather, Cleber longed to return to Japan because he believed that there, where there were the "perennial possibilities of something different, something new" (Jackson 2013: 1), he could more easily pursue his ambitions for a more comfortable and secure future.

Like his siblings, Cleber had had to interrupt his studies to move to Japan in the first place. Although he did not regret having left Brazil when he was younger, he had mixed feelings about whether the decision had been a good one for his family overall:

Sometimes I see good things about it and sometimes bad things. I see the part where I didn't continue my studies, even though I loved school. I see that if there hadn't been the whole debt problem because of my uncle, we would have continued to have a good life here and I would have stayed in school. But at the same time that I see all that, I see what would have happened if we'd stayed in Brazil. If we'd stayed in that kind of good life I don't know if we would have learned as much. I don't know if we'd be as close to God. Who knows what kind of person I'd be. If my parents had gone to Japan and never come back to get us—in the first years they left us behind, my brother Jefferson started stealing things—if we'd stayed far from our family, maybe I would be worse off. Or if no one had gone to Japan, I think maybe we'd be more spoiled. So there are the good sides and the not-so-good sides of having gone.

By the time I met him, however, Cleber was more preoccupied with helping his family return to Brazil. His parents were both in their fifties and were tired of working in factories in Japan. They planned to use the property where their construction shop once stood to put up a new building and rent out parts of it to small businesses: "My parents are tired, they're getting old. I want to help them out financially so that they can retire and be at peace in Brazil. My Mom worked until two or three years ago but then she got in a car accident and started having back problems. She can't stay on her feet very long, and in Japan it's either that or nothing."

Cleber's older brother William (twenty-four when I met him at a church event in Aichi in 2011) was fourteen when he first joined his parents in Japan. For the first few years they were in Japan, William and Cleber went to an Evangelical school run by Americans in Aichi, which has since closed. After their parents ran into disagreements with the administration, however, both William and Cleber were pulled out of the school and encouraged to work. William grew accustomed to making his own money, and for three years worked in factories in Gunma without any family members nearby. He bought his own car and spent most of the money he earned traveling and hanging out with friends.

William had been to Brazil four times since leaving at the age of fourteen: once to evangelize in Bahia for nine months, another time to visit his grandparents, and the third time to complete his high school diploma. The fourth and last time he had gone was in order to check on his parents' construction project. When I met with him in Japan again in 2013, he hoped to gain more international experience before returning to Brazil to join the rest of his family there. In fact, William had recently returned from an English course in Australia and was saving to go back by living with his uncle near Nagoya and working twelve-hour shifts (1,050 yen an hour) at a *bentō* (boxed lunch) factory:

> I want to do an exchange program and learn more English because you have to have some kind of skill to go back to Brazil with. What I don't want to do is stay in Japan working in factories. If you study and do something else, you don't deserve to work in a factory for the rest of your life. Especially for us foreigners in Japan—you work here until you're old and then what, what are you going to do? You can't work in a factory once you're old. I see that happening to my parents, they worked and worked, but they don't have much from all these years because they were so busy helping us out too, and now they're old and tired and they just want some peace. So the only answer is for them to go back to Brazil and let us kids help them out for a change.

Indeed, by early 2014, after studying for a time in Australia, William was back in Mato Grosso do Sul working for a local tourism company and helping his parents and other siblings. When he was still in Japan and I asked him if he thought life would be difficult in Brazil, he said that no, since he had already been several times before and had an idea of how things worked, unlike his sister Raquel who had been in Japan since the age of nine and attended only Japanese school there. At the time, the main reason William saw himself staying longer in Japan was not because he felt increasingly Japanese, but because he had worked there since the age of seventeen and, like Cleber, grown used to the material comforts of Japan:

> In Japan you have access to things. You have a good salary and things are a lot more accessible than in Brazil. There you have a low salary and things are really expensive. It's a great country to live in because you have freedom and you have time, but compared to Japan, you don't have money. When you come here young like I did you learn to spend money. You don't have the mindset to save. Lots of young people got used to how easy Japan is and don't want to leave. That's what happened to me.

William believed that he and his parents stayed as long as they did in Japan because of family, and the comforts they achieved for themselves there. Since all of his siblings were in Japan, and they had access to a comfortable life there, it made sense for the Pereiras to stay. Now that William and his four siblings had reached adulthood, though, he believed his parents could begin paying attention to their own dreams for retirement in Brazil. Return to Brazil made sense for them as a family, since William and his brothers and sister could rely on their parents for a place to stay, social capital in the city of Campo Grande, and the support network of extended relatives. As both William and Cleber believed, it was also their turn to give back to their parents, who were getting too old to work as hard as they once did.

In the end, then, family and religion were important forces guiding the Pereiras's decision to migrate to Japan, to stay there, and then to return to Brazil. For Wania, though her age and physical stamina were clearly limiting factors in how long she could realistically continue working in Japan, she understood return to Brazil as, above all, the will of God. As for Stefanie, Wania's eldest child, she too returned to Brazil so that she and her husband Kenichi could live close to his relatives in the interior of São Paulo, and so that their young daughters could grow up among other Evangelicals, and with the option of attending a good private Brazilian school. Although Stefanie had not studied past high school, she had learned enough English through the American Evangelical school in Aichi and on her own that she could work for a decent enough salary as a private language teacher in Brazil. Kenichi, who had worked for four years in a car parts factory and then three years as a garbage collector in Japan, was at the time still trying to find work at a Toyota factory in Brazil. During the financial crisis of 2008–2009 he took advantage of not being able to work and studied Japanese as hard as he could. Now, he hoped that the linguistic capital he had accrued in Japan might make up for the fact that he had limited education and professional skills.

Wania's son William, in turn, even though he recognized the importance of material comforts as a primary factor in choosing to stay in Japan or not, ultimately decided to return to Brazil because of his parents and siblings. As for Wania's other children, family was key in their decision to return. The fact that Raquel did not speak fluent Portuguese and had little memory of Brazil, or that Cleber wanted to look more Japanese and missed the opportunities for work and travel that he had found in Japan, did not mean that they would stay in Japan without their parents and siblings. Even though they were old enough to try out life on their own there, family was a significant enough factor to keep them—at least for the time being—in Brazil. Moreover, although they were drawn to the material comforts available to them in Japan, they were also aware of the limits to their social mobility should they decide to stay there. By returning to Brazil, the Pereiras hoped to build a better life for themselves than that which they imagined possible, in the long term, as labor migrants in Japan.

OTHER EXPERIENCES OF RETURN

Although the decision to return—just like the decision to migrate in the first place—was often tied to the context of family, individual members of the same family usually experienced it differently. On the one hand, especially for those who moved to Japan as adults, Brazil still represented an important focus of nostalgia; many of these migrants, even before the global financial crisis hit, viewed return to Brazil as a distinct possibility or goal.

On the other hand, as Brazilians have come to occupy an increasingly long-term position in Japanese society, particularly for those raised in Japan, return to Brazil is difficult, if not impossible, to imagine. As Paul Green, an anthropologist who worked with Brazilian youth in Japan in the early 2000s, notes, young migrants often do not share a myth of return with the old. What is more, older migrants may have "built a future in Japan for the sake of their children and yet dreamed of going back to a homeland that was very much in their hearts and nostalgic memories" (2010: 524), not necessarily their children's. Thus, family considerations, as well as differences among generations, are essential in analyzing Brazilians' experiences of circular migration and return.

The Pereiras's experience of return to Brazil, though framed in terms of religion, had much in common with that of returned *dekasegi* in general. In most cases, no matter how Japanese and/or Brazilian people felt, return to Brazil—as well as the decision to stay there—had less to do with ethnic self-identification than it did with a constellation of factors including work opportunities, age and health concerns, and, of course, family constraints and support. What is more, the various generations of a single family necessarily experienced return migration differently. Another example of a multigenerational family, the Furutas, shows how children of Brazilian labor migrants, having spent many years in Japan, often had a difficult time transitioning to life in Brazil compared to their parents.

THE FURUTAS

Born in Brazil to Japanese parents in 1945 and the eldest of six children, Toshi Furuta had worked to support his younger siblings instead of attending university. In 1989, immediately after Japan's immigration reforms were announced, he dressed in a suit and tie and went to the Japanese Consulate in São Paulo to request a tourist visa to Japan. The official in charge granted a visa to Toshi and his wife Sayako, both *nisei*, their youngest daughter Joana, their son Edson, and Edson's wife and one-year-old daughter, allegedly on the condition that the seven of them should return in a few months and let him know how the trip went. Once in Japan, the Furutas quickly found factory jobs in Aichi and ended up staying there for the next thirteen years. Toshi and Sayako's other two sons joined them later and, like Edson, stayed in Japan even after their parents and sister Joana returned to Brazil in 2004. "To this day, that poor official is still waiting for us!" Yoshi laughed, as I sat down to dinner one evening with the Furutas in São João do Rio Preto, in the interior of São Paulo.

Joana's two older children, Shirly and Kazu, were both born in Japan, and were twelve and thirteen when they returned to Brazil with their parents and grandparents in 2004. Shirly and Kazu had been to Japanese school in Japan before spending several years in a Brazilian school, and even years later both spoke Portuguese with a slight Japanese accent. They finished high school in Brazil and after that, Kazu stayed in his room for months and would not speak with anyone in the family. As Joana explained to me in Portuguese:

> He resents that we took him out of Japanese school. He says he would have stayed and gone to university there if we had let him. He didn't pass the *vestibular* [entrance exams] here, has trouble with Portuguese, and got discouraged. He wants to go back to Japan because he thinks life is easier and better there. We tried to do what is best for our children, but right now, Kazu still doesn't understand that. He wants to go back to work but the Consulate told us there's no way he can on his own as a *yonsei* [fourth-generation Nikkei]. We got his passport renewed and everything, but we still haven't figured out a way for him to go. Maybe it would be good for him to go and see that life is not that easy there, then he would understand.

Joana's hope was that by returning to Brazil, Shirly and Kazu would go to university, though neither of them—at that point in their early twenties—had done so yet. Shirly did attend a technical school in Brazil, where she trained to work in a beauty salon, but Kazu had not worked or studied in years. In Japan, he would have been considered a NEET (not in education, employment, or training), since according to his mother, he still spent most of his time playing computer games or reading manga in Japanese: "At least now he hangs out with Brazilian friends who like anime and cosplay, and attends cosplay conferences in São Paulo with them, instead of staying locked up in his room all day."

As we watched the latest soap opera (*novela*) on TV together, Joana (aged forty at the time I interviewed her) told me how divided she still felt about the decision to return to Brazil. "We're torn between a life of luxury there, and a simpler, less strenuous life here." When she and her husband returned to Brazil in 2004, they were able to live in the same two-story house they lived in now, and that all of the siblings and parents had bought together with savings from Japan. They also bought other property on the same block, and rented it out to small businesses. For their first few years in Brazil, the Furutas bought and ran two car-washing businesses nearby, but eventually the owner of the land wanted to reclaim his property and they shut them down. By the time I visited them in 2012, they had taken over a small contracting franchise that hired domestic workers. They did not make a lot of money, they confided, but they made enough to get by on.

In her late thirties, Joana had been diagnosed with lupus, another factor preventing her and her family from ever moving back to Japan. Factory work was hard on the body, and since she grew tired so easily, she could not imagine returning to assembly line work. She also worried about who would take care of her parents as they aged, especially since her three older brothers still lived in Japan and had every intention of staying there.

During my visit to São João do Rio Preto, Joana and I drove out in the family's old Chevrolet truck to the Furutas's *sítio* (farmhouse) that they bought with money saved from Japan. "The idea of this place was to reunite the whole family here, but no one wanted to come back except us," Joana explained. As we walked around the land, checking in on the pigs and chickens, and picking *ponkan*, a type of orange brought to Brazil by early Japanese emigrants, Joana's father Yoshi appeared wearing large rubber boots and a cowboy hat. "We have everything here, we just don't have money!" he laughed.

As had been the case of the Pereiras, for the Furutas the decision to return to Brazil was intertwined with various family constraints and opportunities. Yoshi and his wife, both advanced in age, wished to retire to an easier life in the Brazilian countryside, rather than continue to work in factories in Japan. Their daughter Joana and her family decided to return with them, since they could all live together in the same house and support one another. Joana's children, however, did not share the same dreams as their parents and grandparents of building life anew in Brazil. Having grown up in Japan, when they first arrived in Brazil they were more comfortable speaking Japanese than Portuguese, and struggled to adjust to the Brazilian school system. Although Joana's intention in returning to Brazil had in part been to increase her children's opportunities, they had not furthered their studies the way she hoped. Kazu, in particular, missed Japan and felt trapped by his parents' decision to bring him back with them. However, as a fourth-generation Nikkei-Brazilian, he did not have the option of moving alone to Japan, due to the fact that at the time only Japanese descendants up to the third generation and their dependents qualified for a Nikkei visa to Japan.

Like the Pereira children, then, Joana's son and daughter did not easily feel at home in Brazil. In fact, children of *dekasegi* often suffered once they returned to Brazil, particularly if they did not feel comfortable speaking Portuguese. Many Brazilians in Japan could not easily imagine returning to Brazil precisely because they were concerned that their children would struggle to adapt to a culture and language they had not grown up around. On the other hand, if they stayed in Japan indefinitely, they were afraid their children might never move beyond the life of a foreign, brokered worker.

One *nisei* interlocutor, Rose, who chose to return to Brazil with her three children while they were still in elementary school, said that the most difficult aspect of return had to do with her children's adaptation. As I was discussing the differences between Japanese and Brazilian schooling with her, several months after her family's return to Brazil, Rose explained that her children had already "turned Japanese" through schooling in Japan and that it was important to her that they not forget their Brazilian background. "Brazil is where we belong after all, this is our country," she said in Portuguese. At this, Rose's seven-year-old daughter interrupted in Japanese to say, "But I wanted to be Japanese! I want to go back to Japan!" Though they were slowly adapting to their new school in Brazil, Rose's children—six, seven, and twelve at the time I met them—preferred to speak in Japanese, and deeply missed their teachers and friends in Japan. Their experience of return was very different from their mother, whose primary social ties were in Brazil, and who, after years living in Japan, still felt more comfortable speaking Portuguese than Japanese.

Evidently, for families with children who grew up in Japan, moving back to Brazil was a complicated decision, one that had to do with a variety of concerns including material comforts, language and belonging, and perceived occupational and educational opportunities. Even for those who spoke fluent Portuguese, return to Brazil could be a daunting affair. One fifteen-year-old interlocutor who was born in Japan and had never been to Brazil in her life, though she had always attended Brazilian school in Aichi, told me how her parents were planning to return with her once she finished high school:

Since we have money saved up already, we're going to go back and build something in Brazil. I don't really want to go, though. But I want to because of my studies. I don't want to lose everything here, though, because this is where I grew up. All my friends are here. But in Brazil there's just a lot more opportunity than there is here. I'll be able to go to university there.

Thus, even though she did not herself wish to go to Brazil, and felt she belonged more in Japan, where she had grown up and developed her strongest social ties, she realized that as a foreigner in Japan, educated and fluent primarily in Portuguese, her best option in order to move beyond the life of a brokered laborer was to return to Brazil to study.

Another interlocutor, a thirty-year-old *sansei* woman, who had been in Japan since she was a child and also only ever studied in Brazilian school, opted for an online degree offered via a private university in Brazil. Still, she did not intend to move back to Brazil as long as her parents stayed in Japan. She had tried once before, and felt that without her parents, Brazil was not her home. As she put it, speaking in Portuguese, return to Brazil would be like starting over: "Years ago I still had friends there who might be able to help me out, but they've moved, life has continued on. So that's another barrier keeping me from going back. That's why I say I'll only go when my parents do."

Whether or not *dekasegi* and their children opted to try their luck again in Brazil, then, they rarely made the decision without taking other factors into consideration, including family, future opportunities, and even divine will. The children of *dekasegi* were often bound by the decisions of their parents, who in turn were constrained by the desire to maximize their and their children's life opportunities. As they grew older, the children of labor migrants also had to consider the needs of their aging parents, who themselves often had even older parents or relatives to attend to. These various constraints were as much a part of living transnationally as were the opportunities that moving between Japan and Brazil afforded them.

TO RETURN OR NOT TO RETURN

In 2009, at a workshop on culture shock in São Paulo City for Brazilians recently returned from Japan, I joined a group of ten women and men of various ages for a seminar titled "Big Dilemmas of Return." Raphael, the Nikkei-Brazilian who led the seminar, was trained in psychology and had himself worked in Japan years before. Writing in purple marker, he began the lecture by posing the following two questions on the whiteboard in front of us: (1) What to do? (2) To stay in Brazil or return to Japan? "These are questions you have to ask yourselves," he said in Portuguese, "and questions that may never go away. No matter what, it's important not to confuse *saudade* with *necessidade* [*nostalgia* with *necessity*]. Just because you miss your life in Japan doesn't mean you need to go back there. Similarly, once you're in Japan again, just because you miss Brazil doesn't mean you have to come back here." At this point, a Nikkei woman of about forty, recently returned to Brazil, raised her hand. "In my case, I want to go back to Japan as soon as I can," she explained. "Both Japan and Brazil are my home."

For many transnational Brazilian migrants, then, even though they might have grown up in Brazil and maintained important social and national ties there, return migrating was often a complicated transition. As has been explored throughout this chapter, migrants experienced significant difficulties reentering the educational system or job market (or entering it for the first time), as well as readjusting (or adjusting for the first time) to Brazilian cultural norms, Portuguese language, and a high cost of living coupled with comparatively low wages, resulting in limits to their purchasing power. Stories of returned Brazilians who poorly invested years of savings from Japan, or else experienced unsuccessful business ventures in Brazil, were common, and often spurred migrants to return again to Japan. Marcelo and Carlos Silva of chapter 1, for example, had invested years of savings (including much of their mother's money) upon returning to Brazil, only to find that their uncle had misled them, prompting them to migrate once again to Japan.

Even if return migrants invested in a successful business or found relatively well-paying work in Brazil, however, the reality of transitioning to life in Brazil often meant having less material comforts than were readily available to them as unskilled laborers in Japan. For Wania Pereira's sons, just as for Carlos Silva of chapter 1, this was one of the most difficult aspects of return migrating to Brazil. As another interlocutor put it:

> Many [return migrants] can't get used to Brazil again. They want to have the same lifestyle they had in Japan. So what happens? They eat out for dinner. They go to the grocery store and want to buy everything. No one looks at the prices of things. Because in Japan people buy things and don't even look closely at the price. Now, when you get to Brazil, if you do that, you end up spending double what you would spend in Japan. And then what happens?

Indeed, many interlocutors could not easily adjust to the limitations they experienced in terms of purchasing power in Brazil. One *sansei* migrant in her late twenties, for example, tried living in Brazil with her boyfriend after many years in Japan, only to return to Japan again after six short months:

> I had money saved up from Japan so I could buy what I wanted in Brazil. When I went out with friends there, we went to the mall, and bought shoes, clothes. . . . My friends kept saying "Wow, you're rich, you have so much money," but what they didn't understand was that I ended up spending all my savings. Everything was so expensive and I couldn't earn enough to make it up by working in Brazil, so I decided to return to Japan.

Others found that it was difficult to be financially independent from family in Brazil, and that this was often more frustrating than the decrease they experienced in terms of purchasing power there. One interlocutor, for example, who was in her mid-twenties and had engaged in repeat migration between Japan and Brazil since she was eighteen, said she wanted to return to Japan again because she did not wish to live *de favor* (financially dependent on her parents) anymore: "Finances are a heavy weight in our lives. Unfortunately, even with a university degree in Brazil, it's hard to live apart from your parents, to get away from them interfering with your life." In other words, being financially dependent on family led to social constraints that she could be free of if she were to migrate to Japan again.

CONCLUSION

One might imagine that for Brazilians, return migration to Brazil was a relatively straightforward process. But for Brazilians who grew up in Japan, as well as those who went as adults, it often represented a kind of new beginning rather than a return per se. Of course, fluency in Portuguese, property in Brazil, and strong social and family ties there all helped following the transition from life in Japan. Regardless of how long people had been away, though, return migration required navigating new jobs, new schools, and new social and cultural terrain, and for these reasons it was often experienced as starting anew.

As we saw in the case of the Pereiras, and in lesser detail the Furutas, different members of a single family, though constrained by a common sense of responsibility toward and/or dependence on one another, rarely experienced return in the same way. Brazilians who migrated to Japan as adults, whether or not they felt at home in Japan, had to consider their own future as aging workers, the future of their children and, in some cases, the future of their aging parents. Children of labor migrants, in turn, often identified with the lifestyle they grew accustomed to in Japan, and struggled to find a place for themselves in the social and cultural worlds their parents had left behind in Brazil. While they did not necessarily wish to return to Brazil, family represented a strong pull on the direction their lives took.

Finally, no matter how Japanese and/or Brazilian one did or did not feel, the decision to return migrate often had less to do with ethnic belonging or national orientation than it did with the limitations and opportunities presented by one's personal and family circumstances. In other words, the fact of being Brazilian was not enough to understand Brazilians' return to Brazil, in the same way that being of Japanese descent was not enough to understand their original migration to Japan. If, as researchers and readers, we were to imagine what it means to live transnationally between Japan and Brazil as a richly woven tapestry, ethnicity would, of course, stand out as an important thread throughout. Still, it would be a mistake to stand so close that we could no longer see the other strands—gender, generation, class, family, and, in the case of the Pereiras, religion—with which the story has been, and continues to be, spun. In the next and final chapter, I explore in greater depth how religion both limited and broadened the ways transnational labor migrants and their families between Japan and Brazil made sense of their place(s) in the world.

NOTES

1. In fact, I was not able to find official figures for this. However, among my interlocutors who returned to Brazil or else knew people who had, few appeared to have accepted money from the Japanese government for this purpose.

2. Note the parallel here between Wania's mother's experience and that of Angela (chapter 1), who, when she was still a young woman, was disowned for marrying a non-Nikkei Brazilian.

3. Although many interlocutors spoke of financial troubles (e.g., bankruptcy or debt) leading them to migrate to Japan, it was often a source of embarrassment or shame, and rarely came up in initial conversations.

4. In interviewing Roberto, a Pentecostal Mexican migrant in Boston, Michael Jackson (2013) finds that, while "Emmanuel's and Ibrahim's narratives resist closure, remaining open to the uncertainties of the future, Roberto's religious faith entails, at least in retrospect, an emphasis on divine providence and an expectation that well-being will be finally secured" (198). Similarly, my more religious interlocutors often spoke—despite the uncertainties of their and their children's lives—in terms of divine providence and a guaranteed future.

Chapter 6

Faith in God

We are strangers on this earth. Our place is in church, and in Heaven.

—Brazilian Evangelical preacher in Japan

In June 2010, I attended a *festa junina* celebration in Hamamatsu City, home to one of the largest Brazilian populations in Japan. This event, historically related to midsummer festivities in Europe, and held in honor of St. Anthony, St. John the Baptist, and St. Peter, is celebrated throughout Brazil during the month of June. In homage to rural life, people of all ages dress in stereotypical *caipira*—or country bumpkin—fashion, adorned with oversized freckles, checkered clothes, and straw hats.[1]

Over the last nearly three decades, parallel to the *dekasegi* movement, *festas juninas* have become common in Japan, wherever there is a large enough concentration of Brazilian residents. As noted by other scholars in reference to activities such as samba parades and capoeira demonstrations (see, for example, Tsuda 2003), these events represent opportunities for social communion and the public performance of Brazilian-ness in Japan. Indeed, at this particular *festa junina*, I watched as children square-danced beneath a large Brazilian flag, and the audience, with skewered meat and sweet Guaraná soda in hand, sang the Brazilian national anthem in unison.

This particular day, however, the music struck another note, besides either generically *caipira* (country-style) or alluding to the specific country-ness of the Brazilian nation-state. A middle-aged man in a blue-and-white checked shirt and straw hat, who I later learned was a Catholic priest known as Padre—or Father—Osmar, stepped up on stage with a guitar and began to sing in Portuguese: "He who believed, overcame / He who believed, remained / In the crisis and the pain, life flourished."

169

Padre Osmar, who went to Japan to help Brazilians through their spiritual struggles, wrote this song in the wake of the 2008–2009 global financial crisis. It spoke directly to Brazilian labor migrants who had stayed in Japan throughout the crisis, despite losing their jobs and depleting their savings. More specifically, it spoke to those Brazilians who drew strength from God, and whose spirituality helped them confront the difficulties of migrant life in post-crisis Japan.

For over a century, social scientists have analyzed the function of religion in people's lives. Recently, scholars have carried out important work on the role of spirituality and religion in transnational migration. In the case of Brazil, for example, they have traced how the move toward Evangelicalism, in particular, has grown increasingly significant both at home and among migrant communities abroad (Freston 2008; Marcelli et al. 2009; Margolis 2013; Sheringham 2013; Vásquez 2009). As Manuel Vásquez notes, however, in a 2003 review of works on Evangelical Christianity around the world, many social scientists continue to employ a "social pathology model" of religion, seeing it as a kind of false consciousness or compensation for the despair that comes from being poor or otherwise marginalized from the global economy of desire. Instead, Evangelicalism may be read as a valuable resource in building bonds of solidarity and reciprocity (Peterson et al. 2001), or a positive vehicle through which the marginalized rebuild a sense of self, family, and community, or "new spaces of life" in the midst of anomie and suffering (Shaull & César 2000). Adaptation approaches to the role of religion in migration (e.g., Bonifacio & Angeles 2010; Hirschman 2004; Levitt 2003; Quero & Shoji 2014) further emphasize the agency involved in recreating ethnic-religious spaces as a means of resisting assimilation and/or differential incorporation into a host society.

As seen in the previous chapter, religion was a primary source of direction, comfort, and meaning for Wania Pereira as she moved her family, first to Japan, then later back to Brazil. Throughout the course of fieldwork, many of my interlocutors described how religious faith helped them navigate a hard-hit economy and the daily drudgeries of work, and how it guided their relationship to leisure time and sociality, material wealth, and even their decision to migrate (often back and forth) between Japan and Brazil. In this chapter, I explore the role of religion—especially Evangelicalism/Neo-Pentecostalism—as it related to the *dekasegi* experience more broadly. Rather than read it in terms of either false consciousness or a purely positive, agentive force, I demonstrate the ways in which religion, like family, both constrained and lent meaning to migrants' lives. Specifically, I focus on the ways my interlocutors used religion, especially Evangelicalism/Neo-Pentecostalism, as a means of navigating and understanding their position as transnational labor migrants, as well as creating community and sociality outside of either work or school.

RELIGION AND THE RISE OF BRAZILIAN
EVANGELICAL/NEO-PENTECOSTAL CHRISTIANITY

According to the 2010 Brazilian National Census, 64.6 percent of Brazilians reported their religion to be Roman Catholic. This represented a considerable drop from just ten years earlier in 2000, when the number of Catholics totaled 73.6 percent. Even so, Brazil continues to count more Catholics among its citizens than any other country in the world. While the percentage of people declaring "no religion" on the census slowly grew (from 7.4 percent in 2000 to 8 percent in 2010), the number of Evangelical Christians/Neo-Pentecostals[2] in Brazil has increased significantly over the past few decades, leaping from 15.4 percent in 2000 to 22.2 percent in 2010.

Ascertaining the religious makeup of Nikkei-Brazilians in Brazil, as well as of Brazilians residing in Japan, is not nearly as straightforward. As discussed in chapter 1, Brazil's National Census is carried out by the Brazilian Institute of Geography and Statistics (IBGE), and since 1991 responses have been broken down according to five "race/color" categories: *branca*, or white, *preta*, or black, *parda*, or mixed race, *amarela*, or yellow, and *indígena*, or Indigenous. According to the 2010 census, just over 2 million of Brazil's nearly 191 million people, or approximately 1.1 percent of the population, declared itself *amarela*. While scholars such as Simon Schwartzman (1999) find that most of the *amarela* category is in fact of Japanese descent, it is important to remember that Chinese and Korean immigrants and their descendants are also represented in this grouping (Jye et al. 2009; Lesser 1999 & 2013; Shoji 2004 & 2008).[3]

Although it is difficult to calculate the precise number of Japanese and their descendants among Brazil's roughly 2 million citizens of East Asian background, figure 6.1 depicts the religious breakdown of the broader *amarela* category.

Thus, it is possible to see that in 2010, Brazilians of East Asian background (80 percent of whom were likely of Japanese descent) did not differ greatly in their religious makeup from the overall Brazilian population, especially when it came to numbers of Catholics and Evangelical Christians, with the latter representing between a quarter and a fifth of both the overall Brazilian population and the population of Brazilians categorized as *amarela* (yellow). The main difference of note is that while only 2.7 percent of Brazilians declared themselves adherents of "other religions," 7.5 percent of Brazilians of East Asian background did. This can be explained largely by the historical presence of adherents to Buddhism, Shintoism, and other Japanese new religions found among East Asian immigrants and their descendants in Brazil.

Early ethnographic studies of Brazilians in Japan made little note of migrants' religious practices, or the meanings that they acquired throughout

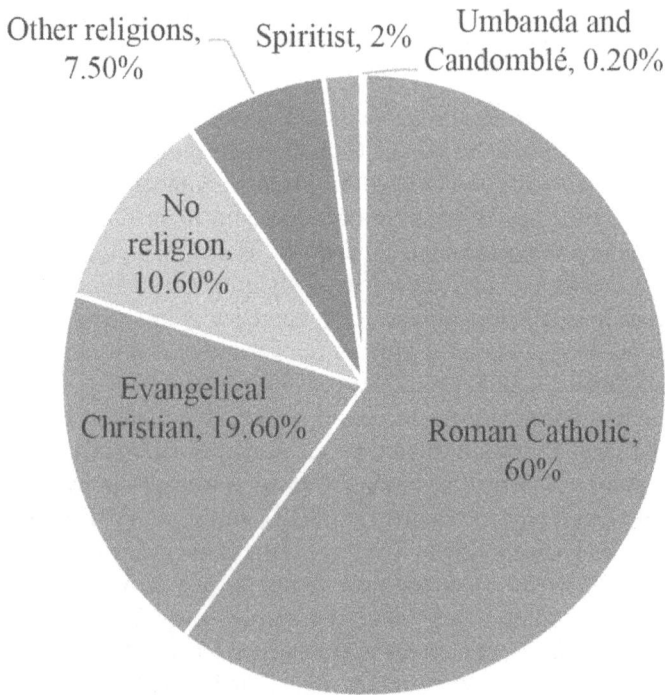

Figure 6.1   Religious breakdown of Brazil's *Amarela* category (adapted from IBGE 2010 Brazilian National Census).

the migratory and settlement processes. Joshua Roth (2002), for example, mentioned only that Catholic Mass was available in Portuguese by the time he conducted fieldwork in Hamamatsu in the mid-1990s, and Takeyuki Tsuda (2003), though he described a kind of religious revival found in Kawasaki and the Ōizumi area during the same time period, only briefly discussed the role of religion in neutralizing the detrimental effects of Brazilians' negative minority status in Japan. Daniel Linger (2001), for his part, described an Evangelical Brazilian family he met in Japan as unusual, given that most Japanese-Brazilians he knew "had little interest in organized religion" (153). More recently, however, scholars have increasingly turned their attention to issues of religion among *dekasegi* in Japan, as in the works of Hugo Córdova Quero (2008), who focuses on gender and faith among Brazilians attending Catholic Church in the Kantō area, Masanobu Yamada (2011), who analyzes the role of Missão Apoio, a Brazilian Evangelical movement born in Japan in 1993, in promoting socialization among Brazilian migrants, Ushi Arakaki (2013), who looks at Umbanda and the importance of the liminal spirit *exú* in helping Brazilian migrants make sense of their place in Japan, and Suma Ikeuchi (2017), who examines the ways in which processes of migration and Evangelical religious conversion intersect among Brazilians in Japan.

The fact that most early *dekasegi* studies mention religious practices only in passing can be attributed in part to the more recent proliferation of Evangelical and Neo-Pentecostal churches around the world, and Japan in particular. Maxine Margolis (2013) argues that the flexible, decentralized nature of Evangelical churches allows them to expand more rapidly than Catholic churches, and Paul Freston (2008) describes Evangelical Christianity as the ideal religion for transnational migrants since it is not tied to a specific location or territory. The spread of Evangelical/Neo-Pentecostal churches in Japan, then, follows a broader pattern of recent growth seen around the world.

As Rafael Shoji (2008) notes, according to a survey conducted by the Evangelical Igreja Metodista Livre (IMel)'s Nikkei Council in Japan, there were an estimated seventy-five Evangelical groups in Japan in 1997. By 2002, the number had reached 200, and in 2007, the magazine *Mensageiro da Paz*, one of the main Evangelical publications for Brazilians in Japan, registered 441 Evangelical missions, not including Neo-Pentecostal movements such as the Igreja Universal do Reino de Deus and the Igreja Internacional da Graça. Among my interlocutors, and corresponding with recent figures for Brazil, approximately a quarter were active Evangelicals/Neo-Pentecostals, while the remaining 75 percent described themselves as (if not always practicing) Catholics, Buddhists, Seichō no Ie adherents, and nonreligious.

Throughout my time in Aichi, I attended services at the Igreja Nacional do Senhor Jesus Cristo/Igreja Yahweh of Israel in Nishio, J-MEAD Japão Missão Evangélica Assembléia de Deus near Okazaki, and Agape in Toyokawa (later named Palavra Viva). I also interviewed people who attended Congregação Cristã no Brasil in Anjō and other, smaller churches in the cities of Ōgaki and Minokamo, Gifu. Even if I had not actively sought out Brazilian Evangelical/Neo-Pentecostal churches during fieldwork in Japan, I would have stumbled on them nonetheless. In Minokamo, for example, where I shadowed workers at a Brazilian-run employment brokerage firm, I noted one day, walking around the neighborhood immediately surrounding the firm, five different Brazilian Evangelical churches within just a few-block radius. Later in the day, driving five minutes further afield, I found two more.

At the time of research, I could not secure official data on the exact number of Evangelical/Neo-Pentecostal Brazilian churches in Minokamo nor, for that matter, other cities in Japan. Many of these spaces were not necessarily visible from the outside, as I learned from other churches I visited in Aichi. What is more, due to fluctuations in the local Brazilian population, churches appeared and disappeared from the local landscape with great frequency, and tended to change names nearly as often. However, it is possible and perhaps useful to give an idea of how many people the churches potentially served. In 2011, when I lived full time in Japan for research, the population of Minokamo that year was estimated at 55,503, of which 2,689 were Brazilian nationals (or nearly 5 percent of the city's population) (Ministry of Justice, Japan). In other words, if I found a minimum of seven churches in Minokamo alone, the figure represented at least one Evangelical/Neo-Pentecostal church per 384 registered Brazilian residents of the same city. Of course, such an estimate does not take into account the fact that only roughly 20 percent of the Brazilians in Japan attended such churches (at which point the number falls to one church per seventy-seven registered Brazilians in Minokamo), or that Brazilians might have attended churches in neighboring cities (or, for that matter, that other non-Brazilians and Latin Americans such as Peruvians or Paraguayans might have and did attend, though the numbers I counted in my own observation of such churches remained negligible).

Clearly, Evangelical/Neo-Pentecostal churches have come to represent an important marker of the Brazilian presence in Japan. To the people attending them, they often served an important role in creating a sense of belonging, even family, in a country that continued to view them as temporary, disposable labor. Sometimes church activities took place in an obviously visible space, with regular Sunday services held in Portuguese. Other times, there were no signs on the outside, and people only knew about the availability of services due to word of mouth. No matter how small or anonymous looking, however, churches scattered throughout Japan helped connect transnational migrants to a broader sense of community and meaning. In this sense, my findings have much in common with Peggy Levitt (2007), who argues that transnationally lived religion is often central to the organization and significance of migrants' lives, and that strong feelings of belonging and shared responsibilities emerge as a result of what she terms "global religious citizenship."

GOD SENT ME A SIGN

Narrating the Decision to Migrate

Leandro and I met every few months in Okazaki, Aichi, to chat over coffee. Born in 1989, he grew up in the interior of São Paulo. Although his mother was Nikkei, he laughed about how often he was mistaken for a *gringo* (foreigner) among Brazilians because of his reddish hair and pink skin tone. His parents migrated to Japan first, in the early 2000s, while he and his sister stayed behind in Brazil. Then, when he was thirteen, Leandro moved to Japan, where he completed high school at a Brazilian school in Aichi before starting to work in a factory. He spoke fondly of the freedom of his childhood, and especially of his Bahian (northeastern Brazilian) grandmother who raised him while his parents worked in Japan. "My grandmother and the church, those are the two things that have really shaped who I am today," he recounted, speaking only in Portuguese.

Leandro was often too busy to meet. Besides working the night shift at a car parts factory, he attended Evangelical services two or three times a week, in a neighboring city, and had just started an online degree from a private Brazilian university in business administration. At the time of my fieldwork he was romantically involved with another member of the congregation who, at sixteen, grew her hair long for reasons of religious faith, and was suspicious of his fraternizing with women from outside the church. Leandro had attended church since the age of six, and his entire family continued to do so in Japan.

In 2007, Leandro returned for a time to São Paulo to attend university, while his parents—by that time divorced—and sister stayed on in Aichi. Once his mother injured her knee, however, and the global economic crisis further reduced her job options, he found himself divided over whether or not to stay in university in Brazil or return to Japan to help his family:

My Mom had to have surgery and she wasn't going to leave Japan for long because my sister was here, she already had my nephew, and my Mom didn't want to be far from them. But I was fine on my own, I was working too in Brazil, so I could help my Mom out from there. There was no problem. Then in 2008 the crisis hit, and people were getting laid off and everything in Japan. My supervisor in Brazil wanted to renew my contract at work and started giving me all kinds of projects to start on but I was worried about my Mom, thinking I should help her out. You can get a different job any time, even a good job, you know, but family comes first. I was pretty confused about what to do.

While family weighed heavily on his mind, and he debated whether or not to leave Brazil, religious faith and direct communion with God ultimately led Leandro to a decision:

At the church I go to, there's this moment where God speaks to us, he talks about our life. You can't just stand up and say I'm going to do this or that with my life, because our church doesn't work that way, the Holy Spirit watches over everything. So I was confused about whether to quit university and my job and go to Japan. What should I do, I asked myself. But then I decided I would go to church and ask God, ask our Lord Jesus Christ what to do: "Do I need to go to Japan or not? If so, I'll quit university for a while and come back to it later.

Or I'll stay on in Japan. But I need to help my Mom." So one day I went to a church service and during the *hora da palavra* [lit. the hour of the word, meaning prayer time], God spoke to me.

At this point Leandro addressed me in the same way he remembered God addressing him, explaining that this conversation happened in his mind, and not in front of anyone else. Based on fieldwork among Evangelical Protestants in the United States, Tanya Luhrmann et al. (2010) note that Evangelical Christians emphasize the dialogic, interactive, and human quality of the relationship between God and self. In this way, God speaks to the faithful either directly through the Bible or "by placing mental images or thoughts in their minds or making their body feel a certain way" (69). Many of Luhrmann et al.'s interlocutors reported recognizing God's voice the way one would a person's voice on the phone. One of my interlocutors in Brazil offered the following explanation for this: "People hear God in music, in others' words, and in their own minds. Everyone has a private way of hearing God." Similarly, Leandro described the experience as a direct and personal conversation between God and himself:

> God spoke to me like this, he said: "You came searching for confirmation, didn't you? You came searching for confirmation and God wants to tell you that I will bless you with my will and that I will fulfill all the wishes of your heart." So I said, "Mom, I think I'm going to Japan." But my Mom said to me: "I'm only going to work a few more months and things are tough here with the crisis and all," and I thought to myself, man, is it really worth going in the end? You can have that kind of doubt, even with God speaking to you.

To guide him through his doubt, Leandro then described entering the *pensamento da igreja*, or the church way of thinking, in which he prayed with others at church as well as on his own at home. As Tanya Luhrmann et al. write of interlocutors in Chicago, "when a decision was consequential . . . it was not uncommon for congregants to spend many weeks praying about the decision and asking other friends in the church to pray about the decision and to talk to them about their prayer experience" (2010: 70). Leandro, consumed with uncertainty over this important decision, spoke of asking God for a clearer sign, and of the experience he had one Sunday afternoon while still in Brazil:

> I went to a youth group worship in my city and there was this *cooperador* [a kind of pastor], and that day the youth *cooperador* wasn't from my city, he was from somewhere else, just to give you an idea of how well God knows our lives. During prayer time, while God was speaking, he [the *cooperador* leading the

prayer and speaking on behalf of God] suddenly changed his tone: "You entered here and you want a sign of life, a confirmation, and God has sent me to say that He has offered His will, and that if you ask for it again He will confirm it every time that you seek it. He will bless you, in that place that you will go." So then it was really clear, right? It was as close as he could get without saying my actual name.

Following this experience, Leandro returned to Japan with certainty and confidence. Arriving in 2008, in the midst of the economic crisis, he found that most Brazilians there were working on short-term, brokered contracts, and expected to be laid off at any moment:

Some had stopped working already, others were unemployed, and people asked me, my friends, my acquaintances, they were like, "What are you doing here?" I said "Well, I came back because of my Mom, and because God confirmed my life, you know." I had that confidence and everyone else was so depressed with the situation here in Japan. Time went by and I got a job really quickly. My Mom got better and she went back to work eventually too. All of this was the will of God.

Leandro was not even twenty when he found himself in this position, far from his family and unsure of whether to leave school or not to help his mother out in Japan. While responsibility for his mother led him to seriously weigh the decision, the belief that God spoke directly to him helped validate the move, despite his favorable prospects in São Paulo and economic difficulties in Japan at the time.

Throughout my fieldwork, it was common for devoutly Evangelical/Neo-Pentecostal interlocutors to narrate migration in this way, as seen in the case of Wania Pereira in the preceding chapter. Rather than view migration as a decision over which they had direct agency, they explained it—like so many other things in their lives—as the result of signs from above. In this way, interlocutors like Leandro and Wania made important decisions for themselves and their family members based in part on religious faith.

The classic *homo economicus* model of migration, which imagines individuals acting out of rational self-interest and primarily only financial concerns, fails to account for the religious and familial forces driving many people in their decisions to move from one place to another.[4] Similarly, studies emphasizing ethnic or national identity above all else run the risk of adopting a *homo anomicus*[5] approach that overlooks the broader social and religious contexts in which people's lives are embedded. As a theoretical tool, Levitt and Glick Schiller's (2004) notion of simultaneity, or multiple embeddedness, helps us move beyond an analysis of the individual migrant to the multiple contexts in which she or he is embedded. In this way we see that Leandro, though he was employed and aware of the potential long-term benefits of continuing with higher education in Brazil, returned to post-crisis Japan because of a sense of family obligation and his own religious conviction that it was the right thing to do. In other words, he was not motivated purely by economic advantages (of which there were few at the time in post-crisis Japan), or a sense of rootedness or ethnic/cultural belonging in Japan in any significant way. Rather, he negotiated his decisions according to the multiple contexts, both social and religious, in which he found himself.

CONVERTING IN JAPAN

Both Leandro, discussed earlier, and Wania Pereira of chapter 5 were already firm in their faith before they migrated to Japan. Still other interlocutors converted (or reconverted) to Evangelicalism/Neo-Pentecostalism once they came into contact with other believers in Japan. As the number of Brazilian Evangelical/Neo-Pentecostal churches continued to grow in Japan over the last decades, so too did the number of converts. For many *dekasegi*, church came to represent an important social space outside of work and school, one where they could be accepted and included, and where they could form alternative communities to the ones offered on assembly lines or in classrooms.[6] These religious communities, though they offered an alternative of sorts, were not, however, removed from the local contexts in which they grew. As the following anecdotes demonstrate, Brazilian churches, like Brazilian schools in Japan, were shaped according to the particularities of the *dekasegi* experience. As a result, they represented a kind of hybridized space, borrowing cultural elements from both Japan and Brazil, as well as the global Evangelical movement. At the same time, they offered congregants opportunities for social and community participation—in short, a sense of belonging that transcended national boundaries.

   One pastor I grew to know in Japan, Edmilson, had been there for nineteen years, fifteen of which he spent attending church, and seven years serving as a pastor. He worked in a factory during the week and preached on weekends, together with his wife. Originally from São Paulo, Edmilson's mother was one of fourteen children of Japanese emigrants, and his father was from Bahia, in northeastern Brazil. Although Edmilson was raised an Evangelical, he had always fought against the church, especially during his problematic teenage years. When I met him, he gave the impression of being a regular, family-oriented man in his mid-forties, proud of his seven-year-old daughter who always paid 10 percent of her allowance as a tithe toward the church.

During church services, however, Edmilson spoke at length, in Portuguese, of his less than exemplary background:

> When others find out about my past they ask me incredulously, "You used to walk around with weapons on you? You got into fights?" But yes, I was like that. I was a Japanese who wasn't Japanese, my eyes were the eyes of a Japanese from Paraguay [meaning a "fake" Japanese, since in Brazil goods from Paraguay are considered inferior or fake]. You know, because all Japanese are supposedly so upstanding, come first in the class, sit in the front row, care about what the teacher says, stay by their side. I wasn't like that. When I was young, I used to sit in the back, I messed around, I skipped class. I did a lot of wrong things in my life. I walked around with weapons a number of times.

After a time working in Japan, Edmilson's uncle brought him to church, where he felt God speaking directly to him. From that moment on, he considered God the saving grace in his life, the force that administered to his heart:

> If I look back on my past, I never want to live through it again, a past of such sadness, solitude, coldness. . . . My heart was sad and bitter, and no one knew what I was going through. Something that really impacted my heart, though, was when I came to a church for the first time in Japan. God revealed all this to me through what was being preached. On that very day. When I was with my friends from the factory I smiled, I went out with them, went to parties, drank, did everything. But I would get home and that emptiness that was inside me would take over my heart. People are happy when they're out with friends, with family, when they get their salary, go to a party, go out with someone. But inside? God takes away the sadness in our heart. He takes the bad things from our hearts and transforms our lives. The emptiness inside us, that black hole, many times it's in our soul, and it's the lack of God, that bread that nourishes us. If we are believers, if we accept Jesus Christ, how can that kind of black hole exist in our hearts?

For Edmilson, as for most of my religious interlocutors, faith represented the spiritual nourishment that work and friends could not provide on their own. Beyond the menial and the material, and beyond even social and family networks, people found in God a sense of meaning that transcended both their daily lives and the geographical and cultural divides between Japan and Brazil.[7]

In Edmilson's case, he believed he had a calling from God to stay in Japan and keep the church going, and that God had spoken to another pastor specifically to tell him not to leave Japan any time soon. He was waiting for a sign, therefore, before considering returning to Brazil. Edmilson had met his wife in church and completed a three-year online course in theology from Brazil while living in Japan. He believed that his role as pastor was to show others how God cared for his life, and how He gave him a sense of purpose. "Here in Japan work takes a lot of time and people make a lot of money so they don't want to come to church. But I want to dedicate my life to God," he told me.

Although Edmilson was in the unique position of pastor, and therefore had special reason to emphasize his conversion to Evangelical Christianity as a turning point in his life, many of the religious services I attended in Japan included at least one public *testemunha* (testimony) of someone who had converted to the faith. The testimonies I heard often included a narrative of drinking, drugs, and a single-minded drive to make money in Japan, and ended with finding God and therefore purpose outside life in the factory. Some of the people I heard testify, including Edmilson, had been exposed to Evangelical churches before coming to Japan, while others had not. Like him, though, once converted, it was common for the church to become the central—or most meaningful—reason for staying in Japan.

Another interlocutor, Melina, who I grew to know in Brazil, also converted to Evangelicalism in Japan, and continued attending church upon her return. She experienced what she described as a strict upbringing with first-generation immigrant parents from Japan in Dourados, Mato Grosso do Sul. A mother of three, she completed a degree in architecture in Londrina, in southeastern Brazil, where she met her Italian-Brazilian husband. When I visited her in her home in Campo Grande, Mato Grosso do Sul, there was an old, unused drawing board propped up in her living room, dating from the time she was still a student. She explained that she had left with her husband for Japan in 1996, partly because he had lost his job and partly because she wanted money to open an architecture firm upon their return. Melina's parents had gone to work in factories in Japan, and she knew that—although they helped her pay for university—her younger brother (the only son out of four) would inherit most of what they left behind. If she were going to earn a larger amount of capital to buy new architecture equipment and set up a firm, Japan was her best chance.

Originally, Melina and her husband planned to spend only three years working in Japan. Within the first six months, however, Melina fell ill. Before that, she had been asked by the factory boss to double as a translator for other Brazilians, while performing easier tasks on the assembly lines. Although she was horrified to be singled out, she was one of the only Brazilians who spoke passable Japanese, and had no choice but to do as he asked. Soon, coworkers began sabotaging her at work, jealous perhaps that she was given an easier time on the line:

> Because of that, I started to get sick. Every day people were trying to hurt me, make mistakes on my machines and make it look like it was my fault. I got

really upset, depressed. I cried all the time, I was stuck in bed and I couldn't even walk. The doctors said there was nothing they could do for me. Thankfully there was an Evangelical couple living nearby, they always called on me and spoke to me about God. Soon I realized that I only felt good when I was around them, not anyone else. You only feel good with people who really have God in their hearts, you see that they don't do things like that. So I was always with this couple, I went to an Assembléia de Deus church with them once a month, it was two hours away, because at the time there wasn't one where I lived. Now there are so many in Japan. I ended up accepting Jesus because of that situation we found ourselves in. But, oh, how happy I was when I went to church! How much happiness I felt to be there.

The strength she found in religious faith led Melina back to work, and after four years in a factory, her first child was born. Together with her husband and newborn son, she returned to Brazil, where they bought an apartment. However, there was trouble with the previous owner of the apartment, who had failed to pay the bills, and Melina and her husband ended up ensnared in a complicated and expensive legal battle as soon as they acquired it. Like Wania Pereira in chapter 5, though, Melina glossed over the financial troubles she experienced, and instead spoke to me—primarily in Portuguese—of the role God played in her return to Japan in 2000, after her second child was born:

Actually God started to use prophets while I was in Brazil, prophets who said I had to go back to Japan. But I thought, how strange, why do I need to return? Materially speaking we didn't need anything else. But then I started to think, they must mean in the spiritual sense, to work for the Lord, to recruit souls, to dedicate my life to people who need help. So that's when God put this in my heart, to go to Japan just to help in His work. I couldn't work anymore because I had two kids already and was pregnant with a third, so I went just in this sense, to go and help with the Lord's work in Japan.

Whether Melina intended to or not, she ended up staying another twelve years in Japan, raising three children and working for the church while her husband supported them with his factory salary. Before leaving Japan the first time she had testified in church that God helped cure her while she was sick and, as a result, other people who were suffering began to convert as well. Later, when she returned, the church was struggling to retain its members and it was then that she understood her role in helping sustain God's work in Japan.

Both the pastor Edmilson and Melina converted to Evangelical Christianity in Japan, and ended up devoting much of their time to church. In the case of Leandro, although he was already firmly religious before moving to Japan as a teenager, he too spent a great deal of his free time outside of work helping with the church. Of the interlocutors I knew to be practicing Evangelicals/ Neo-Pentecostals in Japan, it was not unusual for them to spend three to four evenings a week engaged in church services, youth groups, volunteer activities, and so on. Church created a larger sense of purpose, lending meaning and direction to everything from the decision to migrate and stay in Japan to the experience of returning to Brazil. As Maxine Margolis explains in her book *Goodbye, Brazil: Émigrés from the Land of Soccer and Samba*, Evangelical churches "bestow an enveloping sense of belonging in an otherwise alien society where believers may not speak the language" (2013: 169). In the next section, I turn to religious spaces themselves, and the religious services that labor migrants engaged in.

RELIGIOUS SPACES AND SERVICES

Early on in my fieldwork in Japan, I traveled to Hamamatsu for an interview and, wandering outside the train station, was approached by a tall man speaking English. He was handing out religious pamphlets, and, because I was worried about being late to the interview, I pretended not to understand him. He then asked me if I was Brazilian, pulling Portuguese pamphlets from his front pocket. Within minutes, I was approached by another man, this time Brazilian, who was also handing out pamphlets but from a different Evangelical Church. He spoke to me at length in Portuguese about *Raíz* (lit. Root), a group that claimed to focus on the root of life's problems. "You can't heal a tree by trimming its leaves," he told me, "You have to get to the root," and at this he pointed toward a nearby tree still dressed in October colors.

Wherever I turned during my fieldwork in Japan, it seemed, I came face-to-face with religion. At first, I did not set out to write about Brazilian Evangelical/Neo-Pentecostal churches in Japan, but it soon became clear, as I accompanied my interlocutors in their leisure activities, that any discussion of their lives outside of work and school should include religious spaces as well. My purpose was not to document the specific churches per se, nor to explore the various differences between denominations, though this remains an important project for future researchers. Still, I made a point of visiting various Evangelical and Neo-Pentecostal churches in Japan in order to gain a comparative perspective and to avoid the bias of interviewing members of only a single denomination.

Although many Brazilians continued to explore their spirituality on a more private level, Evangelical churches and religious services in Portuguese were much more prevalent during my fieldwork in Japan than they appear to have been a decade or two ago. Sometimes the signs of religious faith were readily visible—a large, makeshift cross placed in front of a warehouse-turned-church, or pamphlets handed out at a train station—while at other times they were felt only by the people who participated in services held late at night in the privacy of an individual's home.

Services at Evangelical/Neo-Pentecostal churches often followed a familiar pattern. A typical service that I attended regularly at the Palavra Viva Church in Aichi, for example, lasted roughly two hours, from 10 a.m. to noon on Sundays, followed by a communally cooked lunch. Like many of the Brazilian churches in Japan, the space was improvised. This one, once a karaoke club and unmarked on the outside, still contained pink, felt-covered seats and glass chandeliers. As the pastor's wife told me, when they first rented it, the walls were painted black; later she covered them in white curtains from floor to ceiling, and made sure no natural light could enter. The pastor and his wife began renting the church two to three years earlier—before that they used a different building in another city, which was later demolished—initially for 200,000 yen/month (approximately US$2,000) from the Japanese owners who lived next door. As a result of financial difficulties following the economic crisis of 2008–2009, however, they had to tell the owners that they could not afford the price, which was then lowered by half, to 100,000 yen/month for use of the space on Sundays.

The first hour of Sunday service usually consisted of music, with fifteen to twenty congregants singing along as the pastor and a few other musicians performed on stage. The second hour the pastor spent in sermon, the first half with readings from the Bible and a lesson rooted in the familiar, day-to-day lives of the congregants. At some point, usually halfway through the service, the pastor would ask us to stand and continued speaking to the accompaniment of an electric keyboard. The music continued in the background, and the pastor switched from speaking to us directly to speaking to God in a kind of rhythmic prayer, a wall of sound, every few beats of Portuguese punctuated with the word *Senhor* (Lord). With eyes closed, the congregants began swaying, back and forth, both hands raised at their sides, palms to the ceiling, often with tears streaming down their cheeks. I tended to stand with my eyes closed but not more. The pastor's words then turned into a song, a kind of soft Christian Rock, adding to the emotionally soothing atmosphere of the room. Then, almost as suddenly as it had begun, the music stopped, congregants shouted Amen, and sat down again. At this particular church, the pastor would ask for a financial offering, or the tithe that was expected of everyone present—10 percent of what they received from God, although no one ever seemed to contribute such a high amount.

Across churches, work was a common reference point during sermons, and at this particular service offered entirely in Portuguese, the pastor compared the challenges of factory life to the difficulties of living as a good Christian:

> Most of us who come here don't have degrees, but there are some lawyers, engineers, people with degrees in Brazil, who paid for university and studied so much just to become a factory peon. They go in front of a machine and see that everything is written in Japanese. But if they don't try to figure it out they know they'll lose their job. They don't speak Japanese but if they don't try, they won't succeed. Living Christianity is the same thing. People come to you and share with you the word of God. And you know *you* have to make the first step forward.

At the same time, people were encouraged to keep their faith while on the line, despite all their frustrations with work:

> Our spiritual jails often make us feel small, but they break when you adore God. Communion with God is such a marvelous thing. When you're working on the line, working a *yakin* [night] shift, that adoration starts to come to you and you start praying, you don't even see the pieces you're making. *Iine* [how nice, he said, using the Japanese expression in an otherwise mostly Portuguese sermon]. You're working and you don't even notice the shift is over. You go home happy. Now if you start getting mad at everything, wishing that a machine would break down so that you could go home early, or that your boss would fire you, that someone would fall sick and call to ask you to go get them, if you think, "I'm going to kick my *hanchō* [boss] in the shins so I can leave, I'm going to do something, I swear, I'm going to scream, ARRRR!" Despair in the factory. It's not like that. Despair leads us to that, but the Lord puts us in quieter waters.

Still at other times, congregants were reminded of the importance of setting time aside to commune with God, no matter how hard or long they worked:

> We dedicate ourselves so much to work. Not that it's wrong for you to work and do *zangyō* [overtime]. I don't want to say that to you because I do *zangyō* too. But I want to say that you can, inside your work time, have communion with God. Or if you like, a nicer time, when you arrive home, take a bath—or better yet, go as you are because God won't see whether you smell bad or not—go into your room, get down on your knees, or wake up earlier, devote yourself to God in the morning. Or, if you're on a *yakin* [night] shift, then when you wake up in the afternoon. But set aside time for the Lord. It's an essential part of our lives.

Besides the opportunity to find greater meaning in life, churches also offered a sense of community, especially during special events such as weddings, birthdays, and so on. Oscar, one of my students at the Brazilian school where I worked, for example, held his eighteenth birthday party at a three-story church in Anjō, which included a room for services, a Bible School room with attached sewing room, and a kitchen and reception room, the latter of which was decorated in balloons that particular day. Oscar, dressed in a suit and tie, personally greeted the fifty to sixty people present, most of them connected directly to the church. His parents thanked God for their son's life, and for everyone present—"You are our family here in Japan." Then they sang praise to God and led the guests in prayer before eating, snapping photographs, and slicing into a religious themed cake.

Other religious events took place in the privacy of people's own homes, often lasting until late in the night. One rainy Saturday evening, for example, I took a train to meet Sachie, twenty-one at the time and the single mother of a five-year-old girl. Sachie picked me up in the boxy car she owned and we headed straight to her *danchi* (a government-subsidized apartment building), signs in the parking lot warning in Portuguese against illegal parking. That night, the preachers from her church offered a special sermon in her small, one-bedroom apartment. Sachie had prepared a meal of heaping lasagna, but we would not eat until the sermon ended at 10 p.m. Friends and relatives of Sachie's came and went throughout the evening, a total of 26 guests crowded into the fluorescent-lit living room and kitchen. When I arrived, the *genkan* (entranceway to a Japanese home) was already filled with shoes of all shapes and sizes. Only one of the guests present was Japanese. He worked in the same factory as Sachie's friend and had started attending church with them, even though he did not speak Portuguese. The Brazilians present that evening joked around that the Japanese guest was Cambodian because of his slightly darker skin (actually he had come to Aichi from Kyūshū—Japan's southernmost main island—he told me).[8] People also joked that another Brazilian in the room was Filipino because of the way he looked, though everyone was welcomed and encouraged to feel at home, including myself.

The preacher began the sermon by saying, "This here is a family, and the people of God are a united people." Sachie's friend translated from Portuguese into the ear of his Japanese guest. People sat on the floor, at the kitchen table, wherever they could find room. The preacher's wife then started everyone singing in Portuguese, "God is Here," while his brother accompanied on guitar. The sermon began: "Here in Japan, our minds stop. Working in a factory we quit thinking. But we need to stop and reflect. I know a lot of people here don't have friends. We've got to develop our friendships." A tall man in his twenties, who had arrived midway through the sermon gunning a loud hot rod outside, interrupted to say: "Jesus is my only friend." Sachie's stepmother added: "It's important to only make friends with those who go to church."

At this point Sachie chimed in what had become a lively group discussion where all opinions were heard: "Well I have friends outside the church, like her," she said, pointing to me. "I think it's important to bring other people into contact with each other too." Then her father, who worked as a truck driver and did not go anywhere without a blue headset blinking from his ear, asked: "Japanese men can relieve themselves of problems at *sunakku* [hostess bars], why can't we [i.e., Brazilians] have more of that kind of thing in our day-to-day lives? Many people suffer depression here and need to relieve their problems. What can we do?"

A young man who ran a driver's school in nearby Chiryū and had been leaning against the wall quietly, dressed in worn slacks and a white button-up shirt with his initials embroidered in green and yellow (typical Brazilian colors, because of the national flag) on the cuffs, stepped forward: "How many friends have we lost since knowing Jesus, because we walk a different path now? We've taken off our piercings, changed our way of dressing, speaking, using makeup . . . Jesus saved me but saying that makes my old friends back away. We need to make new friendships with our old friends," he said, and applause spread throughout the room. Once she could be heard above the crowd, the preacher's wife resumed:

> We, we people of the Word, we really do change our way of dressing and all when we come to accept Jesus. You have to be careful who your friends are. If you say things to people in the factory you don't know well, before long everyone there knows your business. But two wrongs never make a right, remember that. Here in Japan we're discriminated against and persecuted, but you can't treat others like that just because they do wrong to you. The Bible is our manual. And we here [pointing to herself and her husband], we're here to help you. We want to see young folks here grow up with the word of God, not just say to themselves, "I'm here in Japan, I'm going to make money," and then not think about other things.

Then the preacher's wife switched tracks: "Is anyone here afraid of the world ending?" Another guest in his early twenties, who had just returned from a month in Brazil and was conspicuously suntanned during such a grey time of year in central Japan, answered with a laugh: "Well, I'm trying to save up money to move back to Brazil, so if the world ends, what the Hell's the point of all this?"

In this brief scene, multiple elements arose that I commonly heard voiced among *dekasegi*, religious or not. For one, there was the need for social connectedness, especially as many migrants in Japan found themselves without the usual networks of family, friends, and acquaintances that they or their families had in Brazil. For those who attended church, it often provided them with a built-in social structure that they could not easily find in their day-to-day lives in Japan. As one fourteen-year-old Afro-Nikkei-Brazilian interlocutor put it, having grown up in Japan speaking primarily only Japanese but suffering discrimination and constant questioning based on her appearance, for her the Evangelical Church she attended represented an *anshin suru basho*, a place she could feel safe: "Everyone there has known me since I was small. They're like a family," she explained to me in Japanese.

The need for social connectedness was often also tied to a desire to be heard and accepted. Sachie's father, for example, hinted at the role that hostess bars play in the lives of some Japanese men, serving as a kind of culturally sanctioned emotional and psychological outlet for people suffering from depression or other problems in their personal lives (Okura Gagné 2010). For most Brazilian men in Japan, however, hostess bar "therapy" was not a viable option, in part because, like Sachie's father, they did not have the time or money and could not express themselves fluently in Japanese, and in part because of cultural norms (e.g., a Brazilian woman might not readily accept her partner paying money to talk with hostesses late into the night about personal problems). More regular talk therapy was also not easily available to *dekasegi* and their families, since few accredited Portuguese-speaking therapists and psychologists practiced in Japan, and in the cases they did, usually only in select, urban centers. Religious services, however, whether they took place in churches or more improvised settings such as people's homes, were accessible and accepting, and provided interlocutors with a safe space to relieve their hearts and minds among peers. For this reason, Melina, who was described earlier in this chapter and who suffered from debilitating depression during her first stay in Japan, found comfort and healing in church where medical doctors could not help her.

Still, at the same time as Evangelical/Neo-Pentecostal communities allowed migrants to expand their social networks and even relieve their suffering, they also limited certain interactions, especially if they were with people outside the faith. Sachie's stepmother, for example, believed that she and fellow church congregants should only socialize with people of the same religious outlook. Despite the fact that Sachie disagreed, citing my presence at the service as an example of how important it was to mingle with people from outside the faith, many devout Evangelicals/Neo-Pentecostals I met during fieldwork believed in the importance of limiting their social interactions to those of the same religion. On the other hand, as the owner of the driver's school pointed out, because of their religious beliefs and behavior, practicing Evangelicals were at times also discriminated against by fellow, nonreligious Brazilians. Whereas once he might have found acceptance and community among other Brazilians his age in Japan—for example, the people he worked with—as soon as he adopted the "way of Jesus" (a habitus that among Evangelicals/Neo-Pentecostals usually involved quitting drinking, dressing more conservatively, and so on), this man felt that he *lost* his connection to most other people around him. Certainly, it was common for those very devout interlocutors of mine to express a kind of social disconnect from people who did not share or respect their beliefs. Thus, while religion often served as a form of social connection and expansiveness, it also limited migrants in their contact with people of another (or no) faith.

Finally, as the pastor and his wife alluded to in their sermon at Sachie's, belief in God served as an important balm to migrants' frustrations with work and their need to find meaning outside of making money. In Melina's case, it lifted her out of depression and gave her a sense of purpose for being in Japan other than work, and for Edmilson, it filled the "black hole in [his] heart" and steered him away from a life of crime. Often, interlocutors equated depression/loss of meaning with delinquency, and explained how the Evangelical/Neo-Pentecostal churches in Japan helped pull people out of both. As one interlocutor who regularly attended an Assembléia de Deus church in Gifu told me, in Portuguese: "We only work, that's all we do. And at work the people I know think bad things, and do bad things—they do drugs, rob cars. Church takes you away from that, it puts you on a path to God. And God transforms the lives of people who do drugs. Many people at my church have changed a lot, they don't smoke or drink anymore." Thus, religion, and especially Evangelical faith, represented more than a sense of community or family. It was also transformative in helping Brazilian migrants in Japan find greater meaning in their lives, and served as an important vehicle in overcoming depression and what they considered destructive or deviant behavior.

NON-EVANGELICAL/NEO-PENTECOSTAL MIGRANTS

Clearly, not all migrants between Japan and Brazil believed in the "path of Jesus" as the answer to problems such as loneliness, alienation, or apathy. For people involved in Evangelical/Neo-Pentecostal churches to the extent that they were, free time was largely organized around church-based activities and events. But for other, nonreligious interlocutors, church was either irrelevant or largely unfamiliar. One of my students at the Brazilian school, for example, told me how her family tried attending Evangelical Church when they first arrived in Japan. She liked it because she found it less rigid than Catholic Church, but her family stopped going and so did she. Another student, who worked in a factory immediately after graduating from grade 12, was surprised to encounter so many religious people working on the line with her:

Most of them are Evangelical and most of them were already converted before coming to Japan. And in conversations, religion is always present. God is the explanation for everything. "God saved my life, God wanted it to be like that, God knows everything, God is great, God this, God that." I know I shouldn't be talking like this but for a non-religious person like me it does get annoying, you know? But I think the problem is not God at all. Perhaps what really annoys me is their resignation.

Indeed, as described earlier in this chapter, God was often invoked to explain the most important decisions and events in people's lives. For someone such as the student here, this simply did not make sense, as she did not share the same beliefs. Other interlocutors were even more critical of the churches, complaining that it was a business scam, robbing people of their savings and keeping them from focusing on work, as did this *nisei* woman in her sixties, who had lived in Japan for over twenty years but was most comfortable speaking in Portuguese:

I think Brazilians like the church here because they can get dressed up fancy, have a beautiful environment, get together and talk and hang out. People will laugh at them if they dress up like that and go somewhere else. They think they are important dressed up like that. Where else can they feel that way? Most of the people who come here come because their businesses went bankrupt or they didn't make enough money to eat. So they come here and church is a special event. They have the opportunity to learn music, they're accepted. There's a good side to it because it helps people who have drinking and drug problems. They're very united, they care for church members in the hospital and all. On the other hand, people bring money to the church and have to give over part of their salary. The church is like a business. You've seen how many there are? And the pastors never studied theology, they're ignorant, they just became pastors once they got here. I personally cannot devote my Saturday and Sunday to the church. Why would you come to Japan to work and leave work to the side to go to church? The church grew here because everyone here has money to give to it, and it gives structure and direction to people. But factory life is Monday to Saturday. We came here to Japan to work. I think that if you have to work to structure a family, then you go to work, you don't go to church. God is everywhere, so you don't have to go to church. But you should work.

For the people who attended Evangelical or Neo-Pentecostal services and events, however, church provided them with exactly that which they found lacking elsewhere in their lives and which this interlocutor criticized them for enjoying: the opportunity to dress nicely (not in factory or school uniforms), to participate in and move up within the church structure with little regard for their education or background, to learn things they might not easily be able to otherwise (e.g., musical instruments), to socialize with like-minded people, to celebrate life events, to give meaning to their life decisions, and generally to create community and a kind of alternate family for themselves.

Still, for a nonbeliever such as the interlocutor quoted earlier, the main question was: Why come to Japan to work and leave work to the side to go to church? In fact, this question points to the very contradiction at the heart of the *dekasegi* movement. On the one hand, Nikkei-Brazilians were encouraged to work in unskilled labor in Japan on a temporary basis—a kind of flexible and fleeting labor force—and, in the overwhelming majority of cases, they never intended to stay more than a few years in Japan. Even the Japanese term *dekasegi* points to this temporariness. On the other hand, many Brazilian labor migrants and their families ended up staying in Japan, sometimes for years or decades, while others engaged in repeat, or circular migration between Japan and Brazil. No matter what the original intention, it soon became clear that most *dekasegi* were not a temporary presence; nor were they necessarily immigrants to Japan, in the sense that they might eventually leave, either to Brazil or elsewhere, or continue to move back and forth between the two.

No matter how long they stayed in Japan, however, or how many times they returned to it, Brazilian labor migrants and their families longed for more than just money in the bank. The answer to the question of why one would come to Japan to work and leave work to the side to go to church is the same, then, as it is for any human being seeking diversion and meaning in life. Brazilians who attended church in Japan did so because they could connect with and meet other people outside of school or work, speak freely in Portuguese, celebrate life events, relieve themselves of emotional and psychological pain, and find acceptance and belonging in a place where, next to majority Japanese, they were necessarily positioned and treated as outsiders.

Even for those who did not engage in the regular activities associated with Evangelical/Neo-Pentecostal churches, faith in God or a greater purpose lent meaning to migrants' lives, as well as to the repetitive, menial, and socially undervalued work they carried out in Japan. One *nisei* factory worker in her fifties, Elsa, for example, was brought up Catholic in Brazil, but in Japan she attended monthly meetings in Portuguese of the Seichō no Ie faith. Seichō no Ie, a new religious movement originally from Japan, consolidated itself institutionally among Japanese immigrant colonies in Brazil in the second half of the 1930s, and is commonly considered a "life philosophy" rather than a religion per se (Shoji & Usarski 2008).

Elsa first came across Seichō no Ie when she was a teenager in Brazil. Her parents wanted her to be a seamstress, since learning to cook and sew would allow her to "marry well." Because there were few options near where they lived in the interior of Paraná, she was sent to Maringá, a city with a large population of Nikkei-Brazilians and a special seamstress school set up by Seichō no Ie. There, Elsa learned "manners, how to live with in-laws, etc." Still, it was only in Japan that she became a regular adherent of the faith. When I saw her during her breaks from work at a tofu factory in Gifu, I noticed her pausing before drinking even tea or a bowl of miso soup. Later she explained in a mix of Japanese and Portuguese that she always paused to thank God for even the smallest of gifts:

> When I work I think a lot about God. I pray [*faço oração*] for everyone I work with as soon as I enter the factory. I pray for the person who drives me to work, for the car that carries me, for the cars next to us. I thank the factory, and I thank the employment brokerage firm that employed me. I am thankful for the work I have, and the spirit that protects the factory. Every day I thank the machines and the products that come of them. The work I do doesn't come from me, it's God working through me, and I pray that the people who eat the tofu I make will be blessed with energy, health, and prosperity. Even if I'm doing dirty work, or have to be transferred or laid off, I am glad for it.

As Elsa explained, this kind of positive thinking, particularly the act of being grateful and praying for the wellbeing of others, helped her get through her days. It allowed her to focus on more positive things than petty factory fights, or the pain she felt from standing on her feet all day, and in this way, resembled what Edmilson spoke of in his sermon when he said that, through prayer, "the Lord puts us in quieter waters." In other words, faith in God allowed people the strength, in the midst of day-to-day drudgery or emotional suffering, to focus on a higher meaning.

Like many Evangelical interlocutors, Elsa also had faith that there was greater purpose to life, and that changes always happened for a divine reason. Where Melina believed she had been sent back to Japan in order to spread God's word, for example, Elsa also believed that she was in Japan because of God's greater purpose:

> As long as I'm in Japan, it's because I have a mission here to complete. For example, I worked twelve years at a car parts factory and I was fired because my mission there came to an end. The day I have to go back to Brazil it's because my mission in Japan will have ended, it'll be time to go back. Everything has a beginning and an end. I leave it in the hands of God, because I don't know what tomorrow will bring, I don't even know what the next hour will bring.

Thus, for Elsa, faith in a greater purpose in life helped her make sense both of losing her job, and of staying (or not) in Japan. More broadly, belief in God and a higher purpose served as an important source of strength for migrants facing both the challenges of day-to-day life "on the line," as well as the difficult decisions of whether to move between Japan and Brazil. Even though nonreligious or non-Evangelical/Neo-Pentecostal migrants might not relate to this outlook, it was a significant force in helping religious migrants make sense of their lives, in the grand scheme, as well as in the present moment.

CONCLUSION

Though they originally moved to Japan to work, Brazilian labor migrants and their families—whether they stayed for the short or long term, or engaged in circular migration over the last several decades—inevitably sought more to their lives than higher wages. In the nearly thirty years since the *dekasegi* movement began, life happened, as well as labor, and Brazilians in Japan found themselves concerned with a host of other concerns besides work: how best to prepare their children for the future, whether in Japan or Brazil or elsewhere, how to achieve a greater sense of purpose and meaning in their day-to-day lives, and how to find a sense of belonging and acceptance in a country that, for the most part, still allocated them to the position of temporary, foreign laborers.

As seen in chapter 2, obtaining material symbols of middle-class status provided some labor migrants and their children with feelings of fulfillment. In the case of the Silva family of chapter 1, working or studying to secure the family's future provided Angela and her children with a sense of greater purpose. For the Matsudas of chapter 3, owning a house, rooting themselves as a family in local Japanese society, and going as far as to naturalize to Japanese citizenship offered them meaning and achievement outside of work. Finally, for the Pereira family of chapter 5, a combination of religion and family connectedness served to lend direction and purpose to their migrations between Japan and Brazil.

In this chapter, we saw how religion, particularly Evangelical/Neo-Pentecostal churches, played a strong role among a substantial subset of the Brazilian population in Japan. For the 20 percent or so of my interlocutors who identified as Evangelical/Neo-Pentecostal Christians, churches or other, more private religious services served as important loci for the creation of community and sociality outside of work/school. Faith in God and a higher purpose also allowed them to understand and narrate their decision to move to Japan, to stay there, or to return to Brazil, as the logical next step in a life guided from above. In short, religion was, for many people, a crucial component of what it meant in practice to live transnationally between Japan and Brazil.

At the same time as it provided strength and meaning, however, religion also acted as a constraining force in people's lives. For some people, it meant that, because God intended it, they left good jobs or educational opportunities behind, or even that they lost or limited their friendships with nonreligious peers. Still for other Brazilian labor migrants and their children, they decided to stay in Japan because God needed them to spread His word or help maintain or expand His churches, or because they regularly offered their savings to the church and could not afford to return to Brazil. Whether it constrained or fulfilled, for many of my interlocutors, religious faith, like family, was an important thread wound through people's lives, one that connected individuals to broader contexts—structures and socialities—and shaped their personal trajectories together with other motifs such as ethnicity, class, and gender.

NOTES

1. Expressions of *caipira*-ness also drew on regional identities of the many Nikkei-Brazilian migrants who grew up in the "interior" of Brazil (i.e., in the cities and towns beyond state capitals).

2. As Paul Freston (2001) notes, the terms *protestantes* and *evangélicos* are used interchangeably in Brazil, though the vast majority refer to what English speakers call Evangelicals/Neo-Pentecostals.

3. In 1987–1988, the São Paulo Humanities Research Center calculated that there were 1,228,000 Brazilians of Japanese descent, including those of mixed descent (see Tsuda 2003: 57). By 2010, the Centro de Estudos Nipo-Brasileiros estimated that this number had reached 1,600,000. In other words, in 2010, approximately 80 percent of Brazil's *amarela* population was of Japanese descent.

4. Academics and government officials are not the only ones to describe economics as the primary driver behind certain migration patterns. As Nicole Constable (1999) points out, based on her fieldwork among Filipina migrant workers in Hong Kong, "money is also the easy answer, the generally most acceptable answer, and to some extent an automatic and incomplete response" (212) made by interlocutors, and that "if taken as the only answer, economic motivations obscure other more painful, less comfortable, less socially acceptable, but equally important—and sometimes contradictory—answers that linger below the surface" (ibid).

5. I borrow this term from Manuel Vásquez (2009), who uses it in reference to Émile Durkheim's concept of an anomic individual's lack of strong social ties and sense of collective belonging.

6. Similarly, Joshua Roth (2002) notes that because Brazilians in Japan rarely found value and meaning at work, many found alternative sources of value in outlets such as conspicuous consumption and religious practice (17).

7. Joshua Roth (2002) found a similar phenomenon occurring not at church, but at a Brazilian cultural center in Hamamatsu. This center was ostensibly founded "as

a haven from the contractual relationships that permeated most migrants' lives in Japan; by appealing to values more permanent and meaningful than those represented by money, he attempted to establish the center as a moral community" (98).

8. Japan's southern islands, including Kyūshū, Shikoku, and the Ryūkyūs (the largest of which is Okinawa), are among the country's poorest. Stories and jokes depicting southern Japanese as darker skinned, poorer, and/or more provincial are not uncommon.

Conclusion

Brazilian transnational labor migrants and their families, because of their position in and of both Japan and Brazil, challenge narrow assumptions of what it means to be Japanese (as well as Nikkei), and what it means to be Brazilian. Over the last nearly three decades, the so-called *dekasegi* movement has moved beyond a simple binary of destination settlement or temporary sojourn, creating a framework for multiple life trajectories and variable ways of expressing ethnicity and belonging. Language, dress, diet, work routines, leisure habits, marriage, and other elements of lifeways are now used in intricate and shifting combinations to express a range of ethnic identities and national orientations. Across countries, these lifeways have been shaped by the contexts of family, work, education, and religion, and have been variously experienced as women and men, young and old, and simultaneously working and middle-class laborers in a global economy of desire.

Early studies of *dekasegi* were concerned with the idea of home, reflected in titles such as *No One Home* (Linger 2001), *Brokered Homeland* (Roth 2002), *Strangers in the Ethnic Homeland* (Tsuda 2003), and *Searching for Home Abroad* (Lesser 2003), and how ethnicity affected individuals' experiences of national (non)belonging. What was home, these works asked, for people who were considered neither really Japanese nor Brazilian—and, I would add, for many of the third- and fourth-generation Japanese-Brazilians, not fully Nikkei? Furthermore, what was home for people who were neither fully immigrants nor temporary migrants but often engaged in back-and-forth or repeat migration between Japan and Brazil, and/or with significant ties in both home and host societies?

A standard anthropological conception of home likely includes elements such as physical property, a family or social unit occupying such a place, the location where one lives permanently or from which one originates, and even the place where something flourishes or is most typically found. As I found in my research, home was built out of far more than property or ethnic/national expression and belonging; it was also constructed through family networks, schools, and religious spaces, as well as material comforts and security, and a sense of expanded future opportunities.[1] Each of these elements, always intersecting with gender, generation, and class, provided migrants with a range of constraints and possibilities, in which they were embedded, and through which they explored their position as variably flexible and inflexible in Japan, Brazil, and beyond. Brazilian labor migrants and their children were not lost or without a real home in the world. Rather, I have aimed to show the ways in which they actively and variably created, expressed, and enacted multiple, ongoing forms of belonging across national boundaries. As with Nicole Constable's (1999) description of "plural visions" among transnational Filipina migrants, or Jorge Duany's (2011) work on the "bifocal lives" of Caribbean-Americans, I found that Brazilian *dekasegi* and their families variously saw themselves belonging in, if not to, multiple places (Watson 2014). As Michael Jackson (2013) puts it: "[Migration] is not a matter of being between two worlds, but of being dismembered—no longer being fully integrated into a familiar community. And so the migrant is obliged to re-member himself, to constantly piece together, like a bricoleur, new *assemblages* from the various aspects of his past and present selves" (205).

In order to more deeply explore the ways in which *dekasegi* and their families variously "re-membered" themselves and expressed belonging in Japan and Brazil, I dedicated a chapter to each of three different families involved in the ongoing labor migration movement between the two countries. By exploring the long-term experiences of these families, I aimed to incorporate a life course approach to the study of migration, demonstrating the extent to which national orientations and expressions of ethnic and cultural belonging shifted over time, shaped by the constantly changing local contexts of, among other things, family, work, education, and religion. Chapter 1 focused on the Silvas, a family residing partly in Japan and partly in Brazil; chapter 3 followed the Matsudas, who settled long term in Japan to the point of naturalizing as Japanese citizens; and chapter 5 traced the Pereira family's return to Brazil. This triptych served to illustrate, on the one hand, different possibilities along the horizon of belonging and ethnic/cultural expression, as well as to complicate the very binaries of migrants versus immigrants, Japanese versus Brazilian, and even settled versus returned.

In the case of the Silva family, Angela and her three children navigated the constraints and possibilities of transnational life in different ways. After many years working in Japan, Carlos returned to Brazil in his late thirties to further his studies, investing in a career he hoped would support his mother and siblings down the road. Marcelo, because he had begun working in factories in Japan at such a young age, and was less interested in school than Carlos, felt too old to invest in a new career. Though he longed to return to Brazil, he stayed in Japan to help his mother and support Carlos from afar, and because he knew that, without education or relevant skills, he could maintain a much more comfortable lifestyle in Japan than he could in Brazil. By the time I met him, he was already in his mid-thirties, and no longer felt connected to the *dekasegi* peers he had once spent so much time socializing with. His sense of being lost had little to do with "ethnic alienation" or a "rebellious ethnic counteridentity" (Tsuda 2003), however. Rather, he was frustrated and alienated after years spent in factories in Japan for finally running up against the reality of his employment and social/romantic limitations in both Japan and Brazil. In other words, he had lost the hope of a breakthrough.

Jessica, for her part, had little memory of Brazil and could not imagine returning there. The fact that she was fluent in both Japanese and Portuguese, and had found a way into white-collar work in Japan, meant that she had escaped the segmented labor system through which most Brazilians continued to be employed. Like Marcelo, she was aware that her options in Brazil were limited, and that Japan offered her a more comfortable life, even though in many ways she, too, felt like a partial outsider there. Despite recognizing as an adult that she would never be accepted as fully Japanese in Japan, her sense of belonging shifted over time. When she was in her mid-teens and attending Japanese school, she felt confused about her ethnicity; later, through her experiences as an athlete and in the working world, she came to embrace and creatively use *both* her Japanese and Brazilian identities. Finally, Angela, though she was nearing sixty and tired of her life in Japan, stayed on in order to help Carlos through the end of medical school, and to provide both short and long-term stability and care for Marcelo and Jessica. For her, staying in Japan had less to do with ethnic attachment than it did with her sense of obligation to her children. Thus, beyond simply ethnic or national orientation, family considerations, as well as concerns about social mobility and material comforts, led Angela and her children to construct home(s) out of both Japan and Brazil.

The Matsuda family, for their part, had been in Japan for as long as the Silvas but, as the years passed, they aimed increasingly to make a home for themselves in Japan. Marcia and Elio owned their apartment in Aichi and, together with their three children, they naturalized to Japanese citizenship in 2011. Though their trajectory as a family was markedly different from that of the Silvas, they too were influenced by a combination of factors besides ethnic or national orientation, including lifestyle comforts and aspirations, family concerns, and imagined future opportunities in both Japan and Brazil.

Although they did not originally intend to stay in Japan for as long as they did, Marcia and Elio grew increasingly comfortable with the commodities and security of their lifestyle there. At the same time, their children grew up attending Japanese schools, and spoke little Portuguese. When their youngest son was diagnosed with leukemia as an infant, the Matsudas felt fortunate that—even though they were not Japanese and earned a living working in factories—they had access to high-quality and affordable national health care. As the years went on, and they received additional help from their parents and other relatives who also moved to Japan to work, they felt little need to return to Brazil. What is more, they were concerned that their children, because of their limited Portuguese, would have a difficult time adapting to life should they return one day to Brazil. Sayuri and Tomoko, for their part, did not continue on to university, and earned decent wages working in factories in Japan. Sayuri, for example, could afford to live away from her parents, own a car, and enjoy many other material comforts—all of which, with only a middle school education, would be next to impossible in Brazil.

Still, even as the Matsudas's children passed as Japanese and eventually became Japanese citizens, the family remained flexible in various ways— through food, language use, and so on—and they kept their Brazilian passports stowed away as "back-up" in case they needed them one day. Once she met her Brazilian husband, Sayuri grew more interested in communicating in Portuguese and, for the first time, considered the option of returning to Brazil. Tomoko, for her part, discovered that she could capitalize on being perceived as Brazilian to work at City Hall, though eventually her lack of Portuguese abilities rendered the work unviable. Even Takuya, who never knew Brazil and easily passed as ethnically and culturally Japanese, was now known at school for his family's history of migration and his mother's tasty Brazilian treats. Although he displayed little interest in learning Portuguese, he did not experience the same shame (or shaming) over his Brazilian background as Sayuri and Tomoko had earlier on in their lives. Each in their own way, then, navigated the possibilities and constraints of making a home for themselves as long-term residents in Japan, even as they remained variously tied to Brazil.

Lastly, for the Pereira family, return to Brazil, though framed by Wania as religiously inspired, was influenced by a number of factors besides divine will, including work opportunities, age and health concerns, material comforts, and, of course, family constraints and support. Wania Pereira was similar to Angela Silva in that, though *nisei* and living in Japan for years, she continued to feel like an ethnic outsider there and preferred the idea of returning "home" to Brazil. She and her husband stayed in Japan as long as they did not only because God wished it but also in order to keep the family together and to save for their retirement in Brazil. Once their five children reached adulthood, however, return to Brazil made sense for them as a family, since they owned property and had the support of extended relatives and friends there.

For Wania and her husband, age and physical stamina, as well as educational and linguistic barriers, were limiting factors in how long they could realistically continue working in Japan. Once they decided to return to Brazil, their children quickly followed suit. Their oldest daughter Stefanie and her husband preferred to raise their young daughters near family, and were concerned that if the girls grew up in Japan attending Japanese school, they would reject both their Brazilian and Evangelical backgrounds. William, for his part, even though he was reluctant to give up the material comforts he found in Japan, decided to return to Brazil (for the time being, anyway) to be near his parents and siblings. Cleber also decided to return to live with his family in Brazil, although he considered his "Japanese side" to be a form of positive social and cultural capital and missed the opportunities for work and travel that he had found in Japan. The Pereiras's youngest children, Jefferson and Raquel, who did not speak fluent Portuguese and had little memory of Brazil, did the same. Thus, regardless of how they variously expressed Japanese-ness and/or Brazilian-ness over time, the idiom of family, as well as God, served to guide the Pereiras's life trajectories, first in creating a home in Japan, and then in re-making one in Brazil.

What these three families have in common is the *dekasegi* movement itself, a migratory phenomenon in which people who prove Japanese ethnic descent have been channeled to Japan via a brokered labor system. Still, as we have seen, approximately three decades after the *dekasegi* movement began, the possibilities for ethnic expression and national orientation were as varied as they were shifting. At the same time, work/lifestyle options and ideas of "the good life" (Castles et al. 2014; Fischer 2014), as well as family, education, religion, and other means of "social remittances" (Levitt 1998) shaped the lives of Brazilian migrants and their children in their identities and aspirations, as well as their actual decisions to migrate, settle, and return.

Chapters 2, 4, and 6 of this book operate together as a second triptych illustrating the broader *dekasegi* experience, and placing the experiences of the Silvas, Matsudas, and Pereiras in further context. In chapter 2, I examined the role of work—unskilled, brokered labor—in Japan and what it has come to represent to Brazilian labor migrants in terms of purchasing power, class status, and social (im)mobility in a transnational context. By narrowing in on an employment brokerage firm—particularly in light of a factory fight—I illustrated how the segmented labor system through which most Brazilians continued to work in Japan both mediated problems for its workers and held them back as part of the irregularly employed precariat in Japan. I also explored how, for many migrants, working in Japan came to represent the achievement or maintenance of middle-class subjectivity and consumption, even while it limited or reduced their long-term social mobility across national borders. Finally, within this context of transnational labor migration, I highlighted the potentially different meanings of (im)mobility for women and men, rather than treating it as a genderless and therefore undifferentiated experience.

In chapter 4, I explored the ways in which the children of *dekasegi* were generally encouraged to work in unskilled labor in Japan or leave for what was imagined to be a better future in Brazil. Educational institutions, by orienting students to return to Brazil or stay in Japan, reinforced their position either as temporary migrants (ethnically differentiated, via Brazilian schools) or immigrants (assimilationist, via Japanese schools), and tended to reproduce the labor/social relations of their parents. At the same time, however, whether they were educated in Japanese or Brazilian schools in Japan, 1.5 and second-generation youth creatively and strategically navigated the particular set of limitations and opportunities they faced as the children of transnational migrants, educated in nationally oriented institutions, and subject to globally desired lifestyles of consumption and mobility.

Finally, in chapter 6, I looked at the ways in which religion, especially Evangelicalism/Neo-Pentecostalism, provided additional constraints and possibilities for those migrants devoted to their faith. For many *dekasegi* and their children, religion, like family, served as a means of navigating and understanding their position as transnational labor migrants, as well as creating community and sociality outside of family, work, and school. Whether they stayed in Japan or returned to Brazil, then, the church served as a kind of spiritual home that transcended national borders. Members could flexibly move from an Evangelical/Neo-Pentecostal church in Japan to one in Brazil, and find acceptance and a sense of belonging in both places. At the same time, though, these presumably global types of churches were embedded in local social/cultural structures, such that the Evangelical/Neo-Pentecostal churches and spaces frequented by Brazilians in Japan were shaped by—as well as targeted at—the specifically *dekasegi* experience.

In all of these chapters, one can see the ways in which transnational migrants achieved belonging and membership through a multiplicity of factors: physical property, educational credentials, language, work routines, religious spaces, material comforts and commodities, and social and family networks. At the same time as they found home(s) in Japan and Brazil, however, Brazilian migrants and their children faced considerable barriers in terms of social mobility both within Japan and upon their return—real or imagined—to Brazil. Similarly, transnational affiliation and mixed ethnic identities did not necessarily reflect the ability to move smoothly or flexibly between countries. Thus, in the cases presented, I aimed to illustrate the various "frictions" (Tsing 2005)—including those inherent in structures of family, work, education, and religion—that, at the same time as they pro-vided migrants with a sense of belonging and home, also channeled global migration flows, as well as individual experiences, in complex, delimited ways.

GENDER, GENERATION, AND CLASS

Throughout the book, I aimed to explore the ways in which gender, genera-tion, and class intersected with Brazilian migrants' expression of ethnicity and belonging, and affected their (im)mobility within and across national boundaries. Many women migrants, for example, earned lower pay than men in Japan, even if they performed the same or comparable labor, and/or were equally educated. At the same time, for some women, especially those who previously found themselves financially dependent on their families or who were expected to take care of them rather than join the workforce full time, migrating to Japan represented significant advances in terms of social free-dom, material comfort, and financial self-reliance.

In terms of generation, few studies of Brazilian labor migrants in Japan have accounted for the differences among the first, 1.5, and second genera-tions. A notable exception to this is the work of Paul Green, whose article "Generation, Family and Migration: Young Brazilian Factory Workers in Japan" (2010) demonstrates the loyalties and tensions that exist between working parents and working siblings in Japan. Based on ethnographic fieldwork in and around Nagoya in the early 2000s, Green provides an understanding of migration from the perspective of teenage and young adult Brazilian migrants, "illustrating the extent to which the ideals, values and motivations of young, often single migrants may differ to those of parents intent on building a future for themselves and their (school) children in Japan" (ibid: 517). This work is fundamental in showing how the children of *dekasegi* do not necessarily wish or plan to return to Brazil like their parents do. In other words, many young Brazilians in Japan today experience migra-tion and belonging in ways that are very different from those who moved there as adults.

In my own research in Japan and Brazil, I found much in common with Green's work among Brazilian migrant youth. In particular, there was a marked tension not only between the goals and aspirations of different gen-erations of Brazilian labor migrants but also between the relative flexibility and inflexibility of their lives. In Green's study, for example, he shows how moving to Japan (and, I would add, back to Brazil) provided a way for young migrants to free themselves from overbearing relations with family members. At the same time as I observed this, however, I also found that, as a result of cutting their education short (whether in Japan or Brazil), many young Brazilians experienced both limited mobility in Japan and significant difficulty in returning to work in Brazil. Thus, for younger generations, mobility and immobility intersected at different angles with cultural belonging and detachment than had been the case for their parents.

The issue of linguistic capital was particularly important in understanding the different experiences of first versus 1.5 or second-generation Brazilians in Japan, as well as when they returned to Brazil. Many of the parents I interviewed considered Japanese-Portuguese bilingualism to be the ticket to their children's obtaining better jobs in both Japan and Brazil. In reality, however, few 1.5 or second-generation Brazilian youth actually felt comfortable using both languages, while those who did often obtained better jobs, usually as interpreters or cultural go-betweens in Japan. Much of these children's future mobility, as well as their ethnic orientation, in fact centered upon whether they were educated in Japanese or Brazilian schools, or a mixture of the two. Still, even for those who were relatively fluent in both Japanese and Portuguese, or primarily in Japanese, they often faced ethnic discrimination and/or difficulties related to low social status in Japan. Those who were fluent in Portuguese, for their part, did not necessarily wish to leave Japan, nor did they have an easy time navigating the job market or higher education in Brazil. In this way, linguistic and cultural capital (not to mention economic capital accrued through brokered labor) did not necessarily translate to social capital or smooth patterns of mobility across national borders.

In a discussion of different generations of *dekasegi*, one must account not only for those who grew up in and of Japan and Brazil but also those who have grown older across these same borders. Many of the people mentioned in this book were already in their forties to sixties at the time of research, and were concerned with their health and physical strength, as well as aging parents in Brazil. The precarity of working in temporary, brokered labor in Japan for years on end was further heightened by advanced age. Even if they identified strongly with Brazil and wished to return "home," however, many migrants found that they were limited not only by their age but also by a lack of educational credentials and/or professional skills.

Like gender and age, class and class status were salient factors in an analysis of the *dekasegi* experience in Japan and Brazil. As Ayumi Takenaka notes, "In the process of their incorporation into Japanese society, South Americans became synonymous with *dekasegi* workers" (2010: 225). Thus, no matter how long they stayed in Japan, South Americans were associated with the *dekasegi* mentality of wanting to earn a maximum amount of money and return home with it, meaning that they were seen as both hard workers and as lacking loyalty due to frequently changing jobs. In addition, because they were often viewed as *dekasegi* (temporary workers, as opposed to, say, immigrants), Brazilians were rarely considered a permanent part of the Japanese social fabric. In the end, their vulnerable class position deprived them of a sense of motivation and career aspirations, which made it more difficult for them to move up the socioeconomic ladder in Japan (ibid: 228). Because they had few concrete plans and objectives and were often uncertain about staying in Japan, Brazilians (particularly those who did not go through the Japanese education system at all) tended not to learn much Japanese over time. As Paul Green notes, "by living in the moment of the next barbeque or unplanned pregnancy, some young migrants treat Japan as a non-place through which the transient nature of their everyday experience of displacement becomes a permanent feature of their existence" (2010: 530). This suggests that Brazilians' vulnerability and uncertain position in Japan stemmed, therefore, both from their class position and the fact that they continued to view themselves and be viewed—primarily by the Japanese government but also by members of their local communities—as temporary, transient, and disposable.

Certainly, from what I found, class identities and aspirations played a marked role in people's decision to migrate to Japan, to stay there, and to return to Brazil. Through the process of labor migration to Japan, many Brazilians experienced greater purchasing power, financial independence, and material comforts than they could as blue or white-collar workers in Brazil. At the same time, however, as members of the brokered precariat in Japan, with limited opportunities for educational or occupational advancement, they felt trapped by their position as manual laborers there. Still, were they to return to Brazil, they would be hard-pressed to achieve or maintain the same lifestyle they and their children had grown used to in Japan over the years. In other words, increased economic capital did not necessarily translate into social or cultural capital either in Japan or Brazil. Thus, despite the limitations involved, many migrants opted to stay in Japan in part because of the possibilities it presented in terms of a coveted and comfortable middle-class lifestyle.

FINDING HOME(S) IN JAPAN, BRAZIL, AND BEYOND

In 2005, Tarō Asō—then minister for internal affairs and communication—announced that Japan, a country with "one culture, one civilization, one race, and one language, is a country like no other" (*Japan Times*, October 18, 2005). This was hardly the first time that a prominent Japanese politician pronounced Japan both ethnically and linguistically homogenous. In 1986, for example, Prime Minister Yasuhiro Nakasone actually denied the presence of minorities in Japan, claiming that the country was able to maintain high educational standards due to its lack of internal diversity. The notion of homogenous Japan is, of course, a product of twentieth-century history and, as Eiji Oguma (1995 & 1998) has shown, became especially entrenched as an ideology following the Second World War and the loss of Japan's colonies.

As the number of resident foreigners in Japan steadily grows, parts of the nation have in actuality become "internationalized" through the presence of foreign workers. According to Nelson Graburn et al., in their introduction to the volume *Multiculturalism in the New Japan*, "it became increasingly difficult to uphold a model of homogenous Japan from the 1980s, although the belief that Japan is, always has been, and should be homogenous directs right-wing public policy makers" (2008: 7). No matter what people do or do not believe about Japan's internal diversity, today the nation includes nearly two million officially registered foreigners, constituting approximately 2 percent of the total population.[2] Scholars in and of Japan increasingly use the term *tabunka kyōsei* (lit. many cultures living together) to describe the symbiosis and solidarity of multiethnic society there. As Japan continues to grow even more diverse (see, for example, Komai 1999), the question of how foreign residents such as Brazilians carve out spaces of belonging for themselves in the face of homogenizing discourses is an important one.

While in Japan the state repeatedly denies or submerges issues of ethnic minorities, in Brazil, the 2010 National Census revealed for the first time that a majority of the Brazilian population now considers itself nonwhite. At the same time, the commonsense notion of what it means to be truly Brazilian includes elements of European, African, and Indigenous descent but rarely accounts for people of other ethnic backgrounds. As former President Luiz Inácio Lula da Silva stated in 2010, during a public speech celebrating the Brazilian Agricultural Research Corporation (EMBRAPA), "We [Brazilians] are the result of a triple mixture, in other words a genetic mix purified in three continents that resulted in the people that we are. I don't know if there is a people equal to us, but better there is not, nor more purified [*purificada*]."[3] Lula's words echo the trajectory of popular intellectual and anthropological thought in Brazil that spans from Gilberto Freyre in the 1930s to Darcy Ribeiro in the 1990s, and focuses on the unique identity of a nation formed through the fusion of three distinct "races." Although he made the opposite claim from that of Japanese Prime Minister Asō, still President Lula framed the nation in terms of an authentic Brazilian "people"—one imagined to be a mix of white, black, and Indigenous, but not, for example, Nikkei. What, then, does belonging mean to Brazilians of other ethnic backgrounds, especially those who have engaged in more recent migrations around the world?

Nikkei-Brazilian transnational labor migrants and their families present a particularly interesting case for analysis, since in many ways they are *both* Japanese and Brazilian, temporary migrants and immigrants, and flexible and inflexible citizens of the world. On the one hand, they are fairly flexible in the sense that their ethnic heritage allows them access to a special visa that is not granted to members of other ethnic groups/nationalities wishing to work as unskilled laborers in Japan. On the other hand, however, their social mobility in both Japan and Brazil is still restricted by such factors as the segmented labor system in Japan, limited access to bilingual and higher education, and a lack of positive linguistic capital. For those people "caught" between Japan and Brazil, I have tried to articulate not only how mixed identities played out in their day-to-day lives but also how transnational migration presented them with a particular set of both possibilities and limitations—flexibility and inflexibility—in finding home(s) across national borders. In this way, I find much in common with the work of scholars such as Pardis Mahdavi (2016) and Deborah Boehm (2012), who see flexibility and inflexibility, or even structure and agency, as part and parcel of the same process that is *living transnationally.*

As transnational Brazilian migrants and their children continue to navigate the various possibilities and limitations available to them through family, work, education, and religion, and the ways in which they are both flexible and inflexible in Japan, Brazil, and beyond, their range of ethnic expression and national orientation grows ever more complex over time. Especially for those Brazilians raised and/or educated in Japan, their mixed identities challenge either/or assumptions about who is really Japanese, and who is Brazilian. As one teenage interlocutor told me, speaking in a mix of Japanese and Portuguese: "I was born in Japan and always grew up here. Brazilians say I seem Japanese, but Japanese say I seem Brazilian. As for me, I don't really know. I think I'm *ryōhō* [both]." In other words, although she was labeled as either/or and had never lived in Brazil, this young woman identified as both Japanese and Brazilian.

Another interlocutor who grew up almost entirely in Japan and attended only Brazilian school before beginning to work in a factory at age sixteen expressed her mixed identity in this way, speaking only in Portuguese: "I have a Brazilian heart. I don't consider myself Japanese-Japanese, but I do to a certain degree because of how long I've been here. I've been here nearly my entire life, so I do partly consider myself Japanese. What makes me sad, though, is that I still don't know how to speak Japanese that well. So I think, well, but I am Brazilian after all." Yet another young woman, who grew up primarily in Japan attending only Japanese school, told me in Japanese: "I'm like this Brazilian who speaks mostly only Japanese, and I have this face that looks Japanese, I don't really stick to nationality, but *tashika ni burajirujin kana* [I guess I am Brazilian]."

Other interlocutors saw their mixed identities not so much as *both* Japanese and Brazilian but in fact *neither* of the two; rather, they saw themselves occupying a third, and altogether different space. As one woman in her early forties put it, speaking in Portuguese, "Here in Japan we've become this community that's neither Japanese nor Brazilian. We're Brazilians who have had to adapt to Japanese customs." Another interlocutor, seventeen, who grew up between Japan and Brazil and spoke more English than Japanese, said she felt Brazilian, but did not really like Brazil or want to return there: "Sometimes I feel like I'm actually kind of American, a little bit of everything." Her classmate, nineteen at the time I interviewed her, and having grown up in both Japan and Brazil, told me that though she looked Japanese and spoke fluent Japanese: "I don't consider myself Japanese. I'm Brazilian, but one who doesn't plan to stay in Brazil." She was in fact fluent in both Japanese and Portuguese but did not feel fully at home in either language:

> I want to escape them both. I don't mean I necessarily want to escape home, or Japan, but in some way I want to go somewhere that is more comfortable. Because I've never been really comfortable anywhere. Growing up I wanted to create my own world, or something new that would make me feel secure, and like it was mine. That's when I discovered English. I have a lot of affection for English. Many people prefer to confide in a friend, but I chose something better, another language. I invested in it. I feel most comfortable when I'm writing or reading English, like it's my world, and I'm welcome in it. So maybe I'm wrong to want to escape my two nationalities, my origins, and to go somewhere else, or maybe I'm actually right. Everyone has the right to start something new, don't they?

This young woman, then, discovered a sense of home and belonging not in family or educational and/or religious structures but in language. Interestingly, she did not feel this way about Japanese or Portuguese but, instead, a third language—English.

Indeed, contrary to the aspirations their parents had for them, a growing number of 1.5 and second-generation "Zainichi Brazilians" did not imagine their job/life opportunities or cultural attachments to lie solely in Japan and/ or Brazil. Rather, they imagined and desired a more global, mobile future, one where neither Japanese nor Portuguese, but English operated as the most useful and valuable linguistic currency in the world. While the Japanese government and local international centers offered increasing opportunities for foreign laborers to learn Japanese for free, many of the young Brazilians I spoke with in Japan preferred to spend their leisure time (as well as whatever disposable income they had) on private English lessons. The ability to speak English, it seemed, represented the necessary linguistic capital to potentially move beyond Japan and Brazil, and, consequently, to a desired "third space" of global mobility/flexibility. As in the examples of the former law student in chapter 2 or William Pereira in chapter 5, Australia was often cited as a desirable alternative destination, one where Brazilian youth imagined they could escape both the "Third World" status of Brazil and what they perceived to be the rigid social and cultural barriers of Japan.

Finally, as demonstrated throughout this book, transnational migrants and their families rarely conceived of themselves as having arrived at a final destination, whether they were moving to the "host" society for the first time or returning "home" for the fifth time. No matter where they found themselves at any given point in time, life circumstances and aspirations changed and people who were once considered "settled" moved away, while others who intended to move to a host society for only a short time stayed there for years. Still others who "returned" to their country of origin (in this case Brazil) could very well migrate again to Japan, or else to another place altogether. While Brazilian labor migrants' flexibility was limited by a host of factors, both within and across borders, they engaged in an ongoing, ever-shifting process of place-making that challenged fixed, singular ideas of ethnic/national affiliation, as well as temporary versus permanent models of migration.

Thus, I found that, while early studies of *dekasegi* in Japan were immensely instructive in their historical contextualization, as well as their analysis of mediating institutions and the relations between majority Japanese and minority Brazilians, the general focus on ethnicity served at times to obfuscate other important elements of migrant lifeways such as family, education, and religion, as well as gender, generation, and class. Of course, an advantage of conducting fieldwork more than two decades after the *dekasegi* movement began was that migrants and their children already had the time to grow up and grow old across national borders, such that I could adopt something of a life course approach to migration where earlier scholars could not. Perhaps for this reason, I found that my interlocutors engaged in a kind of transnational belonging as opposed to either complete cultural assimilation or differentiation, the latter of which was framed by Joshua Roth (2002) as "oppositional fluorescence" and by Takeyuki Tsuda (2003) as "ethnic resistance."

Rather than view Brazilian transnational labor migrants and their children as "caught" between countries or cultures, then, as they have so often been portrayed by social scientists, journalists, educators, and policy makers, my research instead locates them *in* and *of* both Japan and Brazil, as well as the global economy of desire. For many Brazilians, especially those who grew up partly or primarily in Japan, the important question was not whether they were Japanese *or* Brazilian, temporary migrants *or* permanent immigrants, but rather what it meant to make homes out of both countries, and what this might tell us not only about ethnicity and belonging but also about globalization and transnational migration more broadly.

NOTES

1. Hope is as essential to migrating as it is to a sense of well-being. As Edward Fischer (2014) notes, "Living up to the expectations of particular values is in many ways the stock and trade of human existence; and it is this forward-looking, aspirational quality that gives meaning to much of what we do, affluent and impoverished alike" (6). Sara Friedman (2015), in her work with the Mainland Chinese spouses of Taiwanese citizens, shows how a sense of belonging is both spatial and temporal, and includes a sense of the future: "And the future, a source of hope as well as anxiety, demands a particular form of immigrant commitment expressed through both productive and reproductive contributions to a new home" (171).

2. This figure does not include long-standing ethnic minorities such as the Ainu or Ryūkyūans, individuals who have naturalized as Japanese citizens, or people of mixed descent who possess Japanese citizenship. Thus, while such statistics do not yet exist, a survey of people's ethnic identity or heritage (as opposed to their legal status or citizenship) would reveal a far greater degree of internal diversity in Japan than the current 2 percent of foreigners suggests.

3. See article by Tânia Monteiro in *Estadão*, April 29, 2010.

Epilogue

In the summer of 2018, thanks to a faculty research grant from Yale University's MacMillan Center, I returned to Japan and Brazil to follow up with the labor migrants and their families I had begun working with nearly a decade earlier, in 2009. Stopping by the Okazaki International Center in Aichi again for the first time in five years, I was greeted by many familiar faces, including Japanese, Brazilian, Chinese, and Filipino employees I had come to know there over the years. One of the Brazilians working at the Center had since naturalized with her family to Japanese citizenship. Like the Matsudas of chapter 3, she felt that naturalization would make it easier for her children to get a good job later, especially since the family planned to stay in Japan for the foreseeable future. Another Brazilian employed by the Center told me how Brazilians were once again coming or returning to Japan to work because of the difficult economic situation in Brazil in recent years: "But they intend to stay a long time now. They're more motivated to learn Japanese than earlier waves of *dekasegi*. Lots of them are coming with their kids now and putting them in Japanese school." To prove her point about the recent upturn in Brazilians, she printed out some statistics from the city government showing an increase in Brazilian residents in Okazaki every month thus far for the year 2018. Indeed, despite the steady drop in Brazilian residents in Japan since the global financial crisis of 2008–2009, since 2016 their numbers had gradually increased again, so that by the end of June 2018, the total population reached 196,781 (see figure E.1[1]). While this number remains well below their peak of over 300,000 in 2007, still it suggests that Brazilian labor migrants and their families continue to view Japan as a viable place to live and work.

Of the three key families I followed and wrote about over the years—the Silvas, the Matsudas, and the Pereiras—all of them continued to cultivate ties, whether social, economic, legal, familial, or cultural, in both Japan and

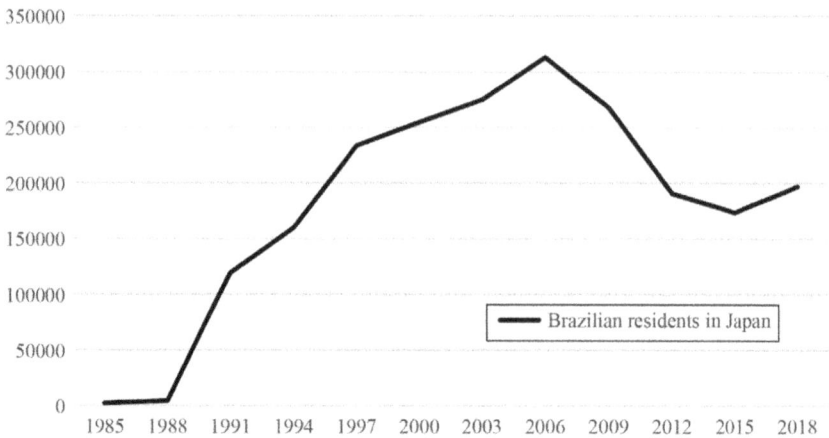

Figure E.1   Number of Brazilian residents in Japan, 1985–2018.

Brazil. Returning to see them five years after I formally completed my dissertation fieldwork in 2013, I found that, as was the case for me, too, many things had changed in their lives, while many things had also stayed the same. What follows is a brief account of both the shifts and the continuities I observed.

THE SILVAS

In 2018, Angela was still living in the same two-bedroom apartment in Gifu with her second son, Marcelo, who was by now forty-three. Angela had closed her employment brokerage firm nearly two years before but, since she could not stand staying put or out of work, was traveling regularly to Yokohama to help her daughter Jessica with her new job there. Marcelo still worked at the same factory as before and, like his mother, was investing most of his savings in a sprawling, luxurious property they had purchased as a family in Presidente Prudente, in the interior of São Paulo State. Carlos, Angela's eldest son, who was now completing his residency as a pediatrician in Brazil, planned to move into the house first. Angela and Marcelo eventually planned to join him there, while Jessica remained firm in her desire to stay on in Japan.

Driving around Minokamo with Angela and Marcelo on Marcelo's day off, we took stock of the many Brazilian churches that had closed since I was last there in 2013. This made sense, given that the number of Brazilian residents in Japan had steadily decreased between 2007 and 2015. The recent uptake in Brazilian residents beginning in 2016 was still not obvious from the outside. Yet to Angela and Marcelo, it was nevertheless noteworthy. Like the staff I visited at the Okazaki International Center, Angela and Marcelo were both quick to point out how Brazilians were once again coming or returning to Japan to work.

Dropping in at the same small Chinese restaurant we used to regularly eat at together—the tables were still as sticky, I noted, and the spring rolls and fried shrimp still as greasy and delicious—our conversation soon turned to the future, as it was apt to whenever Angela or Marcelo reflected on their current situation in Japan. Angela explained that she had not yet returned to Brazil because she wanted her eldest son Carlos to settle into his medical practice there first. Marcelo concurred: "I don't want to die alone in Japan, so I'll move when my Mom does, but first I've got to help Carlos out financially, keep sending him money until he's established." When I inquired as to how much Carlos really needed help financially at this point, Angela clarified that it was not just a matter of keeping up with basic needs, it was also about keeping up appearances: "You know how it is, when you're a doctor, everyone expects you to be of a certain standing, to participate in social events, spend money on nice clothes, outings. . . . We've got to send him a lot so he and his wife and daughter can keep up with the people they're surrounded by." Besides wishing to stay in Japan with Marcelo and thereby support Carlos not only in his professional but also his class and status aspirations, Angela hinted at another reason she had not yet returned to Brazil despite having closed her employment brokerage firm two years before: "I've always worked," she said, "I've always been independent. I can't imagine just being a well-to-do lady (*madame*) at home, taking care of grandchildren or something." In other words, although Angela had technically achieved all that she needed in order to comfortably retire in Brazil, Japan still offered her a sense of purpose and productivity that she was hesitant to give up.

As for Marcelo, he too hinted at other reasons why a return to Brazil was not an immediate priority: "To my childhood friends there, I'm dead socially. Meaning that I'm not married, I don't own property of my own, I don't have a profession. As long as I stay here, though, at least I'm not in debt, and I can pay my bills." Much like I remembered from the last time I had seen him, Marcelo continued to spend most of his time outside work sleeping and browsing social media from home. "I really don't go out anymore," he said, "what would be the point of that?"

While Marcelo's day-to-day life had stayed much the same, his sister Jessica's had changed more significantly. In early 2014, she moved to Yokohama to take a job as an interpreter and assistant to Brazilian professional soccer players. Around the same time, she also began a long-distance undergraduate degree in English and Portuguese from a private Brazilian university, UNIP (Universidade Paulista). When I saw her again in 2018, shortly before she turned forty, she was only a few exams away from completing the degree.

Most of her coursework for UNIP was online, but she made occasional trips to the university's branch office in Hamamatsu, as well as to Nagoya and Tōkyō for sit-down exams. Although she did not live near any classmates, she communicated regularly with other students in her program in both Japan and Brazil via WhatsApp. Still, Jessica found the structure of the distance degree challenging: "I was really discouraged and wanted to quit, I didn't really know anyone, and I wasn't integrated. Distance degrees are much harder than when you study in person, there's no one to ask questions to," she explained. However, one classmate in particular, a Brazilian woman in her thirties who lived in Nagoya and had spent many years working in factories and pachinko parlors in Japan, encouraged Jessica to stay in the program on the many occasions that she considered dropping out: "We studied together online, via video or voice chat until late at night, and she really kept me motivated," Jessica explained.

Why had Jessica decided, well into her thirties, to pursue an online university degree from Brazil while continuing to work and live in Japan?

> Because you never know what tomorrow will bring, what you'll need. A diploma will give me more independence to do what I want to do. I didn't get a job I applied for at Mitsubishi in 2012 because I didn't have an undergraduate degree. And I couldn't move up any further in my job at the international center, even though I passed the 1-kyū [highest level] of the Japanese-Language Proficiency Test [JLPT][2] that year. I can't stop, I have to keep evolving somehow.

Whether or not an online degree from Brazil will ultimately help Jessica move into different lines of work in either Japan or Brazil is an open question. For now, she appears relatively satisfied with her interpreting job in Yokohama, which she obtained without a university degree:

> I like that in this job I'm always learning. I don't just translate literally (*chokuyaku*) between Japanese and Portuguese. I have to translate in a way that is culturally acceptable to both sides, the Brazilian players and the Japanese bosses, so that they can see eye to eye and agree. I've found a niche for myself here. The Japanese respect me because I'm fluent and understand their culture, their customs. The Brazilian players respect me for the same reason.

In other words, with or without a university degree, Jessica feels uniquely qualified to carry out her current job. Unlike her brother Marcelo, who continues to work on a factory assembly line, she feels useful and respected in her work, even irreplaceable. This leads her to feel at home in Japan in ways that the rest of her family does not. Although she is unlikely to return to Brazil any time soon, the fact that she now has a university degree adds a perceived layer of security to her life should she seek out further job opportunities in either Japan or Brazil.

Finally, while Angela and Marcelo may not feel as at home or as mobile or integrated in Japan as Jessica does, they clearly have reasons other than economic for staying there. To them, life in Japan offers a relative independence and sense of purpose they are both afraid of losing should they return to Brazil. Thus, while they continue to foster and prepare for a possible future in Brazil, they extend their present in Japan indefinitely. In this way we see that, for the various members of the Silva family, living transnationally is not only—or necessarily—premised upon economic motivations or ethnic, cultural, or national ties but rather a desire to maximize the chances they have of feeling useful, valued, and productive within the various opportunity structures available to them in Japan and Brazil.

THE MATSUDAS

When I visited them again in 2018, the Matsudas were still living in Okazaki. Elio, who had lost his job at a factory in 2011 and tried various lines of work since then, was now working in real estate specifically targeting Brazilian customers, and Marcia still worked on a year-to-year contract at the local city hall translating for and assisting Brazilian residents in their transition to life in Japan. Elio and Marcia picked me up one evening to go to an okonomiyaki restaurant for dinner, briefly dropping by their house on the way. I noticed the potted plants outside their door this time—*arruda, espada de São Jorge, comigo ninguém pode*—all of them typical house plants in Brazil. Takuya, their youngest son, was now eighteen. We caught him just as he was waking up to prepare for the night shift at a nearby textile factory where he had started working shortly after finishing public Japanese high school a few months earlier. He stumbled groggily out of his bedroom to munch on a dinner of *onigiri* (Japanese rice balls) that Elio had prepared for him.

Even though Takuya had been in the academic track of high school, aimed at students planning to attend university,[3] he let his teachers know that he planned to work right after graduating, and they took him out of the entrance examination preparation that his classmates typically had to go through. Elio and Marcia were happy that, unlike their daughters, their youngest child had graduated from high school; however, they did not push him to continue with his studies. As Marcia explained, Takuya was diagnosed with a mild form of autism in middle school, and he had always struggled with academics. "Also, he was used to getting just a few thousand yen of pocket money from us, so you can imagine how exciting it was for him to suddenly be earning all this

3

money at the factory. We didn't want to pay for him to go to university if he wasn't really that interested anyway," she clarified further.

When we arrived at the restaurant, Elio and Marcia's daughters, Sayuri and Tomoko, were already there with their partners. Sayuri, now in her early thirties, had a three-year-old daughter bouncing on her knee. Since the last time I saw them, Sayuri and her partner Rafael had bought a house not far from Elio and Marcia, and they were both still working in a nearby factory. Tomoko, now twenty-eight, was sitting next to her new Japanese-Brazilian boyfriend, Alex. "They're stuck to each other like glue," Elio laughed, pointing out how affectionate this "Brazilian relationship" had made his middle daughter. It was my first time meeting Alex, and I soon gathered that he had been moving back and forth between Japan and Brazil over the past ten years and that he was now working in a factory near Okazaki.

Tomoko, for her part, was currently working as a bookkeeper for a Japanese employment brokerage firm, a job she had secured during a period of unemployment thanks to a course she took for free at Hello Work, a government employment service center. Like her sister Sayuri, she spoke primarily in Japanese while her partner responded to her in Portuguese. Now, though, she seemed to understand quite a bit more Portuguese than when I had last seen her, likely as a result of her relationship with Alex. After dinner, as we stood around in the parking lot saying good night, I could not help but note that Tomoko hugged and kissed me in a typically Brazilian manner, as opposed to the light bowing I was accustomed to from her in previous years.

As I learned from further conversations with the Matsudas that summer, everyone in the family had kept both their Japanese and Brazilian passports up to date in the years since I last saw them, although no one had used their Brazilian passports for anything of note. "But we're still Brazilian so at least we have a way of escaping in case things get worse with North Korea," Elio joked, referring to the escalating tensions that resulted after North Korea launched a ballistic missile over Japan in the summer of 2017 (Choe & Sanger 2017). In Takuya's case, because he had retained Brazilian citizenship and was now of voting age for the first time, he was required to vote in the upcoming 2018 Brazilian presidential elections in order to comply with Brazilian law. "We registered him to vote but he literally has no idea who to vote for," his parents laughed, amused at the fact that their son, who was born and raised entirely in Japan and was in fact now a Japanese citizen, had to choose between Brazilian presidential candidates he did not have the faintest idea about. Thus, the Matsudas continued to live their lives as dual citizens, maintaining just enough legal connection to Brazil to safeguard their status as citizens there, while going about their day-to-day lives in Japan with the peace of mind that Japanese citizenship afforded them.

Still, I wondered, had anything significantly changed for the Matsudas in the years since they had naturalized to Japanese citizenship? The answer, I found, was by and large: no. Certainly in terms of occupational or socio-economic mobility, Japanese citizenship had not made much of a difference for them. Elio and Marcia were still working in temporary positions tied to the local *dekasegi* community, as were their two daughters Sayuri and Tomoko. Even Takuya, who, of the various immediate family members, had progressed the furthest in the Japanese educational system, was now working in the same kind of factory work his parents had first come to Japan for. While Japanese citizenship may have guaranteed the Matsudas a sense of security and a degree of legal capital that other Brazilians in Japan generally do not have (e.g., the right to vote, an easier time taking out loans, and visa-free travel to many countries around the world), still it did not noticeably affect their cultural or social capital. Furthermore, since Elio and Marcia's children could already choose to pass as Japanese based on their linguistic and cultural know-how, their names, and their appearance as ethnically Japanese, naturalizing to Japanese citizenship made little to no difference in terms of how they were treated in day-to-day interactions with majority Japanese.

Naturalization rates remain low among foreign residents of Japan, especially for "newcomer" minority groups such as Brazilians of Japanese descent. According to figures from the Japanese Ministry of Justice, between 1952 and 2017, of the approximately 500,000 foreigners who naturalized Japanese, nearly three-quarters of them were descendants of former Korean colonial subjects; naturalization in Japan today occurs primarily among those of Korean and Chinese ancestry (Ramos 2018). For the few Brazilians such as the Matsudas who do naturalize to Japanese citizenship, the decision has primarily to do with affirming one's sense of belonging in Japan, without necessarily forfeiting one's rights and privileges in Brazil. Even if, going forward, a greater number of Brazilian residents in Japan begin naturalizing as Japanese, their social acceptance and mobility there will have much more to do with factors such as ethnic background and appearance, cultural and linguistic habitus, educational trajectories, and occupational status than it will with the state of their citizenship(s).

THE PEREIRAS

Landing in Campo Grande in August 2018, I found the city sprinkled in pink ipé flowers in much the same way that cherry blossoms blanket Japan every spring. The Pereiras were now living a block away from their previous house in a building still under construction. Wania and Walter had decided to rent out their older property and divide the new building they had bought into two apartments, one for them and their youngest daughter Raquel, and the other for their oldest daughter Stefanie to live in together with her husband Kenichi and their two young daughters. In the building adjacent to the new family home, Stefanie and Kenichi now owned and ran an ice cream and açaí parlor they had opened three years earlier with savings from Japan.

While the Pereiras in many ways considered their return to Brazil in 2012 to be "for good," several members of the family had in fact continued to move back and forth to Japan for work in the years since. Walter, for example, had gone to work in Japan again for several months in 2015, with the intention of saving more money for retirement. Because Wania did not wish to join him there, however, he soon returned to Brazil and to his job shelving and stocking goods at a local grocery store in Campo Grande. Since I last saw her in 2012, Raquel had also been back to Japan to work. In her case, she spent two and a half years living with an aunt (one of Wania's sisters) in Komaki, Aichi while working in a factory nearby. During that time, she was able to renew her permanent visa and, although she preferred the "easiness" (*facilidade*) of life in Japan, ended up returning to Brazil in order to be near her parents again. Since returning again to Campo Grande, she spent most of her time working at her older sister Stefanie's ice cream and açaí parlor and studying for the Brazilian equivalent of a GED. More than anything, she was now dreaming of how to be closer to her *sansei* boyfriend whom she had met through a missionary course she took together with Walter when she came back most recently from Japan, and who lived hundreds of miles away in the city of Campinas.

Although other members of the Pereira family had not returned to Japan for work in recent years, each of Wania and Walter's three sons had also been back at least once since 2012, either to renew their permanent visa or to pursue religious activities there. In fact, when I visited the Pereiras in Campo Grande again in 2018, Jefferson was in Japan at the time in order to renew his permanent visa. Cleber, too, who had now been working for several years in a relatively stable administrative position in Campinas, São Paulo State, had returned to Japan just the year before to renew his permanent visa. Finally, William, who had since married a non-Nikkei Brazilian and was living with her near Curitiba, in the state of Paraná, planned to return to Japan the following year to renew his own permanent visa. William had also been back to Japan once in 2016, in order to lead an Evangelical mission there for several weeks. Wania and Walter had joined him there at the time, too, though only for as long as the mission lasted.

Of the Pereira children, only the eldest daughter Stefanie had not returned at all to Japan since 2012, whether for work or otherwise. As a result, unlike her four siblings, she had lost her permanent visa there. "I have no intention of going back to Japan anyway," she explained while scooping a heavy cup of ice cream for me from behind the counter of her small business. "It's easier to make money there, but we've got our shop now, and the kids are happy in school here, they'll have more opportunities if they stay in Brazil, I think."

Despite the fact that none of them were currently working in or planning to work in Japan, Wania and Walter's other four children had made sure to return to Japan often enough over the years to keep their permanent visas there up to date. In a sense, this was a similar strategy to what the Matsudas had done; even though they did not necessarily plan to move back to Brazil, still the Matsudas kept their Brazilian citizenship and legal paperwork there in order. This allowed them the added security of an exit option, should they need or wish to leave Japan for some reason. Similarly, the Pereira children, though they were all based in Brazil now, took precautions so as not to cut their official ties with Japan. This allowed them the possibility of an easier entry option to Japan, should they ever decide to reside there again—as Raquel had already done, for example, as recently as 2016.

Wania Pereira, meanwhile, had let her permanent residency in Japan wane. She worked in book keeping at the same grocery store in Campo Grande where her husband Walter was employed, and when I asked her about retirement plans, she replied: "God hasn't revealed what I will do yet. But who knows, I may go work in Japan again if it means I can work for God in some way, or else use the money I make there to help my children." Despite the fact that she had no concrete plans or intentions of ever returning to Japan for work, still she understood it to be a potential future option even though she was now nearing the age of sixty.

Thus, just as the Silvas and the Matsudas continued to maintain ties and possible entry/exit options in both Japan and Brazil, so did the Pereiras. For all three families, living transnationally was an ongoing process, one that involved a continuous negotiation of the social, institutional, and aspirational landscapes spanning Japan and Brazil. As their stories show, the *dekasegi* movement between these two countries is far from over, and what may one day appear to be permanent settlement in Japan or a final return to Brazil can easily change the next. Similarly, Japanese-ness and Brazilian-ness constantly shift and overlap, as opposed to being fixed or discrete identities. Now that a "culture of migration" (Massey et al. 1993) is firmly in place between Japan and Brazil, formed out of legal and economic but also social, familial, and religious conduits, it is unlikely that vicissitudes in the global economy or environmental catastrophes such as Fukushima will bring this back-and-forth movement to an immediate halt. *Dekasegi* and their families will continue living transnationally for the foreseeable future, tracing and retracing the various routes enabled by their roots.

NOTES

1. Numbers are drawn from the Immigration Bureau of Japan and Japan's Ministry of Justice websites, and include Brazilians born in Japan who have not naturalized to Japanese citizenship. Naturalization rates among Brazilians in Japan are still low, and—unlike the case of Zainichi Koreans—do not account for a significant decrease in the number of registered Brazilian residents there. Note that at the time of writing, data was only available through the first half of 2018, whereas for previous years I have drawn from end-of-year data. Still, it is unlikely that Japan's new residency program—in effect since July 2018—for fourth-generation (or *yonsei*) Nikkeijin will draw large numbers of applicants due in part to its restrictive nature (see, for example, Toyama 2018).

2. The JLPT is a standardized Japanese language test that, like the TOEFL or IELTS tests for English, is used by potential employers or admissions officers to gauge proficiency among non-native speakers. As of 2009, the test has five levels, with Level 1 (or 1-kyū) being the highest.

3. As Yoshio Sugimoto (2014) succinctly summarizes, in Japan "high schools are divided into two main groups: those providing general education with the expectation that a significant proportion of their students will advance to universities and colleges, and those specializing in vocational education (such as for agriculture, industry, and commerce) on the assumption that their students will enter the job market of their specialization on completion of their studies" (127).

Bibliography

Adachi, Nobuko. 2006. "Theorizing Japanese Diaspora." In *Japanese Diasporas: Unsung Pasts, Conflicting Presents, and Uncertain Futures*, ed. Nobuko Adachi. 1–20. New York: Routledge.

Allison, Anne. 2013. *Precarious Japan*. Durham, NC: Duke University Press.

Althusser, Louis. 1971. *Lenin and Philosophy and Other Essays*. New York: Monthly Review Press.

Amit, Vered. 2014. "Inherited Multiple Citizenships: Opportunities, Happenstances and Improvisations among Mobile Young Adults." *Social Anthropology/Anthropologie Sociale* 22(4): 396–409.

Appadurai, Arjun. 1996. *Modernity at Large: Cultural Dimensions of Globalization*. Minneapolis: University of Minnesota Press.

Arakaki, Ushi. 2013. "Japanese Brazilians among Pretos-Velhos, Caboclos, Buddhist Monks, and Samurais: An Ethnographic Study of Umbanda in Japan." In *The Diaspora of Brazilian Religions*, ed. Cristina Rocha and Manuel A. Vásquez. 249–270. Leiden: Koninklijke Brill NV.

Aronsson, Anne. 2015. *Career Women in Contemporary Japan: Pursuing Identities, Fashioning Lives*. New York: Routledge Contemporary Japan Series.

Asakawa, Akihiro (浅川晃広). 2003.「在日外国人と帰化制度」 *(Naturalization and Foreigners in Japan)*. Tōkyō: Shinkansha.

"Asō Says Japan is Nation of 'One Race.'" 2005. *Japan Times*, 18 October 2005, accessed 1 March 2018. http://www.japantimes.co.jp/news/2005/10/18/national/aso-says-japan-is-nation-of-one-race/#.U-D-yYBdXZA.

Befu, Harumi. 2001. *Hegemony of Homogeneity: An Anthropological Analysis of Nihonjinron*. Melbourne: Trans Pacific Press.

Bennett, Tony. 2007. "Habitus Clivé: Aesthetics and Politics in the Work of Pierre Bourdieu." *New Literary History* 38(1): 201–228.

Blalock, Hubert M. 1967. *Toward a Theory of Minority Group Relations*. New York: Whiley.

Bloemraad, Irene, Anna Korteweg, and Gökçe Yurdakul. 2008. "Citizenship and Immigration: Multiculturalism, Assimilation, and Challenges to the Nation-State." *Annual Review of Sociology* (34): 153–179.

Boehm, Deborah. 2012. *Intimate Migrations: Gender, Family, and Illegality among Transnational Mexicans*. New York: NYU Press.

Bonacich, Edna. 1982. "A Theory of Middleman Minorities." In *Majority and Minority: The Dynamics of Race in American Life*, ed. Norman R. Yetman and C. Hoy Steele. 270–281. Boston: Allyn and Bacon.

Bonifacio, Glenda Tibe, and Vivienne S. M. Angeles. 2010. *Gender, Religion, and Migration: Pathways of Integration*. Lanham, MD: Rowman & Littlefield.

Borovoy, Amy. 2010. "What Color is Your Parachute? The Post-Degree Society." In *Social Class in Contemporary Japan: Structures, Sorting, and Strategies*, ed. Hiroshi Ishida and David H. Slater. 170–194. New York: Routledge.

Bourdieu, Pierre. 1977. *Outline of a Theory of Practice*. Cambridge: Cambridge University Press.

———. 1990. *Reproduction in Education, Society and Culture*. London: Sage Publications.

Brazilian Institute of Geography and Statistics (IBGE). 2010. "Censo 2010" (2010 Census), available at https://censo2010.ibge.gov.br/.

Brubaker, Rogers, and Frederick Cooper. 2000. "Beyond 'Identity'." *Theory and Society* 29:1–47.

Caldeira, Teresa. 2001. *City of Walls: Crime, Segregation, and Citizenship in São Paulo*. Berkeley: University of California Press.

Castles, Stephen, and Alastair Davidson. 2000. *Citizenship and Migration: Globalization and the Politics of Belonging*. New York: Routledge.

Castles, Stephen, Hein de Haas, and Mark J. Miller. 2014. *The Age of Migration: International Population Movements in the Modern World*, 5th edition. New York: The Guilford Press.

Chiavacci, David. 2016. "Migration and Integration Patterns of New Immigrants in Japan: Diverse Structures of Inequality." In *Social Inequality in Post-Growth Japan: Transformation During Economic and Demographic Stagnation*, ed. David Chiavacci and Carola Hommerich. 233–249. New York: Routledge.

Choe, Sang-Hun and David E. Sanger. 2017. "North Korea Fires Missile over Japan." *New York Times*, 28 August 2017, accessed 29 July 2019. https://www.nytimes.com/2017/08/28/world/asia/north-korea-missile.html.1

Choo, Hae Yeon. 2016. *Decentering Citizenship: Gender, Labor, and Migrant Rights in South Korea*. Stanford, CA: Stanford University Press.

Cohen, Robin. 1997. *Global Diasporas: An Introduction*. London: University College London Press.

Constable, Nicole. 1999. "At Home but Not at Home: Filipina Narratives of Ambivalent Returns." *Cultural Anthropology* 12(2): 203–228.

Conway, Dennis, Robert B. Potter, and Godfrey St. Bernard. 2008. "Dual Citizenship or Dual Identity? Does 'Transnationalism' Supplant 'Nationalism' Among Returning Trinidadians?" *Global Networks* 8(4): 373–397.

Cordero-Guzmán, Robert C. Smith, and Ramón Grosfoguel. 2001. *Migration, Transnationalization, and Race in a Changing New York*. Philadelphia, PA: Temple University Press.

Cresswell, Tim. 2010. "Towards a Politics of Mobility." *Environment and Planning D: Society and Space* 28(1): 17–31.

Daniels, Roger. 1988. *Asian America: Chinese and Japanese in the United States Since 1850*. Seattle: University of Washington Press.

Dikötter, Frank. 1992. *The Discourse of Race in Modern China*. Stanford, CA: Stanford University Press.

DiMaggio, Paul. 1979. "Review Essay: On Pierre Bourdieu." *American Journal of Sociology* 84(6): 1460–1474.

Duany, Jorge. 2011. *Blurred Borders: Transnational Migration between the Hispanic Caribbean and the United States*. Chapel Hill: The University of North Carolina Press.

Endoh, Toake. 2009. *Exporting Japan: Politics of Emigration to Latin America*. Champaign: University of Illinois Press.

Faier, Lieba. 2009. *Intimate Encounters: Filipina Women and the Remaking of Rural Japan*. Berkeley: University of California Press.

Faist, Thomas. 2007. "Introduction: The Shifting Boundaries of the Political." In *Dual Citizenship in Global Perspective: From Unitary to Multiple Citizenship*. 1–23. Basingstoke: Palgrave Macmillan.

Ferguson, James. 2006. *Global Shadows*. Durham, NC: Duke University Press.

Fischer, Edward. 2014. *The Good Life: Aspiration, Dignity, and the Anthropology of Wellbeing*. Stanford, CA: Stanford University Press.

Fiset, Louis, and Gail M. Nomura. 2005. *Nikkei in the Pacific Northwest: Japanese Americans and Japanese Canadians in the Twentieth Century*. Seattle: University of Washington Press.

Foster, James Eric, Suman Seth, Michael Lokshin, and Zurab Sajaia. 2013. *Unified Approach to Measuring Poverty and Inequality: Theory and Practice*. The World Bank: World Bank Publications.

Foucault, Michel. 1995 [1975]. *Discipline and Punish: The Birth of the Prison*. New York: Vintage Books.

Freston, Paul. 2001. *Evangelicals and Politics in Asia, Africa and Latin America*. Cambridge: Cambridge University Press.

———. 2008. *Evangelical Christianity and Democracy in Latin America*. New York: Oxford University Press.

Freyre, Gilberto. 2003 [1933]. *Casa-Grande e Senzala: Formação da Família Brasileira Sob o Regime da Economia Patriarcal* (The Masters and the Slaves: A Study in the Development of Brazilian Civilization). Recife: Fundação Gilberto Freyre.

Friedman, Sara. 2015. *Exceptional States: Chinese Immigrants and Taiwanese Sovereignty*. Berkeley: University of California Press.

Fujiwara, Noriko (藤原法子). 2008. 「トランスローカルコミュニティー：越境する子ども・家族・女性・エスニックスクール」 *(Translocal Community: Transborder Children/Family/Women/Ethnic Schools)*. Tōkyō: Harvestsha.

Fukuoka, Yasunori. 2000. *Lives of Young Koreans in Japan*. Melbourne: TransPacific Press.

Funakoshi, Minami. 2017. "Foreigners in Japan Face Significant Levels of Discrimination, Survey Shows." *Reuters*, March 30, 2017, accessed March 7, 2018. https://www.reuters.com/article/us-japan-discrimination-foreign/foreigners-in-japan-face-significant-levels-of-discrimination-survey-shows-idUSKBN1720GP.

Gladney, Dru. 1998. "Introduction: Making and Marking Majorities." In *Making Majorities: Constituting the Nation in Japan, Korea, China, Malaysia, Fiji, Turkey, and the United States*. 1–9. Stanford, CA: Stanford University Press.

Glick Schiller, Nina. 1999. "Transmigrants and Nation-States: Something Old and Something New in the U.S. Immigrant Experience." In *The Handbook of International Migration: The American Experience*, ed. Charles Hirschman, Philip Kasinitz, and Josh DeWind. 94–119. New York: Russell Sage Foundation.

Glick Schiller, Nina, Linda Basch, and Cristina Szanton-Blanc. 1992. *Towards a Transnational Perspective on Migration: Race, Class, Ethnicity, and Nationalism Reconsidered*, ed. Nina Glick Schiller, Linda Basch, and Cristina Szanton-Blanc. New York: New York Academy of Sciences.

Goodman, Roger. 1990. *Japan's 'International Youth': The Emergence of a New Class of Schoolchildren*. Oxford: Clarendon Press.

Graburn, Nelson, John Ertl, and Kenji Tierney. 2008. *Multiculturalism in the New Japan: Crossing the Boundaries Within*. New York: Berghahn Books.

Green, Paul. 2010. "Generation, Family and Migration: Young Brazilian Factory Workers in Japan." *Ethnography* 11(4): 515–532.

———. 2012. "Explorations of Difference in a Homogenous Field: Intermarriage and Mixedness amongst Brazilian Migrants in Japan." *Anthropological Notebooks* 18(2): 17–25.

Haines, David, Makito Minami, and Shinji Yamashita. 2007. "Transnational Migration in East Asia: Japan in Comparative Focus." *International Migration Review* 41(4): 963–967.

Harrison, Simon. 2003. "Cultural Difference as Denied Resemblance: Reconsidering Nationalism and Ethnicity Author(s)." *Comparative Studies in Society and History* 45(2): 343–361.

Hidaka, Tomoko. 2006. *Corporate Warriors or Company Animals? An Investigation of Japanese Salaryman Masculinities across Three Generations*. Dissertation thesis, School of Social Science, University of Adelaide, 253 pages.

Hirschman, Charles. 2004. "The Role of Religion in the Origins and Adaptations of Immigrant Groups." *International Migration Review* 38(3): 1206–1233.

Hobsbawm, Eric, and Terence Ranger. 1983. *The Invention of Tradition*. Cambridge: Cambridge University Press.

Htun, Tin Tin. 2012. "Social Identities of Minority Others in Japan." *Japan Forum* 24(1): 1–22.

Hurst, Daniel. 2017. "Japan Racism Survey Reveals One in Three Foreigners Experience Discrimination." *The Guardian*, March 31, 2017, accessed March 7, 2018. https://www.theguardian.com/world/2017/mar/31/japan-racism-survey-reveals-one-in-three-foreigners-experience-discrimination.

Iguchi, Yasushi (井口泰). 2007. 「動き出したわが国の外国人政策改革の動向と課題—東アジアの共同体形成を視野に」(Trends and Challenges of the Foreign Policy Reforms Getting Underway in Japan—With a View Toward Forming a Community in East Asia). *Int'lecowk* 62(9): 7–18.

Ikeuchi, Suma. 2017. "Back to the Present: The 'Temporal Tandem' of Migration and Conversion among Pentecostal Nikkei Brazilians in Japan." *Ethnos: Journal of Anthropology* 82(4): 758–783.

Ishi, Angelo. 2011. 「在外ブラジル人としての在日ブラジル人—ディアスポラ意識の生成過程」*(Brazilians in Japan as Overseas Brazilians—the Process of Generating Diasporic Consciousness)*. Tōkyō: Ochanomizu Shobō.

Ishida, Hiroshi, and David Slater. 2010. *Social Class in Contemporary Japan: Structures, Sortings, and Strategies.* New York: Routledge.

Ishikawa, Eunice Akemi. 2005. 「家族は子供の教育にどうかかわるか」(Family Involvement in Children's Education). In 「外国人の子供と日本の教育」*(The Children of Foreigners and Education in Japan)*, eds. Takashi Miyajima (宮島喬) and Haruo Ōta (太田晴雄). 77–96. Tōkyō: University of Tōkyō: Press.

Iyall Smith, Keri, and Patricia Leavy. 2008. *Hybrid Identities: Theoretical and Empirical Examinations.* Leiden: Brill.

Jackson, Michael. 2013. *The Wherewithal of Life: Ethics, Migration, and the Question of Well-Being.* Berkeley: University of California Press.

Jye, Chen Tsung, David Jye Yuan Shyu, and Antonio José Bezerra de Menezes Jr. 2009. "Os Immigrantes Chineses no Brasil e a Sua Língua" (Chinese Immigrants in Brazil and Their Language). *Synergies Brésil* (7): 57–64.

Kajita, Takamichi (梶田孝道), Kiyoto Tanno (丹野清人), and Naoto Higuchi (樋口直人). 2005. 「顔の見えない定住化—日系ブラジル人と国家・市場移民ネットワーク」*(Invisible Residents: Japanese Brazilians Vis-à-Vis the State, the Market, and the Immigrant Network)*. Nagoya: Nagoya Daigaku Shuppankai.

Kariya, Takehiko. 2010. "From Credential Society to 'Learning Capital' Society." In *Social Class in Contemporary Japan: Structures, Sorting and Strategies*, ed. Hiroshi Ishida and David H. Slater. 87–113. London: Routledge.

Kashiwazaki, Chikako. 2000. "Citizenship in Japan: Legal Practice and Contemporary Development." In *From Migrants to Citizens: Membership in a Changing World*, ed. T. Alexander Aleinikoff and Douglas Klusmeyer. 434–471. Washington, DC: Carnegie Endowment for International Peace.

Kearney, Michael. 1995. "The Local and the Global: the Anthropology of Globalization and Transnationalism." *Annual Review of Anthropology* 24: 547–565.

Kelly, William. 1993. "Finding a Place in Metropolitan Japan: Ideologies, Institutions, and Everyday Life." In *Postwar Japan as History*, ed. Andrew Gordon. 189–238. Berkeley: University of California Press.

Kim, Bumsoo. 2006. "From Exclusion to Inclusion? The Legal Treatment of 'Foreigners' in Contemporary Japan." *Immigrants & Minorities* 24(1): 51–73.

Kim, M. 1995. "Zainichi Kankokujin no Gakureki to Shokugyo [Education and Occupation of Korean Japan]. *Annals of Human Sciences* 16: 39–56.

Kim, Yondal (金英達). 1990. 「在日朝鮮人の帰化」 *(The Naturalization of Zainichi Koreans)*. Tōkyō: Akashi Shoten.

King, Angela. 2004. "The Prisoner of Gender: Foucault and the Disciplining of the Female Body." *Journal of International Women's Studies* 5(2): 29–39.

Komai, Hiroshi (駒井洋). 1999. 「日本の外国人移民」 *(Foreign Migrants in Contemporary Japan)*. Tōkyō: Akashi Shoten.

Kondo, Atsushi. 2002. "The Development of Immigration Policy in Japan." *Asian and Pacific Migration Journal* 11(4): 415–436.

———. 2005. "Migration and Law in Japan." *Asia & the Pacific Policy Studies* 2(1): 155–168.

Kymlicka, Will. 1995. *Multicultural Citizenship: A Liberal Theory of Minority Rights*. Oxford: Oxford University Press.

Landman, Karina, and Martin Schönteich. 2002. "Urban Fortresses: Gated Communities as a Reaction to Crime." *African Security Review* 11(4): 71–85.

Le Bail, Hélène. 2012. *"Migrants Chinois Hautement Qualifiés au Japon: Mobilité Transnationale et Identité Citoyenne des Résidents Chinois au Japon" (Highly Qualified Chinese Migrants in Japan: Transnational Mobility and Citizen Identity among Chinese Residents in Japan)*. Paris: Les Indes Savantes.

LeBlanc, Robin. 1999. *Bicycle Citizens: The Political World of the Japanese Housewife*. Berkeley: University of California Press.

Lesser, Jeffrey. 1999. *Negotiating National Identity: Immigrants, Minorities, and the Struggle for Ethnicity in Brazil*. Durham, NC: Duke University Press.

———. 2003. *Searching for Home Abroad: Japanese Brazilians and Transnationalism*, ed. Jeffrey Lesser. Durham, NC: Duke University Press.

———. 2013. *Immigration, Ethnicity, and National Identity in Brazil: 1808 to the Present*. New York: Cambridge University Press.

Levitt, Peggy. 1998. "Social Remittances: Migration Driven Local-Level Forms of Cultural Diffusion." *International Migration Review* 32(4): 926–948.

———. 2003. "You Know, Abraham was Really the First Immigrant: Religion and Transnational Migration." *International Migration Review* 27(3): 847–873.

———. 2007. *God Needs No Passport: How Immigrants are Changing the American Religious Landscape*. New York: New Press.

Levitt, Peggy, and Nina Glick Schiller. 2004. "Conceptualizing Simultaneity: A Transnational Social Field Perspective on Society." *International Migration Review* (38): 2–39.

Linger, Daniel. 2001. *No One Home: Brazilian Selves Remade in Japan*. Stanford, CA: Stanford University Press.

Liu-Farrer, Gracia. 2013. "Chinese Newcomers in Japan: Migration Trends, Profiles, and the Impact of the 2011 Earthquake." *Asian And Pacific Migration Journal* 22(2): 231–257.

Loveman, Mara, Jeronimo O. Muniz, and Stanley R. Bailey. 2012. "Brazil in Black and White? Race Categories, the Census, and the Study of Inequality." *Ethnic and Racial Studies* 35(8): 1–18.

Low, Morris. 2012. "Physical Anthropology in Japan: The Ainu and the Search for the Origins of the Japanese." *Current Anthropology* 53(S5): S57-S68.

Luhrmann, Tanya Marie, Howard Nusbaum, and Ronald Thisted. 2010. "The Absorption Hypothesis: Hearing God in Evangelical Christianity." *American Anthropologist* 112(1): 66–78.

Mahdavi, Pardis. 2016. *Crossing the Gulf: Love and Family in Migrants Lives*. Stanford, CA: Stanford University Press.

Maia, Suzana. 2012. *Transnational Desires: Brazilian Erotic Dancers in New York*. Nashville, TN: Vanderbilt University Press.

Manzenreiter, Wolfram. 2017. "Squared Diaspora: Representations of the Japanese Diaspora Across Time and Space." *Contemporary Japan* 29(2): 106–116.

Marcelli, Enrico, et al. 2009. *(In)Visible (Im)Migrants: The Health and Socioeconomic Integration of Brazilians in Metropolitan Boston*. San Diego, CA: Center for Behavioral and Community Health Studies, SDSU.

Marcus, George. 1995. "Ethnography in/of the World System: The Emergence of Multi-sited Ethnography." *Annual Review of Anthropology* 24: 95–117.

Margolis, Maxine. 2013. *Goodbye Brazil: Emigrés from the Land of Soccer and Samba*. Madison: University of Wisconsin Press.

Massey, Douglas S., J. Arango, G. Hugo, A. Kouaouci, A. Pellegrino, and J. E. Taylor. 1993. "Theories of International Migration: A Review and Appraisal." *Population and Development Review* 19: 431–433.

McCowan, Tristan. 2004. "The Growth of Private Higher Education in Brazil: Implications for Equity and Quality." *Journal of Education Policy* 19(4): 452–472.

Minami, Thiago Amaral. 2012. "The Social Costs of Labor Migration and Global Recession on Brazilian Schools in Japan." In *The Immigration & Education Nexus: Comparative and International Education* (Volume 12), ed. David Urias. 227–242. Rotterdam: SensePublishers.

Ministry of Justice, Japan. 「在留外国人統計」 (Foreign Resident Statistics), available at http://www.moj.go.jp/housei/toukei/toukei_ichiran_touroku.html.

Mino, Tamaki. 2008. *Anatomy of Ijime (Bullying) within Japanese Schools*. Dissertation thesis, University of Queensland, 190 pages.

Monteiro, Tânia. 2010. "Lula Diz Que o Brasil Está Enfrentando Países Ricos" (Lula Says that Brazil is Confronting Rich Countries). In *Estadão*, April 29, 2010, accessed July 29, 2014. http://economia.estadao.com.br/noticias/geral,lula-diz-que-brasil-esta-enfrentando-paises-ricos,15965e.

Morita, Kyoko (森田京子). 2007. 「子どもたちのアイデンティティーポリティックス：ブラジル人のいる小学校のエスノグラフィー」 (*Identity Politics of Children: Ethnography at an Elementary School with Brazilian Children*). Tōkyō: Shinyōsha.

Morris-Suzuki, Tessa. 1998. *Re-Inventing Japan: Time, Space, Nation*. New York: East Gate.

Motani, Yoko. 2002. "Towards a More Just Educational Policy for Minorities in Japan: The Case of Korean Ethnic Schools." *Comparative Education* 38(2): 225–237.

Murphy-Shigematsu, Stephen. 1993. "Multiethnic Japan and the Monoethnic Myth." *MELUS* 18(4): 63–80.

———. 2012. *When Half is Whole: Multiethnic Asian-American Identities*. Stanford, CA: Stanford University Press.

Naito, Takashi, and Uwe P. Gielen. 2005. "Bullying and Ijime in Japanese Schools." In *Violence in Schools: Cross-National and Cross-Cultural Perspectives*, ed. Florence Denmark et al. 169–190. New York: Springer Science and Business Media.

Nakamura, Karen. 2006. *Deaf in Japan: Signing and the Politics of Identity*. Ithaca, NY: Cornell University Press.

———. 2013. *A Disability of the Soul: An Ethnography of Schizophrenia and Mental Illness in Contemporary Japan*. Ithaca, NY: Cornell University Press.

Nishida, Mieko. 2017. *Diaspora and Identity: Japanese Brazilians in Brazil and Japan*. Honolulu: University of Hawaii Press.

O'Dougherty, Maureen. 2002. *Consumption Intensified: The Politics of Middle-Class Life in Brazil*. Durham and London: Duke University Press.

Ogbu, John, and Herbert D. Simons. 1998. "Voluntary and Involuntary Minorities: A Cultural-Ecological Theory of School Performance with Some Implications for Education." *Anthropology & Education Quarterly* 29(2): 155–188.

Oguma, Eiji (小熊英二). 1995.「単一民族神話の起源: 「日本人」の自画像の系譜」 *(The Origin of the Myth of Ethnic Homogeneity: The Genealogy of 'Japanese' Self-Images)*. Tōkyō: Shinyōsha.

———. 1998. 「日本人」の境界: 沖縄· アイヌ · 台湾· 朝鮮: 植民地支配から復帰運動まで」 *(The Boundaries of the 'Japanese': Okinawa, the Ainu, Taiwan, and Korea: From Colonial Domination to the Return Movement)*. Tōkyō: Shinyōsha.

Ohnuki-Tierney, Emiko. 1998. "Ch. 2: A Conceptual Model for the Historical Relationship Between the Self and the Internal and External Others." In *Making Majorities: Constituting the Nation in Japan, Korea, China, Malaysia, Fiji, Turkey, and the United States*. 31–51. Stanford, CA: Stanford University Press.

Okano, Kaori. 1993. *School to Work Transition in Japan*. Bristol: Longdunn Press.

———. 1997. "Third-Generation Koreans' Entry into the Workforce in Japan." *Anthropology & Education Quarterly* 28(4): 534–549.

Okubo, Yuko. 2009. "The Localization of Multicultural Education and the Reproduction of the 'Native Speaker' Concept in Japan." In *The Native Speaker Concept: Ethnographic Investigations of Native Speaker Effects*, ed. Neriko Musha Doerr. 101–134. Berlin: Walter de Gruyter GmbH & Co.

Okura Gagné, Nana. 2010. *Salarymen in Crisis? The Collapse of Dominant Ideologies and Shifting Identities of Salarymen in Metropolitan Japan*. Dissertation thesis, Yale University, 427 pages.

Olwig, Karen Fog. 2007. *Caribbean Journeys: An Ethnography of Migration and Home in Three Family Networks*. Durham, NC: Duke University Press.

Ong, Aihwa. 1999. *Flexible Citizenship: The Cultural Logics of Transnationality*. Durham, NC: Duke University Press.

Ortner, Sherry. 2005. "Subjectivity and Cultural Critique." *Anthropological Theory* 5(1): 31–52.

Peterson, Anna L., Manuel A. Vásquez, and Philip J. Williams. 2001. "Introduction: Christianity and Social Change in the Shadow of Globalization." In *Christianity, Social Change, and Globalization in the Americas*, ed. Anna L. Peterson, Manuel A. Vásquez, and Philip J. Williams. 1–22. New Brunswick, NJ: Rutgers University Press.

Pinho, Patricia de Santana. 2009. "White but Not Quite: Tones and Overtones of Whiteness in Brazil." *Small Axe* 29: 39–56.

Pollock, David C., and Ruth E. Van Reken. 2009 [2001]. *Third Culture Kids: Growing Up Among Worlds*. Boston, MA: Intercultural Press.

Quero, Hugo Córdova. 2008. "The Role of Religion in the Process of Adaptation of Brazilians of Japanese Ancestry to Japanese Society: The Case of the Roman Catholic Church." In *Sociedade Japonesa e Migrantes Brasileiros: Novos Caminhos na Formaçãao de Uma Rede de Pesquisadores* (Japanese Society and Brazilian Migrations: New Directions in the Formation of a Researchers Network), ed. Chiyoko Mita, Hugo Córdova Quero, Aaron Litvin, and Sumiko Haino. 79–90. Tōkyō: Centro de Estudos Lusófonos, Sofia University.

Quero, Hugo Córdova, and Rafael Shoji. 2014. *Transnational Faiths: Latin American Immigrants and their Religions in Japan*. Surrey: Ashgate Publishing.

Ramos, Ana Paula. 2018. "Em Busca do Passaporte Vermelho" (In Search of the Red Passport). *Alternativa*, July 12, 2018.

Reed-Danahay, Deborah. 2005. *Locating Bourdieu*. Bloomington: Indiana University Press.

Ribeiro, Darcy. 1995. *O Povo Brasileiro: A Formação e o Sentido do Brasil (The Brazilian People: The Formation and Meaning of Brazil)*. São Paulo: Companhia das Letras.

Rivas, Zelideth María. 2011. "Negotiating Mixed Race: Projection, Nostalgia, and the Rejection of Japanese-Brazilian Biracial Children." *Journal of Asian American Studies* 14(3): 361–388.

Roberts, Glenda. 1994. *Staying on the Line: Blue-Collar Women in Contemporary Japan*. Honolulu: University of Hawaii Press.

Rohlen, Thomas. 1983. *Japan's High Schools*. Berkeley: University of California Press.

Roth, Joshua. 2002. *Brokered Homeland: Japanese Brazilian Migrants in Japan*. Ithaca, NY: Cornell University Press.

———. 2007. "Adapting to Inequality: Negotiating Nikkei Identity in Contexts of Return." In *Creolization: History, Ethnography, Theory*, ed. Charles Stewart. 201–219. Walnut Creek, CA: Left Coast Press.

Rumbaut, Rubén G. 2012. "Generation 1.5, Educational Experiences of." In *Encyclopedia of Diversity in Education*, ed. James A. Banks. Thousand Oaks, CA: SAGE Publications.

Ryang, Sonia. 1997. *North Koreans in Japan: Language, Ideology and Identity*. Boulder, CO: Westview Press.

———. 2000. *Koreans in Japan: Critical Voices from the Margin*, ed. Sonia Ryang. London: Routledge.

Safran, William. 1991. "Diasporas in Modern Societies: Myths of Homeland and Return." *Diaspora: A Journal of Transnational Studies* 1(1): 83–99.

Sasaki, Elisa. 2009. *Ser ou Não Ser Japonês? A Construção da Identidade dos Brasileiros Descendentes de Japoneses no Contexto das Migrações Internacionais do Japão Contemporâneo* (To Be or Not to Be Japanese? Identity Construction of Nikkei-Brazilians in the Context of Contemporary Japan's International

Migration). Campinas: University of Campinas. Dissertation thesis, University of Campinas, 667 pages.

Saulny, Susan. 2011. "Black? White? Asian? More Young Americans Choose All of the Above." *New York Times*, January 29, 2011, accessed November 12, 2012. http://www.nytimes.com/2011/01/30/us/30mixed.html?pagewanted=1&_r=1&adxnnlx=1400084300-HRZHXQxaazqeHVYRqT2Gtg,&.

Schwartzman, Simon. 1999. "Fora de Foco: Diversidade e Identidades Etnicas no Brasil" (Out of Focus: Diversity and Ethnic Identities in Brazil). *Novos Estudos CEBRAP* (55): 83–96.

———. 2004. "Equity, Quality, and Relevance in Higher Education in Brazil." *Annals of the Brazilian Academy of Sciences* 76(1):173–188.

Sekiguchi, Tomoko (関口知子). 2003.「在日日系ブラジル人の子どもたち：異文化間に育つ子どものアイデンティティー形成」(Japanese-Brazilian Children in Japan: Identity Formation of Children Growing up Across Cultures). Tōkyō: Akashi Shoten.

Sellek, Yoko. 1997. "Nikkeijin: The Phenomenon of Return Migration." In *Japan's Minorities: The Illusion of Homogeneity*, ed. Michael Weiner. 178–210. London: Routledge.

Shaull, Richard, and Waldo César. 2000. *Pentecostalism and the Future of the Christian Churches: Promises, Limitations, Challenges*. Grand Rapids, MI: Wm. B. Eerdmans Publishing Co.

Sheringham, Olivia. 2013. *Transnational Religious Spaces: Faith and the Brazilian Migration Experience*. Basingstoke: Palgrave Macmillan.

Shoji, Rafael. 2004. "Reinterpretação do Budismo Chinês e Coreano no Brasil" (Reinterpretation of Chinese and Korean Buddhism in Brazil). *Revista de Estudos da Religião* (3): 74–87.

———. 2008. "Religiões entre Brasileiros no Japão: Conversão ao Pentecostalismo e Redefinição Etnica" (Religions Among Brazilians in Japan: Conversion to Pentecostalism and Ethnic Redefinition). *Revista de Estudos da Religião* 8(2):46–85.

Shoji, Rafael, and Frank Usarski. 2008. "Japanese Religions in Brazil. Introduction." *Japanese Journal of Religious Studies* 35(5): 1–12. Nagoya: Nanzan Institute for Religion and Culture.

Slater, David. 2010. "The 'New Working Class' of Urban Japan: Socialization and Contradiction from Middle School to the Labor Market." In *Social Class in Contemporary Japan: Structures, Sorting, and Strategies*, ed. Hiroshi Ishida and David H. Slater. 137–169. New York: Routledge.

Smith, Michael Peter, and Luis Eduardo Guarnizo. 1998. *Transnationalism from Below*. New Brunswick, NJ: Transaction Publishers.

Standing, Guy. 2012. "The Precariat: from Denizens to Citizens?" *Polity* 44(4): 588–608.

Sugimoto, Yoshio. 2014. "Diversity and Unity in Education." In *An Introduction to Japanese Society* (4th edition). 126–162. Cambridge: Cambridge University Press.

Sugino, Toshiko. 2008. *Nikkei Brazilians at a Brazilian School in Japan: Factors Affecting Language Decisions and Education*. Tōkyō: Keiō University Press.

Takato, Michiyo. 2009. "'Native Speaker' Status on Border-Crossing: The Okinawan Nikkei Diaspora, National Language, and Heterogeneity." In *The Native Speaker*

Concept: Ethnographic Investigations of Native Speaker Effects, ed. Neriko Musha Doerr. 83–100. Berlin: Walter de Gruyter GmbH & Co.

Takaya, Sachi (髙谷幸), Yukiko Omagari (大曲由起), Naoto Higuchi (樋口直人), and Itaru Kaji (鍛治致). 2013.「2005年国勢調査にみる在日外国人の仕事」(A Study on Zainichi Foreigners' Professions in the National Census of 2005). *Okuyama Daigaku Daigakuin Shakai Bunka Kagaku Kenkyūka Kiyō* 35: 39–58.

Takenaka, Ayumi. 2010. "How Ethnic Minorities Experience Social Mobility in Japan: an Ethnographic Study of Peruvian Migrants." In *Social Class in Contemporary Japan*, ed. Hiroshi Ishida and David Slater. 221–238. New York: Routledge.

Takenoshita, Hirohisa. 2010. "Circular Migration and Its Socioeconomic Consequences: The Economic Marginality among Japanese Brazilian Migrants in Japan." In *Asian Cities, Migrant Labor and Contested Spaces*. ed. Tai-Chee Wong and Jonathan Rigg. 156–174. London: Routledge.

Takenoshita, Hirohisa, Yoshimi Chitose, Shigehiro Ikegami, and Eunice Akemi Ishikawa. 2013. "Segmented Assimilation, Transnationalism, and Educational Attainment of Brazilian Migrant Children in Japan." *International Migration* 52(2): 84–99.

Tanno, Kiyoto (丹野清人). 1999.「在日ブラジル人の労働市場——業務請負業と日系ブラジル人労働者」(Zainichi Brazilians' Labor and Lives). *Ohara Shakai Mondai Kenkyu Zasshi* 487: 21–40.

"Teen Sues Ōsaka Pref. After School Forces Her to Dye Natural Brown Hair Black." 2017. *Mainichi Japan*, October 27, 2017, accessed October 18, 2018. https://mainichi.jp/english/articles/20171027/p2a/00m/0na/021000c.

"The Mortarboard Boom." 2012. *The Economist*, September 15, 2012, accessed August 6, 2014. http://www.economist.com/node/21562955.

Toma, Christiane Yuri. 2000. *A Experiência Feminina Dekassegui* (The Experience of Women Dekasegi). Londrina: Editora UEL.

Torresan, Angela. 2012. "A Middle Class Besieged: Brazilians' Motives to Migrate." *The Journal of Latin American and Caribbean Anthropology* 17(1): 110–130.

Toyama, Naoyuki. 2018. "Japanese-Brazilians Snub Tokyo's Diaspora Residency Program." *Nikkei Asian Review*, October 25, 2018, accessed July 12, 2019. https://asia.nikkei.com/Spotlight/Japan-immigration/Japanese-Brazilians-snub-Tokyo-s-diaspora-residency-program.

Tsing, Anna. 2005. *Friction: An Ethnography of Global Connection*. Princeton, NJ: Princeton University Press.

Tsuda, Takeyuki. 2003. *Strangers in the Ethnic Homeland: Japanese Brazilian Return Migration in Transnational Perspective*. New York: Columbia University Press.

———. 2009. "Japanese-Brazilian Ethnic Return Migration and the Making of Japan's Newest Immigrant Minority." In *Japan's Minorities: The Illusion of Homogeneity (Second Edition)*, ed. Michael Weiner. 206–227. New York: Routledge.

Tsumura, Kimihiro (津村公博), and Mayu Nakamura (中村真夕). 2011.「孤独なツバメたち：デカセギの子どもに生まれて」(Lonely Swallows: Living as the Children of Immigrant Workers). DVD: Hamamatsu Gakuin University.

Turner, Victor. 1974. *Dramas, Fields, and Metaphors: Symbolic Action in Human Society*. Ithaca, NY: Cornell University Press.

Urano, Edson. 2004. "Brazilian Migrants and Labour Flexibility: A Comparative Analysis of Japanese Subcontractor Companies." Paper presented at Industrial Relations in Europe Conference (IREC) 26–28 August 2004. Utrecht School of Governance, Netherlands.

Urano, Edson, and Lucia Yamamoto. 2008. "Social and Economic Support among Migrants and Families Left Behind in Transnational Contexts." *International Journal on Multicultural Societies (IJMS)* 10(2): 223–239.

Useem, Ruth. 1973. "Third Cultural Factors in Educational Change." In *Cultural Challenges to Education: The Influence of Cultural Factors in School Learning*, ed. C. S. Brembeck and W. H. Hill. 121–138. Lexington, MA: Lexington Books.

Vásquez, Manuel A. 2003. "Tracking Global Evangelical Christianity." *Journal of the American Academy of Religion* 71(1): 157–173.

———. 2009. "Beyond Homo Anomicus: Interpersonal Networks, Space, and Religion among Brazilians in Broward County." In *A Place to Be: Brazilian, Guatemalan, and Mexican Immigrants in Florida's New Destinations*, ed. Phillip J. Williams, Timothy J. Steigenga, and Manuel A. Vásquez. 33–56. New Brunswick, NJ: Rutgers University Press.

Wagatsuma, Hiroshi, and Arthur Rosett. 1986. "The Implications of Apology: Law and Culture in Japan and the United States." *Law & Society Review* 20(4):461–498.

Watarai, Tamaki. 2014. "Can a *Mestiça* be a *Haafu*? Japanese-Brazilian Female Migrants and the Celebration of Racial Mixing in Contemporary Japan." *Journal of Intercultural Studies* 24(6): 662–676.

Watson, Mark. 2014. *Japan's Ainu Minority in Tokyo: Diasporic Indigeneity and Urban Politics*. New York: Routledge.

Weiner, Michael. 1997. *Japan's Minorities: The Illusion of Homogeneity*. New York: Routledge.

White, Merry. 2003. "Taking Note of Teen Culture in Japan: Dear Diary, Dear Fieldworker." In *Doing Fieldwork in Japan*, ed. Theodore Bestor, Patricia Steinhoff, and Victoria Bestor. 21–35. Honolulu: University of Hawaii Press.

Willis, Paul. 1977. *Learning to Labor: How Working Class Kids Get Working Class Jobs*. New York: Columbia University Press.

Yamada, Masanobu (山田政信). 2011.「デカセギブラジル人の宗教生活 ：エスニックネットワークの繋留点としてのブラジル系プロテスタント教会」(The Religious Life of Brazilian Dekasegi: The Role of a Brazilian Protestant Church in Socially Anchoring an Ethnic Network). In 「グローバル化の中で生きるとは：日系ブラジル人のトランスナショナルな暮らし」 (*What Does It Mean to Live in the Midst of Globalization? The Transnational Lives of Nikkei-Brazilians*), ed. Chiyoko Mita (三田千代子). 195–222. Tōkyō: Sophia University Press.

Yamanaka, Keiko. 1997. "Return Migration of Japanese Brazilian Women: Household Strategies and Search for the 'Homeland.'" In *Beyond Boundaries: Selected Papers on Refugees and Immigrants (5)*, ed. Diane Baxter and Ruth Krulfeld. 11–34. Arlington, VA: American Anthropological Association.

———. 2003. "Feminization of Japanese Brazilian Labor Migration to Japan." In *Searching for Home Abroad: Japanese Brazilians and Transnationalism*, ed. Jeffrey Lesser. 163–200. Durham, NC: Duke University Press.

Index

bounded community, 12
Bourdieu, Pierre, 116–17, 142n1
branca (white), 25–26, 171
Brazil, 8–10; East Asian immigrants
and their descendants, 171; economic
growth, 67; Japanese descent in,
12–13; National Census, 25, 84n16,
171, 204; population, 171, 204;
presidential elections of 2018, 214;
race/color categories, 25–26, 171;
state capitals in, 17–18n6; Third
World status, 67, 207; university
graduates, 51n7; *vestibular* university
entrance exam, 127, 131, 132–34
Brazilian Agricultural Research
Corporation (EMBRAPA), 204
Brazilian Institute of Geography and
Statistics (IBGE), 50n3, 84n16, 171
Brazilian Ministry of Education and
Culture (MEC), 119, *120*, 142n3
Brazilian print media in Japan, 64, 121,
123, 173
Brazilian residents in Japan, 8–10,
13–16; brokered lives, 55–57;
cultural norms, 187; middle-class
subjectivity, 66–69; naturalization,
96–103; negative minority status,
172; passing as Japanese, 104–105;
permanent residency, 87–88, 100–
101; population, 6, *9*, 145, 209, *210*;
religious practices, 171–72; return to
Brazil, 145–66; social (im)mobility,
34, 41–42, 49, 54, 69–74, 201–202
Brazilian-run enterprises, 12, 64, 115,
173
Brazilian schools in Japan, 118–20;
administrators' perspective, 126–27;
bus ride/transportation to, 123–24;
a day at, 124–25; factory work in
Japan, 134–39; mixed Japanese
and Brazilian schooling, 129–30;
possibilities and limitations, 127–39;
preparing students to return to Brazil,
132–34; profiles of students, 127–39;
uniform, 123; and working in Japan,
131–32

bridge between cultures, 21–27
Brokered Homeland (Roth), 195
brokered laborers, 55–57; ethnic
discrimination, 65–66, 72–73; factory
fight, 57–63; gender discrimination,
64–65; marginalization, 60; middle-
class subjectivity, 66–69; single
mothers, 74–80; social (im)mobility,
69–74
Brubaker, Rogers, 16
buchō (manager), 44
Buddhism, 22, 149, 171, 173
buki ni suru (use as a tool), 66
bullying, 22–24, 50n1, 93, 99, 103,
105, 128, 129–30, 134, 139; Jessica
Silva's experience, 22–24
Burajirukei Nihonjin (Brazilian-
Japanese), 107
Burakumin, 3, 5
bus ride/transportation to Brazilian
schools, 123–24
butajiru-jin (insult), 21

caipira (country-style), 169, 193n1
Caldeira, Teresa, 51n11
calor humano (human warmth), 130
Canada, 1–2, 10
capoeira demonstrations, 169
carambola (starfruit), 154
Castles, Stephen, 2, 83n4, 84n20, 199
Catholics. *See* Roman Catholic
Center of Information and Support
for Workers Overseas (CIATE), 13,
146
César, Waldo, 170
Chiavacci, David, 7, 8, 9, 11, 83n10,
101, 102
Chinese: in Japan, 5, 6, 7, 100, 113n9;
in Taiwan, 50–51n5, 208n1
Choe, Sang-Hun, 214
chokuyaku (literal translation), 212
Choo, Hae Yeon, 1
Chubu International Airport, 29, 35
churrasco (Brazilian BBQ), 55, 148
Cidade Morena (Brown City), 148
circular migration, 145, 160

About the Author

Sarah A. LeBaron von Baeyer received her PhD in sociocultural anthropology from Yale University and a BA in East Asian studies from Oberlin College. As lecturer in anthropology and East Asian studies at Yale University and visiting lecturer in transcultural studies at the University of Heidelberg, she has taught classes on contemporary Japanese society and culture, transnational migration, global cities and diasporas, and anthropological field methods and theory. She is currently working on a new research project on overseas voting behavior and support for far-right politics among transnational Japanese-Brazilian labor migrants.

www.ingramcontent.com/pod-product-compliance
Lightning Source LLC
Chambersburg PA
CBHW022306280326
41932CB00010B/1004